D0850738

Satire's Persuasive Voice

# Satire's Persuasive Voice

EDWARD A. BLOOM

and

LILLIAN D. BLOOM

Cornell University Press

ITHACA AND LONDON

Copyright © 1979 by Cornell University

All rights reserved. Except for brief quotations in a review,
this book, or parts thereof, must not be reproduced in any
form without permission in writing from the publisher.
For information address Cornell University Press,
124 Roberts Place, Ithaca, New York 14850.

First published 1979 by Cornell University Press.
Published in the United Kingdom by Cornell University Press Ltd.,
2-4 Brook Street, London W1Y 1AA.

International Standard Book Number 0-8014-0839-3
Library of Congress Catalog Card Number 78-11668
Printed in the United States of America
*Librarians: Library of Congress cataloging information*
*appears on the last page of the book.*

# CONTENTS

arm'd for Virtue when I point the pen,
Brand the bold front of shameless, guilty men,

.  .  .  .  .

TO VIRTUE ONLY and HER FRIENDS, A FRIEND,
The World beside may murmur, or commend.

Alexander Pope, *The First Satire of*
*the Second Book of Horace Imitated*

# ACKNOWLEDGMENTS

During the preparation of this book we have incurred many obligations, and we are grateful that we now have the opportunity to acknowledge them. The John Simon Guggenheim Memorial Foundation provided financial support and encouragement to go on with a task that at times was as intricate and hazardous as a journey through the Minoan labyrinth. The Henry E. Huntington Library responded generously to our requests with a summer grant and with hospitality that we have been permitted to enjoy on a number of occasions. An allocation from the Brown University Faculty Research Fund helped defray the expense of secretarial assistance. Library staffs in the United States and England were unfailingly helpful and courteous: the Brown University Library, the Huntington Library, the Houghton Library of Harvard University, the John Rylands Library of the University of Manchester, the Bodleian Library of Oxford University, the British Library.

We also wish to express our appreciation to the editors of journals who gave us forums for some of the material that follows, and who thereby provided us the incentive to revise our work extensively through modification, amplification, and all the other processes of reconsideration that shape any scholarly criticism. The basic concepts remain the same, however, as when parts of Chapters 1, 3, and 5 first appeared in the pages of *Criticism* (Spring, 1969), the *Huntington Library Quarterly* (November, 1970, and February, 1971), and *Studies in the Literary Imagination* (October, 1972).

Our thanks are also offered to Professor William D. Vanech for his thoughtful reading of an earlier version of this text, and to Noelle Jackson and Nancy Castle for meticulous preparation of the typescript.

EDWARD A. BLOOM
LILLIAN D. BLOOM

*Providence, Rhode Island*

# SHORT TITLES

Addison and Steele,
  *Spectator*
Aristotle, *Rhetoric*

Boswell, *Life*

Cicero, *De Oratore*

Defoe, *Review*

Dryden, *On Satire*

Foxon, *Catalogue*

Hall, *Poems*

Horace, *Satires*

*The Spectator,* ed. Donald F. Bond, 5 vols.
(Oxford: Clarendon Press, 1965).
*The Basic Works of Aristotle,* ed. Richard
McKeon (New York: Random House, 1941).
*Boswell's Life of Johnson,* ed. George Birkbeck
Hill and L. F. Powell, 6 vols. in 8 (Oxford:
Clarendon Press, 1934–1964).
*De Oratore,* trans. E. W. Sutton and Harris
Rackham (London and Cambridge, Mass.:
Loeb Classical Library, 1942).
*Defoe's Review,* ed. Arthur W. Secord, 22 vols.
(New York: Facsimile Text Society,
Columbia University Press, 1938).
"A Discourse concerning the Original and
Progress of Satire," prefixed to *The Satires of
Decimus Junius Juvenalis . . . together with the
Satires of Aulus Persius Flaccus,* trans. John
Dryden et al. (1693).
David Fairweather Foxon, *English Verse,
1701–1750: A Catalogue of Separately Printed
Poems with Notes on Contemporary Collected
Editions,* 2 vols. (Cambridge: Cambridge
University Press, 1975).
*The Collected Poems of Joseph Hall,* ed. Arnold
Davenport (Liverpool: University of
Liverpool Press, 1949).
*Satires, Epistles, and Ars Poetica,* trans. H.
Rushton Fairclough (London and
Cambridge, Mass.: Loeb Classical Library,
1947).

| | |
|---|---|
| Johnson, *English Poets* | *Lives of the English Poets by Samuel Johnson, LL.D.*, ed. George Birkbeck Hill, 3 vols. (Oxford: Clarendon Press, 1905). |
| Johnson, *Poems* | *Poems*, ed. E. L. McAdam, Jr., with George Milne, Vol. VI in *The Yale Edition of the Works of Samuel Johnson* (New Haven and London: Yale University Press, 1964). |
| Loeb *Juvenal* | *Juvenal and Persius*, trans. G. G. Ramsay, rev. ed. (London and Cambridge, Mass.: Loeb Classical Library, 1950). |
| *POAS* | *Poems on Affairs of State: Augustan Satirical Verse, 1660–1714*, general editor George deF. Lord, 7 vols. (New Haven and London: Yale University Press, 1963–1975): Vol. I, 1660–1678, ed. George deF. Lord. Vol. II, 1678–1681, ed. Elias F. Mangel, Jr. Vol. III, 1682–1685, ed. Howard H. Schless. Vol. IV, 1685–1688, ed. Galbraith M. Crump. Vol. V, 1688–1697, ed. William J. Cameron. Vol. VI, 1697–1704, ed. Frank H. Ellis. Vol. VII, 1704–1714, ed. Frank H. Ellis. |
| Pope, *Correspondence* | *The Correspondence of Alexander Pope*, ed. George Sherburn, 5 vols. (Oxford: Clarendon Press, 1956). |
| *Twickenham Pope* | *The Twickenham Edition of the Poems of Alexander Pope*, general editor, John Butt, 11 vols. in 12 (London and New Haven: Methuen and Yale University Press, 1939–1967): Vol. I, *Pastoral Poetry and "An Essay on Criticism,"* ed. Emile Audra and Aubrey Williams. Vol. II, *"The Rape of the Lock" and Other Poems*, ed. Geoffrey Tillotson. Vol. III¹, *An Essay on Man*, ed. Maynard Mack. Vol. III², *Epistles to Several Persons (Moral Essays)*, ed. F. W. Bateson. Vol. IV, *Imitations of Horace with "An Epistle to Dr. Arbuthnot" and "The Epilogue to the Satires,"* ed. John Butt. |

Quintilian

Shaftesbury,
  *Characteristics*

Swift, *Correspondence*

Swift, *Poems*

Swift, *Prose Works*

Vol. V, *The Dunciad,* ed. James Sutherland.
Vol. VI, *Minor Poems,* ed. Norman Ault,
completed by John Butt.
*The Institutio Oratoria of Quintilian,* trans. H.
E. Butler, 4 vols. (London and Cambridge,
Mass.: Loeb Classical Library, 1920-1922).
Anthony Ashley Cooper, 3rd Earl of
Shaftesbury, *Characteristics of Men, Manners,
Opinions, Times,* ed. John M. Robertson,
intro. Stanley Grean, 3 vols. in 1
(Indianapolis, Ind.: Bobbs-Merrill, 1964).
*The Correspondence of Jonathan Swift,* ed.
Harold Williams, 5 vols. (Oxford: Clarendon
Press, 1963-1965).
*The Poems of Jonathan Swift,* ed. Harold
Williams, 2d ed., 3 vols. (Oxford: Clarendon
Press, 1958).
Jonathan Swift, *Prose Works,* ed. Herbert
Davis, 14 vols. (Oxford: Shakespeare Head
Press, Basil Blackwell, 1939-1968).

# Satire's Persuasive Voice

# INTRODUCTION

It is merit enough for a writer on a subject that has been often canvassed, if he can reduce into a short compass whatever hath been said
before, and add something material of his own. Whether I have done
this in the present case, must be submitted to the judgment of the
audience.[1]

Satire is a subject that has been canvassed often and over a
long period. Of that we are as keenly aware as of the succession
of critics who have set courses for us to pursue, from the ancient
past to the present. Although we have attempted to be
chronologically judicious, we have not presumed to write a history of satire. We have, rather, essayed a critical view of
problems—technical and thematic—long perplexing to us and
others. So complex and controversial is satire that its trails are
seldom neatly contiguous or the destinations plainly marked. We
may have followed many of the familiar paths, but we have also
created a few more to be ventured along for whatever fresh
scenery they may provide.

Like the god Mercury, satire is elusive and variable, wearing
many disguises and satisfying many expectations. Even as the
deity adroitly roamed from high to low—as orator and trickster,
as fleet messenger and patron of the market place—so satire has
always demonstrated its adaptability to circumstance and intention. No single norm can accommodate the many possibilities of
a genre or a set of attitudes: satire can be either or both. In this

1. Joseph Trapp, "Lectures XVII, XVIII," *Lectures on Poetry* [1711–1715],
trans. from the Latin by William Bowyer and William Clarke (1742), p. 218.
(Place of publication for all primary sources, unless otherwise noted, is London.)

study we take note of long-recognized prescriptions but do not insist upon conformity. We understand that satire is often personal, vindictive, opportunistic. But we also understand that it is frequently idealistic in more than assertion, that it can be unabashedly didactic and seriously committed to a hope in its own power to effect change. The distance between hope and fulfillment may be vast, and we have cautioned at various points against confusing the formula with the fact: even the best-intended satire does not readily convert desire into action.

The theory of satire as an efficient cause of sociomoral reparation is easier to assert than to prove. Yet, with the idealists on one side and the cynics on the other, a good deal of dispute is periodically generated by an assumption that improvement must (or cannot) be in direct proportion to satiric persuasion. As realistic critics, we are able to apprehend—when the occasion dictates—a pragmatic satiric spirit, unencumbered by ethical and reformist expectations. In this connection, we can look at that writing which means patently to destroy the reputations of adversaries and to humiliate them so that they will be laughed, hopefully, into extinction. When Rochester sets his sights on Sir Carr Scroope, for instance, or Churchill on Hogarth, the private is unmistakably private and the feud in each instance a local one. Such satire entertains even as it retains its spite. The question of reform may be introduced as a red herring, but no one is likely to be taken in by professions that are transparently irrelevant. Like spectators drawn to the scene of a brawl, we are stimulated by personal satire but only rarely involved in it.

We neither discount the aesthetic and historic appeal of subjectively motivated ridicule nor waive our right to enjoy it. At the same time we must distinguish this branch of satire from one less constricted by occasion, topic, or personality. That is, a broader, more compelling dimension of satire exists whose applicability is determined by the breadth of its moral premises. This brings us closer to the possibilities of constructive alteration, although we are not so visionary or so confident of the powers invested in satire as ever to associate it with instant reform. What we suggest, rather, is the capacity of some satire to effect a gradual moral reawakening, a reaffirmation of positive social and individual values. This renewed awareness—probably beyond the grasp anyway of the culprit or *eiron* under fire—is intended for a general mankind capable of moral perception. In an ultimate sense, the moral satirist does not address a specific victim at a specific time, be he Lemuel Gulliver, Sporus, or Orgilio. These, on the contrary, represent the fallen *exempla*, timelessly fictional agents of human vanities, errors, and perversities.

Ideally, the satiric potential for reform continues indefinitely, unaffected by the transience of a literary situation; it connotes the appeal of conscience and justice as universal attributes. From Bishop Hall, as an example, we derive an implication that his "hot-blooded rage" knows neither moment nor reader. Vindictive in tone, he nonetheless thinks of his poetry as a gift of enduring recrimination for anyone "that hears, and readeth guiltily." Many metaphors of satire—thorns, darts, knives, rods, poison—are vividly punitive, suggesting that when men will not respond to reason, they may to force. But again, even if the assumptions of reform are aimed at a particular or immediate transgressor, the challenge is not confined by singularity. The specific malefactor has already done his worst, but he can be held up as an abhorrence. The satirist encompasses an idealized vision that, like a sea gull impaled on a pier to warn off other gulls, wrongdoing—when properly exposed—may deter others from related crimes.

If we think of the satirist as a popular philosopher, Plato is at hand with a useful analogy: his view of the civil punishment meted out for crimes against the state has a corollary in satiric castigation of infractions against manners and the social code generally. When Protagoras speculates on the nature of retribution and its strength to inhibit, the satirist and the ethical philosopher draw a comparable line between the real and the ideal. "For if you will think, Socrates, of the effect which punishment has on evil-doers, you will see at once that in the opinion of mankind virtue may be acquired; for no one punishes the evil-doer under the notion, or for the reason, that he has done wrong—only the unreasonable fury of a beast acts in that way. But he who desires to inflict rational punishment does not retaliate for a past wrong, for that which is done cannot be

undone, but he has regard to the future." Then he hopes that
the example of one who is punished will shame others from
similar wrongdoing.[2]

Satiric reform, it appears to us, is too often treated by critics as
a literal proposition rather than as a conceptual and figurative
one. Periodically, we readers of satire must remind ourselves
that satire is a literary as well as a polemic art. Alecto's whip may
inflict bumps on the imagination or the intellect, but its effect as
a forthright goad to action will be far less apparent than, say, the
birch rod of the benignly tyrannical schoolmaster. The point to
be insisted upon, when considering serious satire, is that punitive intention seldom if ever resolves itself in measurable reform
or deterrence. But paradoxically, if the satire is just, its potential
for useful change may grow beyond the symbolic. The social or
psychological change attributable to satire may be slow in coming; but if it comes at all, that serves obviously as a gain to be
cherished. Such change, further, may be infinitesimal and pro-
visional, dependent upon vagaries of time and place, on an atmosphere receptive to affirmative criticism, and on an inter-
dependence of satire with institutional action—political, religious, cultural.

It would be folly to expect reformation to burst forth from
extensive readings of Juvenal's satires, for instance, or *Gulliver's
Travels, The Vanity of Human Wishes*, or *1984*. On the other hand,
it would be altogether reasonable to look to them for
consciousness-raising, no matter when they happen to be read.
Even before reform, there must be an awareness of such
shortcomings and vanities that erode the quality of human nature. Satire is not functional in the same way that the institutions
of Church and State are: that is, it is not explicitly obliged to
preserve or restore moral and legal standards of conduct. Although it cannot enforce compliance, satire does, indeed, appeal to private decency or social sympathy and even fear, which
link perception to conscience. Like Protagoras, the satirist—as
idealist—believes virtue may be acquired. If overt or implied

2. "Protagoras," *The Works of Plato*, trans. Benjamin Jowett, 4 vols. in 1 (New York: Tudor, n.d.), 4:155.

praise of the good points the way, he uses applause as a legitimate part of his armory. Otherwise and for the most part, he relies upon ridicule and castigation to prompt rejection of whatever may be inconsistent with reason and good nature. If we are moved positively by a satire, we respond to a plea for a return to our senses, moral, intellectual, and aesthetic. The idiom of mockery and outrage may be seen as rhetorical cover for convictions that the satirist would like to share. If folly and vice are to be made distasteful, he must draw deeply from a reservoir of emotional persuasiveness that ranges from the language of scorn to that of indignation. Often, to be sure, the polemicist seems to outrace the artist. The accomplished satirist, nevertheless, maintains literary control. And whatever the depth of his feeling, he professes to expect that the reader will emerge from the satiric experience better equipped than before to fulfill his potential for social understanding and self-knowledge.

The theory, as we said earlier, need not fit the literal expectation if we are in fact hoping to discover workable panaceas. Our vision of the satirist, furthermore, tends frequently to be confounded by the disparity between talent and performance. First-rate satirists are relatively few; the mode has attracted hordes of writers more concerned with their own hunger and notoriety than with principle. When imitators and hangers-on outnumber their masters, we have a particular duty to distinguish between theory as lip-service to a popular dogma and theory as bona fide commitment to realizable ideals. The difference is between satire as entertainment for its own sake or as rationalized spite and satire as an artistic examination of man's failed promise. Most satire, we have found, subscribes in some degree to a need for human obligation. Critical disputes flair continually over the credibility of satiric achievement. Yet, however imperfectly satire is realized in many productions, they provide an extended chain of human identity, stretching between the vulnerable and the noble, that gives a sense of generic agreement.

We argue for the affirmative impulse that is the seal of satire at its best. There is always the risk, we understand, of overlooking a positive aim in the dramatic heat and hyperbole of charged language. And similarly there is always the risk of wish-fulfillment when the disposition is to believe that overstatement is necessarily a formal disguise for good will. But, then, the contrary hazards are courted when the tendency is to disbelieve any assumption of satiric purpose that is not negative. Flourishing critical industries have grown up around varied analyses regarding the intent of Juvenal's Sixth Satire or the Fourth Voyage of *Gulliver's Travels*. What interests us in any debate or reading is open-minded exploration, a quest for the innate quality that we call *humanitas*.

By this we mean the satirist's preoccupation with everything human: man's nature, feelings, inclinations, alienations. It is, further, what we would call a committed preoccupation of the artist as opposed to the aloof perspective of the spectator, although detachment helps to form the literary or graphic work. In this large context, as we see many satirists, severity or harshness of tone need not imply rancor or an absence of social empathy. We think of those satirists who scold and berate, who sound caustic, bitter, and savage because they care enough about man to be angered by his errant betrayals of self and fellow creatures. There is in them an underlying hope, a disguised sense of generosity conducive to dealing with the encrustations of corrupted lives. *Humanitas,* as a kind of shorthand for human nature and all that that notion evokes, is a useful term. But it should not, we insist, be confused with any so-called "soft view" of satire, that is, with the amiably sentimental. There is no implication in *humanitas* of secondary significations like gentility, do-goodism, unthinking kindness. It connotes a view of satire that alerts us to moral lesions and yet stops short of initiating remedial action or organized benevolence. Most satirists would gladly endorse programs of social reform, but without asserting themselves as humanitarians prepared to see them through. The acquisition of virtue is a shared good, but the idiom and strategies and intention of the satirists differ markedly from those of the active "philanthropes." And the satirist who alludes to himself as a surgeon knows (or should know) the limits of his craft and abilities.

As a persuasive art, satire reveals essential parallels with the formal rhetoric codified by Aristotle, Quintilian, and Cicero. Rhetorical prescriptions, indeed, go far toward clarifying the inherent *humanitas* of exhortation, *saeva indignatio,* and derision or ridicule. Juvenal's satires, for instance, embrace an almost systematic repertory of all the prescribed devices, the structural organization, and even the verbal tricks and confrontations of the rhetoricians whose calling he had practiced before he became a poet. Many of the satirists who imitated him—among them Dryden, Oldham, Johnson—likewise understood the relationship between satire and the rhetorical discipline. Important as we take this relationship to be, we have not attempted to write a specialized account of the rhetoric of satire. On a somewhat broader canvas, we have tried to formulate a theory suitable to an understanding of satire's complex aesthetic, of satire as a fiction dependent upon a creative imagination and an image-making faculty. We have divided our materials between theory, and theme and practice.

Starting with the theoretical principles of a genre or a state of mind motivated by authorial dissatisfaction with the ways of the world, we see that satiric "intention," shaped by a moral-didactic impulse, becomes one man's expression of dismay, disappointment, even revulsion. Not unusually, in the opinion of some critics, the satirist's incentive to criticize is resolved in nihilistic abjuration. But to accept this view without qualification is to interpret the satirist and his work in a context of misanthropy. So construed, the fall—if only from worldly grace—is final, irremediable, and deserving of venomous, destructive reaction. Once we allow for instances of self-serving malice, however, we should see satire in a humanistic frame. An extensive body of satire implies that sensitivity to moral stumbling makes rectification a hope and preservation of the good possible. Man and his institutions are the matter of satire and, when the outlook is positive, the satirist addresses his subject not in a static or sentimentalized glow, but in an active spirit of social integrity and continuity, in the language of Truth, Justice, and Reformation.

We also concern ourselves with "shape and order," seeking architectonic tenets relevant to the construction of a satire. Detailed examination of *Absalom and Achitophel* has confirmed our belief that formally conceived satire owes a significant debt to the organization of classical rhetoric. Although they vary with relevance to polemic and literary needs, the satiric and the rhetorical are nonetheless joined by like cultural and ethical goals, the promulgation of virtue, and—more visibly—by structural particulars. The Restoration satirist no less than the ancient orator proceeds according to a careful program entailing a framework of *inventio* and *elocutio,* the requisites for both structure and style. Audiences for oratory and satire diverge, but the similarity of general purpose, as we have stated, promotes a compatible bond of design. And in both disciplines design is quintessential.

Implicit in this schema is a desire to bring the often diffuse materials of satire into a cohesive and probable whole. Consequently, we are enabled to argue for controlled unity in a mode that encourages hyperbole and kaleidoscopic profusion. An important component of such control is a definable point of view, whether that of the satirist speaking in his own voice—both alone and in debate with an *adversarius*—or in the disguised voice of an apologist, ironically naive about the quality of his performance. In other instances of virtuosity, the satirist cements his materials by the use of a multiple point of view, figuratively enacting the roles of prosecutor, defendant, judge, and jury. And as still further evidence of conscious unification, he sets his "plot" in certain *topoi:* particularized urban or salon settings associated with dissolution, abstract places like barren "summits" of futile aspiration, or, on the other hand, pastoral scenes that recall a sound tradition made obsolete in a corrupt present.

In considering "tone and meaning" next, we emphasize the literary nature of satire: evaluating problems of language and attempting an overview of the linguistic resources at the satirist's disposal. These vary in degrees of finesse and obvious exposition, from the subtlety of razor-sharp irony to the hammer-blows of subjective imprecation. No generalization could account for the versatility with which satirists have deployed their verbal batteries. If, however, any one norm of effective satire were to be proposed, we would argue for that whose verbal aptness retains a connection with familiar experience or makes distant experiences as familiar as though we had participated in them ourselves. Satire, after all, is generally prompted by the realistic and the topical; undue opacity becomes a threat to meaning. Durable satire translates the occasional into the historical. But language changes and allusions fade; inevitably there comes a time when annotations function as essential compromises if the pertinence of once localized satire is to continue. Notes, indeed, may please as well as inform; this we discover from Swift, Pope, Fielding, and even Wilkes, whose academic playfulness enhances and ultimately merges into satiric intention.

But above all, the literary quality that brings the satirist close to us—somewhat perhaps in the conversational temper (if not always the moderation) of the Horatian *sermones*—is his tone. This we describe as a "persuasive verbal pitch," a tonality compounded of intellect and imagination, and these connected by emotions, especially of mockery or violent retort. The more agreeable, naturally, is the risible, for laughter tends to obscure, or at least palliate, unpleasantness. Furthermore, if we wish to heed moralists like Shaftesbury and Johnson, ridicule leads to an exposure of inexorable truth. Basic to concern with the laughable is *wit*, a free-wheeling designation in the eighteenth century as pertinent to word-play as to wisdom and reflection. Furthermore, the moral implications of laughter in its various forms are less overt (though not necessarily less serious in concept) than those of indignation, which may be regarded as a tonal opposite. Indignation, notable for linguistic explosiveness, is so overwrought at times as to appear vengeful if not downright sadistic; so responsive to outrageous breaches of custom as to seek comparable levels of revulsion in obscenity and scatology. And yet, as a matter of Aristotelian theory, indignation at human wrongdoing is sustained by pity for those who have suffered at the hands of the unworthy. The intensity of moral rage, according to this notion, coincides with the depth of sympathetic human identification.

The voluminous outpouring of satiric literature between 1660 and 1800 may be attributed to exceptional industry and also to exceptional interest in public issues. As George deF. Lord points out: "No significant event or person in politics, religious affairs, or in court or literary circles escaped notice."[3] And many insignificant events and individuals were also memorialized in satire. Our search through this literature, limited as it had to be, was nevertheless extensive enough to help us chart certain themes that attracted Restoration and eighteenth-century audiences. In the final three chapters of this book, therefore, we have arranged our materials so as to reflect these major currents and also to serve as demonstrations of theories put forward in the preceding three chapters. The topics that have engaged us persistently are controversies related to religion, politics, and manners; and within those categories we have been as representative as possible of conflicting interests and values. For that reason, many of our models will be familiar as monuments of literary history; others will be less well known, even ephemeral.

Our tripartite division will doubtless seem arbitrary at times, mainly because of the interlocking character of much satire. A work that we treat primarily for its religious interest may very well have legitimate claims to attention for its political substance. By the same token, a satire taken up under the rubric of "studied civility" may warrant analysis for its treatment of a political Great Man. Certain topics, also, have a shared validity in more than one chapter. The subject of hypocrisy, as a specific case in point, becomes inevitably prominent in discussions of religion affecting Erasmus, Swift, Cowper, Gibbon, and Burns. But we hardly need be surprised when it reemerges elsewhere in connection with Fielding's theory of manners and fictional characters. If the relevance of ridicule is debated by both proponents and adversaries of religious satire, the same concern confronts us in rationales for political satire. Stereotypes like "holy rage" and "sacred truth" find their secularized way into innumerable satires on parties and manners. And so also do reformist shibboleths crop up with expected regularity throughout all varieties of satire, along with pleas for good nature.

Nevertheless, religious satire and political satire can be distinguished from each other. They deal with specific quarrels of sect

3. *POAS*, 1:vii.

and faction, however much these contentions overlap in an age when a politicized church is an organic arm of the state. In an age, further, when social ceremony is intricately textured within the public fabric, it is difficult to keep clear of religious or political nuance. Despite these reservations, we talk about numerous ways in which satire of manners has a cast that, if not peculiar to itself, is circumscribed by the "unofficial" and the secular. Even as we cling to such distinctions, we are alert to the fact that a decadent taste manifest in misused wealth and luxury parallels a decadent political and religious structure, or at least a structure with visible weaknesses. An aversion to fops and dandies has chauvinistic or patriotic undertones. Feminine immodesty and arrogance are tied to the transgressions of a permissive, licentious society—its theaters and salons, for instance—but the shadow of Court maneuvers hovers constantly. The most specifically cultural mores to be attacked, probably, are related to the intellectual life, to literature and art and scholarship reduced to *pedantry,* an epithet deriding the labors of socially inert hacks and bookmen.

These, seemingly, are all separate pieces in the curious puzzle of eighteenth-century manners. They are, however, pieces belonging to a cohesive whole for the consideration of social satire. The pattern that finally gives them definition—and indeed bears also upon the satiric vision of priestcraft and statecraft—is a duality of *dullness* and *affectation.* In them the satirist makes us see the horror of lives without love, imagination, or purpose; mere existence in which moral stasis and superficial pretense have stamped out vitality and the communion of person with person.

Our focus upon satire of the Restoration and eighteenth century has encouraged us to draw upon Classical and Continental writers absorbed into the English tradition. Horace and Juvenal, Erasmus and Boileau were inevitable choices. Others doubtless could be added. We were attracted, for instance, to possible analogues between Cervantes and the English satirists. It would be difficult indeed to ignore the Cervantes-fever that once seized the Island. Imitators and translators abounded, the essayists thumbed the Spaniard's pages for *mots* and exempla. Butler

found in him a source of parodic inspiration. Fielding extrava-
gantly allowed him the near conversion of "a civilized people in a
nation of cut-throats."[4] For our generic aims the complexity of
Cervantes's fiction holds a dimension far beyond the satiric.
Nevertheless, his creative spirit contains that very quality which
we have called *humanitas,* and which evoked the praise of such as
Johnson and Coleridge.

In the opinion of the former, *Don Quixote,* "a book to which a
mind of the greatest powers may be indebted," is one in which
we see our own identities and aberrations. Few readers following
the fantasized adventures of the knight, "amidst their mirth or
pity, can deny that they have admitted visions of the same
kind. . . . When we pity him, we reflect on our own disappoint-
ments; and when we laugh, our hearts inform us that he is not
more ridiculous than ourselves, except that he tells what we
have only thought." What Coleridge saw in the novelist's inven-
tions was a redemptive grace that had been the guiding principle
of many a satiric ideologue. Cervantes's was "the sweet temper of
a superior mind, which saw the follies of mankind, and was even
at the moment suffering severely under hard mistreatment; and
yet seems everywhere to have but one thought as the undersong—
'Brethren! with all your faults I love you still!'—or as a mother
that chides the child she loves, with one hand holds up the rod,
and with the other wipes off each tear as it drops!" Thus, when
Johnson looks into *Don Quixote,* he peers into a glass that end-
lessly repeats the empathy of its readers. For Coleridge the experience is even deeper, evoking as it does a sympathy with the
entire race. But however differently they respond to the novel,
Johnson and Coleridge agree that an essential aim is rightful
criticism in which, to borrow Koestler's phrase, Cervantes has
taken "a semi-affectionate kick at the heel of Achilles."[5]

4. See Fielding's review of Charlotte Lennox, *The Female Quixote,* in the
*Covent-Garden Journal* 24 (24 Mar. 1752); "Preface," *Joseph Andrews.* Smollett's
trans. of *Don Quixote* appeared in 1755; and in 1784, *A Continuation of the History
and Adventures of the Renowned Don Quixote de la Mancha,* trans. from the Spanish
of Alonzo Fernandez de Avellaneda by William Augustus Yardley.
5. Johnson, *English Poets,* 1:209, and *Rambler* 2; *Coleridge's Miscellaneous Criticism,* ed. Thomas Middleton Raysor (London: Constable, 1936), pp. 99–100;
Arthur Koestler, *The Act of Creation* (New York: Macmillan, 1964), pp. 70–71.

By the time we arrive at nineteenth-century and twentieth-century judgments of satiric theory and practice, the evidence is largely retrospective. Satire by no means withers into moribundity, but we cannot deny that its vital growth now lies well in the past. There are satirists yet to come, but the splendid "Age of Satire" has retreated into history, its concentrated energy no longer the force of a brilliant cultural movement. If we were to accept Roy Campbell's modern tirade, "one of the chief glories of English literature has been dead for a hundred years." Characteristically splenetic, he regarded his own times as "so inimical to satire that there is no depth of grovelling to which its representatives will not descend." Campbell, we must be aware, is grinding a very personal axe in retaliation for a rejected review of Wyndham Lewis's novel *The Apes of God.* Campbell also seizes this opportunity to flatten Bloomsbury gentility, an act—it turns out—of self-esteem because in compensation for ostracism by this one group he places Lewis in a union with Dryden, Pope, and himself: all of them engaged in courageous defense against scurrilous attack.[6]

In a sense, Campbell gives the lie to his contention that satire has long since died. Both he and Lewis, his mentor, are certainly among the most powerful of the moderns, however short their satire falls by comparison with that of the eighteenth century; and however disturbed we may be by the repressive bigotry that they espoused. As an heir of a combative and quasi-sanctified tradition, Lewis comes especially near the mark, as Robert Elliott observes (p. 231), with an image of the satirist as "a hangman . . . a dissector, a surgeon, an executioner, a prophet." On reflection Lewis's comparison of himself with Dryden is, at best, idiosyncratic. The earlier satirist, he asserted, "dispensed with the protective moralistic machinery of the classical satire. It was, in short, not because his opponents were *naughty* that Dryden objected to them, but because they were *dull.* They had sinned against the Reason, rather than against the Mosaic Law."

6. Roy Campbell, preface to "A Rejected Review," in Wyndham Lewis, *Satire & Fiction,* Enemy Pamphlets No. 1 (London: The Arthur Press [1930], pp. 13-14. See the discussion of Lewis and Campbell by Robert C. Elliott, *The Power of Satire: Magic, Ritual, Art* (Princeton: Princeton University Press, 1960), ch. 5.

That is rubbish to be explained away only on the assumption that Lewis had read no further in Dryden than *Mac Flecknoe,* and that poem only superficially. The Juvenalian translations apparently do not count and perhaps *Absalom and Achitophel* is not to be treated as a satire. "If you remove from Satire its moralism, then it has no advertisement value for the victim—then it is doubly deadly, and then also the satirist is doubly hated, by those picked out for attack.... It could be asserted even, that the greatest Satire *cannot* be moralistic at all: if for no other reason, because no mind of the first order has ever itself been taken in, nor consented to take in others, by the crude injunctions of any purely moral code."[7] Thus we find in Lewis (and in his disciple as well) a familiar rationale for antihumanitas. To satisfy this negativism, he inclines radically toward the personal invective of satire in which dullness is often the enemy. But in the word *"naughty,"* he sneers at misconduct as at the trifling antics of a child. Willfully he misinterprets Dryden's idea of immorality as intrinsic to the human condition, as a concomitant of dullness, as a violation of reason and spirit, the spirit both Christian and Mosaic.

We dwell upon Lewis not because he is innately interesting to us as a satirist, but because he is symptomatic of a tenacious battle carried into the twentieth century between the proponents of humanistic, remedial satire and those who negate its possibility. Not only was the moral issue too deeply traditional for Lewis to escape it, he also could not remain consistent with his own satiric claims. Pursuing Lewis's confusions and contradictions, Spender ironically concludes that the subject of *The Apes of God* "is moral indignation, even though Lewis may have no moral axe to grind, and is no politician. But actually this amorality is in itself a moral point of view, because it is related to the old question ... of the position of the artist in society. Lewis's amorality and unpoliticism applies only to the artist: it is not anarchy.... So here we have satire which is moral, although the writer is himself no moralist." And if this seems a bit like rabbinical hairsplitting, then Spender guides us to *Men Without Art,* in which

7. Lewis, *Satire & Fiction,* p. 43.

Lewis himself concedes the operation of "the ethical will" in
"satire of the highest order."[8]
    But for a totally unambiguous commitment to the concept of
*humanitas,* we have the example of Auden, a practical theorist
who places his endorsement in a frame that would have been
familiar to any eighteenth-century reader: "Satire is angry and
optimistic; it believes that, once people's attention is drawn to
some evil, they will mend their ways." What Auden, like many of
his predecessors, proposes is a premise that can be shared with
like-minded people, those whom he stresses as having "the normal faculty of conscience."[9] There may be room for cynical dis-
claimers, both with regard to the reconstitutive powers of satire,
and to the responsiveness in general of individuals to shortcomings about which they have been made aware. We do not question the interest or importance of debate on issues that border
on the ontological. At the personal level our ethical choice is
clear, and that is what we have attempted to argue within the
confines of the book. At the same time we have worked for
objectivity, presenting the other side of the coin when it supports
a particular satirist, his theory and practice.
    Modern satire is obviously a subject for other books, but it is
one we have touched upon briefly for a sense of continuum.
From classical times to the present the vagaries of satire have
been many, dictated by personal and public frictions yoked to
literary and rhetorical fashion. But despite disagreements about
intention and patterns of oscillation, the purposes and even objects of satire have remained astonishingly consistent. And
within our own times also a study of Waugh, Orwell, and Huxley
concludes that though they differed in origin and outlook, each
had a vision of "men as caught up in a horrid circle of dehumanization, futility, madness, evil." Alike in vision, they enjoy
a capacity to convey a sense of positive solutions and a hope for

    8. Stephen Spender, *The Destructive Element: A Study of Modern Writers and
Beliefs* (London: Jonathan Cape, 1935), pp. 207, 209, 212. See also on Lewis's
destructive tendencies, Kenneth Burke, *Attitudes toward History*, 2 vols. (New
York: New Republic, 1937), 1:62–69.
    9. W. H. Auden, foreword to *Sense & Inconsequence: Satirical Verses,* by Angus
Stewart (London: Michael de Hartington, 1972); "Notes on the Comic," *The
Dyer's Hand and Other Essays* (New York: Random House, 1962), pp. 383–84.

reordered lives.[10] Orwell, the most politically dynamic of the three, calls for a "limit to pessimism" when he rejects Malcolm Muggeridge's defeatist book *The Thirties*. And comparably, when he looks to a more distant past, he complains:

Swift falsifies his picture of the whole world by refusing to see anything in human life except dirt, folly, and wickedness, but the part which he abstracts from the whole does exist, and it is something which we all know about while shrinking from mentioning it. Part of our minds—in any normal person it is the dominant part—believes that man is a noble animal and life is worth living: but there is also a sort of inner self which at least intermittently stands aghast at the horror of existence. In the queerest way, pleasure and disgust are linked together.[11]

Orwell has it wrong about Swift because he has made the traditional blunder of confusing the author with his excrementally obsessed personae. No, Swift sees the same positive qualities that Orwell does. It is his creations, rather—obtuse men and women—who are blind to the nobility and worth of existence. But whereas Swift wishes to redirect us by imagination and shocking human symbols away from "the horror of existence" to something better, Orwell's route at the propitious time is the direct one of exposition. In his fiction, he too has a powerful command of fantasy, but at the moment of presenting the theme, he wants it stated without hazard of misunderstanding, even as it is stated here. Ironically, Swift has won a point anyway by causing Orwell to enlarge his vision in an attempt to grasp the very essence of humanity he has overlooked in Swift. So Orwell brings the wheel full circle back to the Irish Dean and the eighteenth century, much closer to him in moral instinct and *humanitas* than he knew.

10. Stephen Jay Greenblatt, *Three Modern Satirists: Waugh, Orwell, and Huxley* (New Haven and London: Yale University Press, 1965), p. 117. For a discussion of these and other modern satirists, see Leonard Feinberg, *Introduction to Satire* (Ames: Iowa State University Press, 1967).

11. George Orwell, "The Limit to Pessimism," *An Age Like This, 1920–1940*, 1:535; and "Politics vs. Literature: An Examination of *Gulliver's Travels*," *In Front of our Nose, 1945–50*, 4:222, both in *The Collected Essays, Journalism, and Letters*, ed. Sonia Orwell and Ian Angus, 4 vols. (London: Secker & Warburg, 1968).

# CHAPTER 1

# INTENTION:
## Satiric Mode of Feeling

In the "Apology" added to the fifth edition of *A Tale of a Tub,* Swift informs his readers that the work is "a satire, that would be useful and diverting." Thereby he synthesizes a prevailing satiric intention, although, like most contemporaries and classical predecessors, he does not insist upon equality between *utile* and *dulce.* Despite the aesthetic pleasure afforded by individual works, satirists and their critics—in explanatory statements, at least—have always justified an overbalance of functionalism. Sometimes tacitly, often overtly, satirists have liked to think of themselves as judges of morals and manners with certain added prerogatives: not only do they pass and execute sentence on the guilty, they cry out against the inequities suffered by the victims. Righteousness, to be sure, may become a liability when the judge is so intent upon redressing injustice that he risks alienating his audience. So the ancient furious Archilochos, for instance, seems more a vengeful killer than a healer.

But this role is plainly exaggeration in which fantasy competes with probability. The issue is forced when "the satirist casts himself as a tough guy giving the bullies their lumps, a warrior . . . drawing his sacred weapon in a heroic last-ditch defence of truth and freedom." The fantasy may overreach the demonstrable, yet that does not lessen the desirability of the striving. As sympathetic critics concur, satire should tend not toward destruction but toward renewal, and even the angriest declamations may be constructively motivated. The equation of morality and satire has indeed become a stereotype. Characteristically, the Juvenalian commentator Holyday asked: "For what is the end of satire but to reform?" And reform cannot take place until inadequacies or failures of will and conduct have been isolated and judged as such. "'Tis an action of virtue," Dryden declared, "to make examples of vicious men. They may and ought to be upbraided with their crimes and follies: both for their own amendment, if they are not yet incorrigible; and for the terror of others, to hinder them from falling into those enormities which they see so severely punished in the person of others."[1]

On comparable grounds—the popular code of *in terrorem*—Trapp rejected Persius as a satirist who wanted "poignancy and sting." Here, the critic said, is one who "does not correct faults so much, as find them; his reproof, at best, is too mild, and more like the evenness of a philosopher, than the severity of a satirist."[2] Deterrence, the practical substitute for outright reformation, had long been argued as a rationale for satiric buffeting. Strongly worded satire, at least according to the premise, might temporarily provide readers with an illusion of transferred reality, a suspension of their own vulnerability. While the scapegoats suffer for varied transgressions, we are asked to believe, the general audience enjoy a feeling of liberation akin to catharsis as though they have nothing to do with animosities, vanities, and absurdities. But this sensation does not last, for reason soon informs that the aim of satire is not to anesthetize but to activate: there is no escaping universal guilt.

Satiric representation, in other words, should be a goad toward positive action, uniting in its readers aesthetic satisfaction and the ache of conscience. Those details that had earlier pleased them—the reproaches and recriminations heaped upon others—are inverted to become a burden of personal faults, a source of moral discomfort and remorse if not of outright pain.

1. Thomas R. Edwards, *Imagination and Power: A Study of Poetry on Public Themes* (New York: Oxford University Press, 1971), p. 86; Barten Holyday, "The Preface to the Reader" (Sig. A), trans., *Decimus Junius Juvenalis and Aulus Persius Flaccus* (Oxford, 1673); Dryden, *On Satire*, p. xxxv.
2. Joseph Trapp, *Lectures on Poetry*, pp. 235–36. For attacks *in terrorem*, see James Miller, *Seasonable Reproof, a Satire in the Manner of Horace* (1735). Cf. *Guardian* 71; *Monthly Review* 32 (1765): 400.

In censuring wrongdoing and foolishness, satire may set in motion the possibility of remedy (which can be the discontinuance
as well as the rectification of error): the innocent, forewarned
and innately scrupulous, are equipped to face their obligations;
the guilty, if capable of repentance, are moved to self-
redemption.

Disposed toward didacticism, satire best makes its points by
attending to sources and instances of failure in human behavior
or institutions. As part of his intention, the satirist criticizes contemporary shortcomings within a context whose values, ideally,
outlast occasions or crises of the moment. Whatever is specious
and debilitating, whatever is morally and socially corruptive,
these he cuts away as the preliminary condition for a cure. But
the disquiet caused by an abrasive satiric text is declared modified by its ultimate meliorism. Even the surgeon's probe can be
endured when the prognosis is favorable, as in the paradoxical
allusion of Pope's speaker to satire that "heals with morals what
it hurts with wit." Or in the vivid imagery of one of Pope's
eulogists:

> Oft Satire acts the faithful surgeon's part;
> Generous and kind, tho' painful is her art:
> Her optics all the dark disease explore,
> Her weapon lances wide the gangren'd sore;
> Deep wounds hypocrisy's fair-seeming skin,
> Where death in ulcerous humors lurks within:
> With caution bold, she only strikes to heal,
> Tho' folly burns to break the friendly steel.[3]

Such therapeutic benefits are more like formal promises than
realizable ideals; but their articulation by the satirist points to his
presumed humanity—his rejection of disabling weakness and
error, his hope for man's restored dignity.

Most satirists are realistic enough to understand that public
response to their complaints may be painfully long in coming, if
it comes at all. To dramatize this realization and also to under-

---

3. "Epistle to Augustus" [Horatian *Ep.* II. i], *Twickenham Pope*, 4:217, l. 262;
John Brown, *An Essay on Satire: Occasioned by the Death of Mr. Pope* (1745), ll.
147–54; cf. ll. 87–88: "Like the nice bee, with art most subtly true/ From
pois'nous vice extracts a healing dew."

score the naiveté and pride of Gulliver, Swift ironically permits his persona to expect the nearly instant reform of his fellow Englishmen. As Gulliver impatiently writes to his cousin Richard Sympson: "Instead of seeing a full stop put to all abuses and corruptions, at least in this little Island, as I had reason to expect, behold, after above six months warning, I cannot learn that my book hath produced one single effect according to mine intentions."[4] Imbued with a comfortless perception, Swift himself avoids such futility. Unlike Gulliver he does not set up a time schedule for human amendment, and he finds temporary release in bleak drollery while he waits. However mirthless Swiftian wit may sometimes be, it is never a disguise for indifference to or despair over man's fate. On the contrary, it deliberately taunts those who might be so wise and yet remain so stupid.

This is a deep and strange idealism, the antinomy of love and hate toward a single object with the ultimate inseparability of conflicting emotions. A *successful* satire engages its readers so that we share the satirist's point of view and his emotional strain. That is, we too recoil from the *alazons* and the self-seekers. Some of these become so plainly identifiable as to arouse suspicion of a vindictive satirist at work, and we do not intend to argue that the creation of a Mac Flecknoe or a Sporus, for example, did not afford their creators a degree of malicious pleasure. At the same time we recognize the expansion of seemingly literal or trifling matters until private disaffection becomes metaphoric statement for large public truths. Basic to this expansive literary experience, we suggest, is the poet's capacity for what Richards has called "tied images," an image-making quality that has the character of "a mental event peculiarly connected with sensation." Dryden and Pope enjoyed this faculty to an unusual degree, and though they indulged themselves in many a nasty swipe at their enemies, they were not assassins. For them, rather, as for the Renaissance poets who influenced them, "images have efficacy to move a reader's affections, to quite properly affect his

---

4. *Gulliver's Travels* in *Prose Works*, 11:6. See also W. B. Carnochan, *Lemuel Gulliver's Mirror for Man* (Berkeley and Los Angeles: University of California Press, 1968), p. 93, and pp. 15-51, "The Context of Satiric Theory."

judgments; they move him to feel intensely, to will, to act, to understand, to believe, to change his mind."[5]

The attack of an Alexander Campbell upon Johnson, by contrast, is memorable only for its expedience and pettiness. It evokes no associations beyond a more or less immediate occasion. Similarly, even Swift's more clever assault upon Partridge puts us on pleasant notice that a *reductio ad absurdum* is safely limited to one man and one set of circumstances. The "mental event" is circumscribed by its very particularity. Mac Flecknoe and Sporus, on the other hand, transcend themselves: "All writing with an overt or hidden satirical purpose . . . juxtapose[s] the grand and the trivial in order to bring out the triviality of the trivial. . . . An image using the figure meiosis momentarily allows the entrance into the poem of the purposes which in satire characterize the whole piece." The images created by Dryden and Pope give no evidence of pity or esteem for their culprits. But the poets do encourage the sympathy and compassion of the reader for those who have been tyrannized by the bad poetry and immorality that prevail as standards of culture and conduct. The satirist's concern is to track down and punish those he deems guilty of culpable error. But he is not merely an instrument of abstract justice. There is always the subjective tendency to associate himself with those who have been hurt by the wrongdoing of others. Implicitly, further, the personal equation is realizable when the satirist confronts actions that while blameworthy are not contaminated by gross cruelty or evil. Only an exceptionally arrogant person would fail to know that the fall from grace is as possible for himself as for the one who has already toppled. If a bond of sympathetic recognition connects the satirist and the victim of injustice, neglect, or selfishness, another less voluntary one provides a tie with the fallen victimizer. Without the indulgence of sentimentality, it seems to us, the satirist enters into an affinity (generic, to be sure, rather than explicit) with the culprit comparable to one expressed by

5. I. A. Richards, *Principles of Literary Criticism* (London: Routledge & Kegan Paul, 1949), p. 119; Rosemond Tuve, *Elizabethan & Metaphysical Imagery* (Chicago: Phoenix Books, University of Chicago Press, 1961), pp. 183, 215.

Boris Pasternak in a nonsatiric context: "No deep and strong feeling, such as we may come across here and there in the world, is unmixed with compassion."[6] The satirist is instinctively help-less to sever the human links even while he is being provoked to inflict the remedial pain of derision or anger.

II

The connotations of the word *satire* have changed so exten-sively that we need to be reminded that its present application is considerably less elaborate and ritualized than it would have been in Roman times or in the eighteenth century. Many of its formal implications have either vanished or been subordinated by affective and conceptual priorities. Commonly, now, *satire* suggests modality, a state of mind or feeling, a critical outlook on some detail or quality of existence. Earlier, however, satire had been responsible for a more complex set of possibilities, convey-ing not only a notion of meaning but of form as well. Classical satire was understood to be simultaneously tenor and vehicle; it absorbed an aggregate of opinions that aimed toward rhetorical and aesthetic distinction and that were organized according to principles of formal structure. When Quintilian, excessively pa-triotic, brags that satire emerges from Roman rather than Greek genius—*Satira quidem tota nostra est*—he obviously has in mind a well-defined genre that can be discussed alongside others like elegy, lyric, tragedy, and comedy.[7]

Although he acknowledges the primacy of formal verse satire such as that of Horace and Persius, he also pays tribute to the older Menippean kind represented by Terentius Varro (ca. 116-127 B.C.), *vir Romanorum eruditissimus*.[8] There is room also, then, for the intellectual, structurally diversified medley that ranges from Petronius and Apuleius to Rabelais, Burton, Swift, and Voltaire. Satire that observes certain organizational and

---

6. *Doctor Zhivago*, trans. Max Hayward and Manya Harari (New York: Panth-eon, 1958), p. 331. For a corrosive extension of this proposition, cf. Kenneth Burke's view of a sadomasochistic intention whereby "the satirist attacks in *others* the weaknesses and temptations that are really *within* himself. . . . [The satirist] *gratifies* and *punishes* the vice within himself. Is he whipped with his own lash? He is." *Attitudes toward History*, 1:62–69.

7. Quintilian, X. i. 93.

8. Quintilian, X. i. 94–95.

metrical principles may be a genre. But fidelity to familiar rules will not determine the conclusive interest or importance of specific satiric writing. Given the semantic flexibility of the key word *satire,* a random construct like Fielding's *Jonathan Wild* advances satiric motivation as fully as does any formal verse satire. The same might be said of other didactic fictions like *1984* and *Brave New World.* The human cosmos is too various, too mercurial, to be limited by the restraints of any one regularized "form."

Additionally, *satire* may be other than a genre; or it may be a part of some other genre. *Satire,* that is, though often connoting a kind, may also convey adjectival attributes. *Roderick Random* and *Tristram Shandy,* frequently discussed in this connection, are novels containing satiric passages. *Bleak House* and *Ulysses* are not satires in the generic sense, and yet they assimilate satiric moments, scenes, and characters. The same could be said of plays by Wilde and Shaw, or of certain poems by Browning and Auden. Nor is the use of satiric interludes—phrases, descriptions, occurrences, analogies—confined to strictly literary performances. There exists a large body of works whose primary purpose is nonliterary polemic. Consider the high incidence of satiric statement in the sermons of Tillotson and Hoadly and in the pamphlets and speeches of Burke. Swift is a splendidly evocative political writer who uses satiric strategies without losing sight of his quarry. He "always prefers to move in a straight line, attacking directly down the middle, dividing his enemies to the left and to the right, passing through them unharmed and leaving them to their mutual destruction." The polemics and militancy are present, as surely as in Juvenal. The *Drapier's Letters* and the *Examiner* essays are not formal satires, to be sure, any more than *Gulliver's Travels* is formal. We may hesitate to call Swift's *Letters* and other journalistic pieces "satires." But we need have no hesitation at all about calling them satiric, just as we confidently identify the *Travels* as *a* satire.[9]

9. Herbert Davis, "Political Satire," *Jonathan Swift: Essays on his Satire and other Studies* (New York: Galaxy, Oxford University Press, 1964), p. 134. Cf. Edward W. Rosenheim, Jr., *Swift and the Satirist's Art* (Chicago: University of Chicago Press, 1963), p. 168, who calls the *Drapier's Letters* "literal polemic" as opposed to satire. See also chs. 4 and 5 below on religious and political satire. For the normative problem of genre, see Elliott, *The Power of Satire,* pp. viii, 185.

At its highest level, the satiric impulse is humanistic, its essence a tough-minded dedication that—to paraphrase Pope—wishes the world well. Satire, when thus broadly motivated, weeps, scolds, and ridicules, generally with one major end in view: to plead with man for a return to his moral senses. The ideal, to be sure, often becomes mere pretense, a transparent screen for verbal hair-pulling, which figures prominently in the satiric outpouring of the eighteenth century. Unbridled vituperation often brought private vendettas into the public domain so that reputations fell with casual regularity. The quarrels themselves have become legendary and beyond need of further examination here. Their impact on and relationship to the satiric temper, however, become integral to the larger problems that we are attempting to treat. One of the most notorious slanging matches on record, between Pope and Lady Mary Wortley Montagu, provides vivid instances of low thoughts in high places. On one occasion, thus, like a devotee of the ancient fliting, Pope abused his "furious Sappho" with charges of lewdness and slander. Though otherwise unnamed, Lady Mary appears to have had no doubt that she was meant and—according to contemporary gossip—retaliated immediately. In exchange for two uncharitable lines, Pope found himself vilified as an "angry little monster" in a "wretched little carcass," his deformity the brand of Cain. Of course, long before 1733 Pope had been mauled by other adversaries for crimes of plagiarism, literary incompetence, ingratitude (to Addison), obscenity, Catholicism, physical infirmity, and so on.[10] "Satire" of this order was as often as not a rambling excuse for blatant malice.

10. For the quarrels involving Pope with Lady Mary and others, see Robert Halsband, *The Life of Lady Mary Wortley Montagu* (Oxford: Clarendon Press, 1956), pp. 140–43; J. V. Guerinot, *Pamphlet Attacks on Alexander Pope: 1711–1744, a Descriptive Bibliography* (London: Methuen, 1969); *Twickenham Pope*, 4:13; *Correspondence*, II, 185. *Verses Address'd to the Imitator of the First Satire of the Second Book of Horace* (1733) may be by Lady Mary, but see Halsband. See also the anonymous retort, *A Proper Reply to a Lady, Occasion'd by her Verses* (1733). For further consideration: *The Female Dunciad* (1728); Sir Butterfly Maggot, *The Gentleman's Miscellany; . . .*, 2d ed. (1730); Leonard Welsted's venomous pamphlet ("A little monk thou wert. . . . A pimp at altars, or in courts a spy!") *Of Dulness and Scandal. Occasion'd by the Character of Lord Timon in Mr. Pope's Epistle to the Earl of Burlington* (1732) [Foxon, *Catalogue*, 1:878]; Mr. Gerard, *An Epistle to the Egregious Mr. Pope, in Which the Beauties of His Mind and Body are Amply Display'd* (1734) [Foxon, *Catalogue*, 1:303, suggests "Gerard" may be Eustace Budgell].

Charged phrasing has also served a great many writers who were disaffected by the world and its follies but who nevertheless were not prepared to turn their backs on humanity. Idealistic in spirit but realistic by avocation and necessity, satirists seldom look for remedies in monastic withdrawal. The idiom of shock and outrage frequently predicates conviction, which the satirist hopes to induce in his readers; and this transfer of emotions can be antecedent to reparation and redemption. Repair, it is almost trite to observe, cannot begin until the rot has been laid bare; and what satire reveals its readers are expected to help eradicate. The immediate incentive for exposure is the author's anger, hatred, contempt, and those other allied passions that Quintilian associated with *pathos*. Such expressions of emotion are in effect the creative spark of *facit indignatio versum*.[11] At times the *indignatio* is so overwhelming that it obscures the *humanitas*. But the reader should beware of subordinating interior purpose to surface effect, especially when the satirist works alterations in tone and theme.

Of a writer like Juvenal, for example, there is a frequent suspicion—even by learned students of his work—that he gloats over the punishment of wrongdoers. Surmise like this is not easily withstood when we confront language so expressive of contempt that it appears to derive from passionate authorial feeling. Juvenal's depiction of the miserly glutton's death (I. 210-19), to cite one example, may indeed send out vindictive echoes:

> Ev'n parasites are banish'd from his board:
> (At once a sordid and luxurious lord:)

This gross creature, "the peacock raw"

> He bears into the bath; whence want of breath,
> Repletions, apoplex, intestate death.
> His fate makes table-talk, divulg'd with scorn,
> And he, a jest, into his grave is borne.

As in these lines, so also in those describing the murder of Domitian (IV. 254-55), a subjective note of exhilaration spills forth:

> But when he dreadful to the rabble grew,
> Him, who so many lords had slain, they slew.

11. Quintilian, VI. ii. 8-20; Loeb *Juvenal*, I. 79.

Or again, Juvenal's grim view of modern man seems unambiguous when he asserts that "serpents now more amity maintain" than do human beings (XV. 202).[12] If all this invites belief in Juvenalian spite, we can also insist that presumptive evidence does not suffice. We must not overlook the reasonable likelihood that the poet meant instances of depravity to be interpreted as symbolic moral exempla, antidotes to enervating selfishness, cruelty, and perversion. In Juvenal as later in Swift, the astringent touch is necessitated by distrust of softer statement: "Being corrective, [satire] tends to compensate excess with excess; if mild reproof and counsel could succeed, the satirist would have nothing to do."[13] Juvenal's vision of the punishment visited upon the glutton, though not so pointedly affective as the depiction by Dante in the third circle of the *Inferno* (Canto VI), centers similarly in a humanistic intention. Juvenal, furthermore, refusing to represent only viciousness, also provides contrapuntal interludes of calm, near-sentimental exposition when he contrasts a lawless present with a virtuous past:

> Oh happy ages of our ancestors,
> Beneath the kings and tribunitial powers!
> One jail did all their criminals restrain;
> Which, now, the walls of Rome can scarce contain.
> [III. 490-93]

Such digressions do not encourage pastoral retreat. Rather they function elegiacally, as complaints that man's capacity for reverence, peace, and love suffers paralysis, its cause an indulgent and bloated modernity.

Neither nostalgia for the past, however, nor indignation with the present completes the moral limits of Juvenal's intention. He directed his commitment to the future, hoping his literary effec-

---

12. See, for example, William S. Anderson, *Anger in Juvenal and Seneca* (Berkeley: University of California Press, 1964). Translations are by Dryden et al.

13. Ernest Tuveson, "Swift: The View from within the Satire," *The Satirist's Art*, ed. H. James Jensen and Malvin R. Zirker, Jr. (Bloomington and London: Indiana University Press, 1972), p. 68. For an example of the antithetical view, that satire does not correct or reform, but merely reveals "incongruities, absurdities," and the like see P. K. Elkin, *The Augustan Defence of Satire* (Oxford: Clarendon Press, 1973), pp. 200-201.

tiveness would one day be felt as a source of individual and communal good. Hume put his finger on a timeless benevolent compulsion: Juvenal, he concluded, wrote satire that would encourage "larger opportunities of spreading our kindly influence than what are indulged to the inferior creation. It must, indeed, be confessed, that by doing good only, can a man truly enjoy the advantages of being eminent."[14]

As Juvenal's English heir, Swift also elaborates on man's failure to acquit himself decently. So blistering is his condemnation of mankind at times, so undeniable his eagerness "to vex the world," that he himself appears devoid of all compassion and humanity. We ask, is *he* in fact the Brobdingnagian king who "cannot but conclude the bulk of your natives to be the most pernicious race of little odious vermin that nature ever suffered to crawl upon the surface of the earth"? Indeed, Swift is not satisfied to let mere descriptive words carry the burden of his nausea and rage; they are only anticipatory. The intensity of feeling mounts in the *Travels,* the savage rhetoric of the second voyage becoming a scenario for the grotesque imagery and actions of the third and fourth voyages. And yet, although the affective impact of the *Travels,* by the time Gulliver reaches the land of the Houyhnhnms, becomes almost unbearable, Swift's intention suggests a regenerative possibility. If he appears to annihilate, he does so only in order to build anew. True, he stands forth as a deadly enemy of fragmented man, of the one whose conduct is mob-controlled or professionalized, dominated by inhumane or irrational desires. But he wishes to substitute for the defaced creature John, Peter, and Thomas, whom he loves because they live and act like integrated persons uniting body and soul, pity and discrimination, faith and reason.[15]

14. David Hume, "Of Benevolence," *Essays Moral, Political, and Literary,* ed. T. H. Green and T. H. Grose, 2 vols. (London: Longmans Green, 1875), 2:175. Cf. W. B. Carnochan, "Satire, Sublimity, and Sentiment: Theory and Practice in Post-Augustan Satire," *PMLA* 85 (Mar. 1970): 260–67; and Thomas B. Gilmore, "The Politics of Eighteenth-Century Satire," *PMLA* 86 (Mar. 1971): 277–80.

15. "A Voyage to Brobdingnag," *Prose Works,* 11:132; to Pope, 29 Sept. 1725, Swift, *Correspondence,* 3:103. R. S. Crane argues that Swift, reacting against the logicians whom he had studied at Trinity College, meant to undermine the concept of man's rationality: "The Houyhnhnms, the Yahoos, and the History of

Those who insist on portraying Swift as a wanton destroyer also insist on reading *Gulliver's Travels* as an autobiographical document rather than as an observant moral fiction in which Gulliver is not an actual person. As a persona, the seaman undergoes a change of mind and soul through which Swift chooses to symbolize England's maladies: the change is from error to error, from an absolute faith in the moral and social standards of a flawed civilization to an unthinking repudiation of humanity itself. Neither way is advocated by the satirist, for, if *Gulliver's Travels* is a distorting mirror, it is one in which readers, profiting from the experiences of the principal, may see their own faults magnified. Ironically, Gulliver concludes sixteen years as a modern Odysseus without having achieved for himself either the wisdom or instruction that he professes to have deeded to mankind. He thinks himself superior to all other Yahoos and yet fails to reconcile himself to the goodness and humane understanding of Captain Pedro de Mendez. Far from being superior, Gulliver demonstrates that he has never surrendered his attachment to that "sublime and refined point of felicity, called, *the possession of being well deceived;* the serene peaceful state of being a fool among knaves."[16] For responsive readers to be identified with obtuseness like this is unflattering, but Swift seems to make the point that self-discovery leading to a reassertion of ethical values—if it comes—will justify their initial anger and hurt. Implicitly, Swift demands that they affirm their Christian legacy and redeem themselves as men whose passions, when directed by reason, are gloriously relevant to human endeavor.

It is not the satirist but his persona who would withdraw from an imperfect society of men to a soulless one of animals. It is not the satirist but his persona who repeatedly shows weakness of ethical perception; and it is the persona who finally proves that *humanitas* has deserted him. The blindness, hence, is not

Ideas," in *Reason and the Imagination: Studies in the History of Ideas 1600–1800*, ed. J. A. Mazzeo (New York and London: Columbia University Press and Routledge & Kegan Paul, 1962), pp. 231–53. Cf. Elliott (p. 215), who treats Swift as a humanist.

16. *A Tale of a Tub* (sec. ix), *Prose Works*, 1:110.

Swift's—he sees all too clearly—but Gulliver's. In shocking us with a bitter tabulation of our own faults and of Gulliver's, Swift means to warn that as the first step in a program of moral rehabilitation we too must see how we can be better. If a satire like his fails to reach us in a positive way, perhaps we are reluctant to align ourselves with Swift, or prefer to ignore the reverberations of a masked love for individuals and a *humanitas* in favor of a spectacular and entertaining misanthropy.

Although his ideals have been endangered by misunderstanding or hostility, the satirist hints that he will never surrender the struggle to make men profoundly sensitive to the imperfections he *must* expose. A latter-day Jacob, he gives the impression of wrestling courageously, not with angels, but with mortals and for their own redemption:

> Lives there a man, who calmly can stand by,
> And see his conscience ripp'd with steady eye?
>
> [215-16]

Whether the satirist, as in these lines from *The Author,* is Charles Churchill or someone less notorious, we know that in theory he commits himself to an ethical role that asserts man's deep need for self-scrutiny. Satire, Auden observes, "pre-supposes conscience and reason as the judges between the true and the false, the moral and the immoral to which it appeals."[17] Yet even as an act of conscience, satire appears often to be the handiwork of a public scold. Unfortunately, when a writer feels that he must beat his audience into a state of active good will, he may produce more bruises than benevolence. Such becomes the risk many satirists have chosen to take, often acknowledging their mission through aggressive metaphors. Umbricius of Juvenal's third satire seems hardly able to contain his belligerence when, in the concluding lines, he volunteers, *saturarum ego, ni pudet illas, / Adjutor gelidos veniam caligatus in agros* ("I shall assist you in the writing of your satires if you consider me worthy of the task.

---

17. *The Poetical Works of Charles Churchill,* ed. Douglas Grant (Oxford: Clarendon Press, 1956); W. H. Auden, "Interlude: West's Disease," *The Dyer's Hand,* pp. 240–41.

And I shall come to your aid across the frozen fields wearing my soldier's boots").[18] The dynamic Roman, fitting out his persona in military attire, serves notice that ideals must not be compromised by a truce.

When Johnson rendered Juvenal's closing lines for *London,* he relaxed the particularized militancy of the original. Artistically, this does not surprise, for he was writing in the deliberative high style that characterizes his poetry. But more important, the softer exposition satisfied his didactic need; it gave him a means to synthesize his argument, to make plain his own plea for the exercise of virtue and good will:

> Then shall thy friend, nor thou refuse his aid,
> Still foe to vice, forsake his Cambrian shade;
> In virtue's cause once more exert his rage,
> Thy satire point, and animate thy page.
>
> [260–63]

By comparison with Juvenal's brusque rhetoric, Johnson's holds back somewhat. The polite exhortation, which suggests his own reflective intelligence, also provides a new frame for the Roman's well-meant but contentious *indignatio.* The explicitly martial tone of Juvenal has vanished, although Johnson has preserved a modified image of angry comrades who can be depended upon to join together in the use of satire for the benefit of mankind, "in virtue's cause." But the reader's feelings need no further prompting, and emotive idiom is no longer pertinent. Having spent his passion in the main text of the poem, Johnson uses the conclusion as a resting place, a locus for the final thoughtful and restrained appeal to conscience. The opening of the poem, which describes Thales' departure in interrelated terms of sorrow and modulated anger, testifies to the poet's good nature; the closing, equally "mournful" lines confirm the consistence of his intention.

Not many satirists in the Juvenalian tradition could match Johnson's verbal moderation. The more common practice was to

18. For the Juvenalian image, cf. letter to Robert Nugent, 14 Aug. 1740, Pope's *Correspondence,* 4:257. *Adjutor,* the favored seventeenth- and eighteenth-century reading, appears in Johnson's Latin text appended to *London, Poems,* p. 61. *Auditor* is now preferred.

adopt a truculent pose that suggested harsh outrage. From such artifice Marston produced a *Scourge of Villainy* (1598), which pulsated with threat:

> Preach not the Stoic's patience to me;
> I hate no man, but men's impiety.
> My soul is vex'd, what power will'th desist?
> Or dares to stop a sharp fang'd satirist?
> Who'll cool my rage? who'll stay my itching fist
> But I will plague and torture whom I list?
>
> [I. ii. 5–10]

He proclaims himself the champion of "fair Religion," and yet he makes it hard to accept an avowal of conscience that must be enforced by the "knotty rod" of satire. Marston's *humanitas* lacks credibility if only because his language, gruffly explicit, elicits inquisitorial fear rather than love or conviction.

Joseph Hall likewise resorted to overstatement in an attempt to be persuasive. Hence the "biting satires" that comprise the second half of *Virgidemiae* (1597–1598) were meant to delineate the ruthless vigor with which man's most serious failings must be treated.[19] Included among these are such transgressions as the pride of inherited greatness, the brutal power of economic oppression and actual warfare, the self-absorption of moral degeneracy and domestic misconduct, the vapid submission to Catholic dogma. To show his aversion to fainthearted complaint, Hall drives home zealous conclusions as though syntax and language are heavy nails to fasten down idea after idea. With the crude directness of "hot-blooded rage," he demands that

> The satire should be like the porcupine,
> That shoots sharp quills out in each angry line,
> And wounds the blushing cheek, and fiery eye,
> Of him that hears and readeth guiltily.
>
> [V. iii. 1–4]

Even more evocative than the "harvest of rods" denoted by *virgidemia* on which Hall based his title, the porcupine quills are aptly metaphoric of the satirist's prickly art. (Later writers—such as John Oldham, Macnamara Morgan, William Kenrick, William

---

19. Hall's satires are also frequently designated *Virgidemiarum*.

Cobbett—borrowed the metaphor or adapted it: "Peter Porcupine" and "Porcupinus Pelagius"; *The Porcupinade, The Porcupiniad, The Porcupine, Porcupine's Political Censor.*) Vividly tactile, Hall's image summoned forth what became a convention, an image of holy rage well barbed.

But not all human failings repel equally or deserve equal castigation. Although never really moderate or conservative in his recriminations, Hall does go through the motions of selective criticism, reserving—he tries to make us believe—his severity for the worst offenses and offenders. To afford a semblance of humanity, he appropriates the subtitle "Of Toothless Satires" for the first three books of the *Virgidemiae.* He thus implies that the weaknesses encompassed in their topics—"poetical, academical, moral"—do not cry out for piercing satire. But he stretches actuality, and there is more mockery than truth in the subtitle. Note, as an instance from the first series, the rancor with which he attacks the contemporary theater:

> Now when they part and leave the naked stage,
> 'Gins the bare hearer in a guilty rage,
> To curse and ban, and blame his likerous eye,
> That thus hath lavish'd his late half-penny.
> Shame that the Muses should be bought and sold,
> For every peasant's brass, on each scaffold.
>
> [I. iii. 53–58]

His tone is not convincingly milder in the "Toothless Satires" than in the "Biting Satires" of the second series. Patently ironical, then, Hall describes the untoothed satires as "gentle," a mild prelude to the sterner poems to follow, like whiplashes on "galled hides."

But Milton, who would not ignore a chance (even belatedly) to repudiate Hall, insisted on the impropriety of gentle satire. Presumably, he chose to gloss over the irony of Hall's categorical scheme. "A 'toothless satire,'" Milton retorted, "is as improper as a toothed sleekstone, and as bullish." Satire that does not bite, in other words, he holds to be anomalous. Inferentially, to pursue the simile, satire, such as Hall describes, is as counterproductive as a defective whetstone that destroys a knife's edge; and it is like a papal bull that—in Milton's Protestant ethic—confronts sin with indulgences. Ascribing to tragedy the origin of satire, Milton took offense at a title that seemed to treat grave matters flippantly. And further, by entering into a debate with the satirist, he had an opportunity to advance their ideological differences. Fiercely religious, Milton wanted "to rip up the wounds of Idolatry and Superstition."[20] Neither Hall nor Milton is malicious, both being virtuous men who mean to eradicate only the morbid and to assert the desirability of moral health and growth. Separated by an unbreachable theological fence, however, they were bound to disagree not only about ideas and faith but about the uses of satire in connection with them.

The image of satire as weapon is conventional and does not necessarily reflect an author's attitude toward his purpose. For that matter, the ingredients of satire are often combined in such an intricate mix of topic, image, tone, and the like that meaning cannot be flatly pinpointed. We can sympathize with the dilemma of one "unspecialized" reader, who concludes that "the satirist may have a bundle of intentions, not altogether harmonious, and he may even be unstable in his distribution of emphasis between his various intentions."[21] The well-taken stricture is a useful warning against insistence on *the* interpretation when more than one may be reasonable. A single-minded or unitary approach can lead only to dogmatism, which works if we can be certain the satirist himself is dogmatic. Furthermore, no convenient gauge exists for determining how tightly the satirist has turned the screw of painful intention or intentions. Each reader must decide that for himself on a private scale measuring his own tolerance to shock, derision, or vexation. For philosophical comfort he may eventually turn to Schiller, who in

20. *Animadversions upon the Remonstrants Defence, against Smectymnuus* [1641] and *An Apology against a Pamphlet call'd a Modest Confutation of the Animadversions upon the Remonstrant against Smectymnuus* [1642], in *The Works of John Milton*, 18 vols. in 21 (New York: Columbia University Press, 1931–1938), 3:114, 317; Pope in "Epigram. Occasion'd by Ozell's Translation of Boileau's Lutrin": "Nor had the toothless satire caus'd complaining, / Had not sage Rowe pronounced it entertaining."

21. Jacob Viner, "Satire and Economics in the Augustan Age of Satire," *The Augustan Milieu: Essays Presented to Louis Landa,* ed. Henry Knight Miller, Eric Rothstein, and G. S. Rousseau (Oxford: Clarendon Press, 1970), p. 78.

1795–1796 speculated that the satirist, by making him react against *empörender Wirklichkeit* (disgusting reality), enables him to transcend the limits of experience and apprehend the ideal. The author's massing of unpleasant particularities prepares the mind for something higher and better than the merely sensuous and temporal. Or, if the reader prefers the homelier resources of literary criticism, inference and analysis inform him that satirists frequently arouse revulsion so that they may stimulate correction. Surely Smollett intended this partially in the naval scenes of *Roderick Random,* which contain hideous enactments of brutality and injustice. Comparably—in a graphic milieu—Hogarth's plates *The Four Stages of Cruelty* (1751) are emblematic of an all-embracing sadism, beginning with the torture of dogs, cocks, cats, and birds and culminating with murder and the dissection of criminals. The cycle depicts the career of Tom Nero from street rowdy to highwayman, thence to thieving murderer of the pregnant Ann Gill, and to his own physical destruction. The grisly irony initiated by the barbarous victimization of animals terminates with Nero himself the eviscerated prey of anatomists and a hungry dog. Hogarth's reformist intention is patent. To clinch the point, however, he deplored his need to describe what offended the sight, "but it could not be done in too strong a manner as the most stony hearts were meant to be affected" by the prints.[22]

When a satirist concentrates meticulous detail upon the ugly and the vicious, as Hogarth does in this instance, his motives verge upon the puritanical in their severity. He bares man's depravity to express his own concern and to attempt sharing that concern with his audience. The indignation is his; but he wishes to implant it among his readers. Similarly, he initiates through satire awareness of a need for improvement; but the individual—reader or satirist—cannot undertake to reform others without a conscious desire for self-betterment. Metaphor

---

22. Johann Christoph Friedrich von Schiller, "Über naive und Sentimentalische Dichtung," *Sämtliche Werke,* ed. Otto Güntter and Georg Witkowski, 20 vols. in 10 (Leipzig, 1910), 17:479 ff. (esp. 510–17); *Hogarth's Graphic Works,* ed. Ronald Paulson, 2 vols. (New Haven and London: Yale University Press, 1965), 1:211–12; 2:plates 201–14.

may serve these ends when, for example, "Ithuriel's spear" is borrowed from *Paradise Lost* as an instrument of satiric exposure and reproach. In a related way, allusion to classical myth, as to that of "Alecto's whip," can sometimes intensify the resonance and meaning of a satiric passage.[23]

The hazards of overuse are of course always imminent, for custom will stale or weaken all but the most forceful images. The quintessential verb "lash" is a rhetorical embarrassment, appearing so repeatedly in satire that it becomes mechanical. Perhaps it cracks out in sadistic purpose, but it soon ceases to be the dreadful tool of vengeance supposed to frighten us. Satire produces other stereotyped weaponry, much of it described in fairly stiff, commonplace terms like "nettles or thorns." Or in a dream allegory (*Spectator* 63) Addison portrays Satire as a dualistic creature wearing "smiles in her look, and a dagger under her garment." Johnson's allegorized Satire (*Rambler* 22), reminiscent of the porcupine similitude, is the conventional son of Wit and Malice, a vindictive archer carrying "a quiver filled with poisoned arrows, which, where they once drew blood, could by no skill ever be extracted." Although Addison and Johnson on occasion retain some of the warlike symbols typical of satire and its descriptive commentary, they do so only formally and without heat. They do not take exception to the moral bases of satiric theory. On the contrary, they acknowledge that ideally satire is a valid means to harass fools and evildoers into reason.[24] They object not to satire but its abuse, protesting that it can become an

23. Wild, "Iter Boreale" [1660], *POAS*, 1:4 (ll. 9-10); "An Elegy on the Much Lamented Sir William Waller, Who Valiantly Hang'd Himself at Rotterdam" [1683], *POAS*, 3:464-65 (ll. 1-16); Swift, "An Epistle to a Lady" [1733], *Poems*, 2:635, ll. 179-80. Cf. Hall, *Virgidemiae*, in *Poems*, bk. V, Sat. 3; and anon., *A Satyr against Common-Wealths* (1684). See also ch.5.

24. For "nettles" and "thorns," cf. Abraham Cowley, "Of Agriculture," *Essays, Plays, and Sundry Verses*, ed. A. R. Waller (Cambridge: Cambridge University Press, 1906), p. 406; and Jean Paul Richter and Samuel Taylor Coleridge, in *Coleridge's Miscellaneous Criticism*, pp. 118 and *n.*, and 441-42. To Arbuthnot, 26 July 1734, Pope, *Correspondence*, 3:419: "To reform and not to chastise, I am afraid is impossible, and that the best precepts, as well as the best laws, would prove of small use, if there were no examples to enforce them . . . to chastise is to reform. The only sign by which I found my writings ever did any good or had any weight, has been that they rais'd the anger of bad men."

underground instrument of libel and malice. They object to levity that derides when gravity is in order or that mocks vice and folly but fails to clear a path to amendment. In *Spectator* 249 Addison, supporting his contention with an epigraph from Menander, held that misdirected laughter harms. Ridicule, if falsely conceived, forces satire to "laugh men" not out of their errors but "out of virtue and good sense," by attacking everything solemn and serious, decent and praiseworthy in human life. When, conversely, ridicule is properly conceived—as in *Don Quixote* and (despite an Addisonian reservation) *Hudibras*—then satire fulfills its just and justifiable intention.

In his own approach to human weakness, Addison attacks the silly and the foolish with laughter so gentle that the line between comedy and satire comes near to being erased. But whether his attack be comic or satiric, he remains a guardian of the "praiseworthy." His meaning, however light the representation, eschews frivolity. Sir Roger de Coverley becomes an object of fun when (in *Spectator* 115) he stands revealed as a vain, indefatigable hunter of small animals whose remains—noses and ears and pelts—he mounts as trophies on salon walls and barn doors. Although Addison writes about the squire's exploits without specific derogation, he forwards an unmistakable moral issue through simple exposition and dramatic contrast. Man as "a compound of soul and body" has the double obligation of employing each day "in labor and exercise, as well as . . . in study and contemplation." By means of a structural trick—planting a description of Sir Roger's activities in the midst of a serious discussion about what constitutes effort and productivity—the essayist mocks the squire's fatuousness, his imprudent expenditure of time and energy. Addison's method dramatizes man's frailty under a thin cover of ethical assumption. The critical point of view is decisively his, but he invites the reader to share it: he supplies the data but the reader makes his own transition from amiable particularization to stern generality. The process is akin to that recently described as "transformational." In other words, a creative collaboration exists between author and reader, in the course of which the latter transforms the literary experience into a personal one. The written work must always remain primary, of course, but each reader reconstructs it in the spirit of his own response.[25]

Aiming, like Addison, toward mild-mannered derision—this time of antiquaries and collectors of trivia—Johnson concentrates upon two rhetorical devices. The first is that of ironical language: for instance, in *Rambler* 82 his supposed correspondent, unwittingly self-betrayed, comments: "I never entered an old house, from which I did not take away the painted glass, and often lamented that I was not one of that happy generation who demolished the convents and monasteries, and broke windows by law." The second related device is that of the significant name to identify personality or occupation. The personality of the correspondent is satirically defined and measured by his name Quisquilius, from *quisquiliae,* "the waste or refuse of anything."[26] As a man he is no more important than the fragile slivers of glass that he collects. In gibing at the innocuous but nonetheless wasteful social behavior of Quisquilius, Johnson makes clear that he is not confined to the Juvenalian accents of tragedy, which appeared in *London* and *The Vanity of Human Wishes.* Like Addison, he shows himself to be a good-natured prose satirist. Through a combination of comedy and polite mockery he hopes to provoke his audience to amused contempt and pity for those who are merely inane and indifferent to their role as human beings.

### III

But not all critics concede generosity to satiric aims. To this day, indeed, some discover in satire a sadistic titillation that gives "the reader a kind of astringent pleasure like an acid drop or a dash of bitters." The satirist, were this explanation to be accepted, draws on a "malicious reservoir"; he produces "a licensed cathartic of envy, hatred, and malice, and all uncharitableness." The premise here is that he has found a valve to release

25. Earl Miner, "In Satire's Falling City," *The Satirist's Art,* pp. 3–27; cf. the comments of Wayne Booth and Wolfgang Iser, "In Defense of Authors and Readers," *Novel: A Forum on Fiction* 11 (Fall 1977): 6–24.

26. See E. A. Bloom, "Symbolic Names in Johnson's Periodical Essays," *MLQ* 13 (Dec. 1952): 333–52 [342].

his own bad temper and, vicariously, the reader's. In precisely such a mood La Bruyère spoke of the writer who falls upon his subjects "to ease him of his resentment." If we were to agree that "the general purpose of satire is not to cure . . . or reform [anyone of] anything," but simply to provide the enjoyment of public floggings, then it becomes little more than a peephole into human degradation. And pleasure in that case becomes a form of perversion for both writer and reader.[27]

Ever since its ceremonial beginnings in primitive cultures, when it had the authority of a curse upon one's enemies, satire was reputed to be nihilistic. But whereas an abundance of such writing can be mustered to support this reputation, we should shun the unqualified generalization. It has become habitual for many critics to see the obviously reductive but not the innately beneficial. The choice, oddly, is sometimes triggered by the satirists themselves. Whenever fervor, though honorable enough, carries forward an assault with a semblance of maenadic zest rather than of rational, imaginative appeal, readers are likely to shrink away. In the figurative ordeal by fire to which certain satirists subjected the errant, they often came closer to destroying than purifying. Sin and folly they made odious, but with such savagery that the rite of purification appeared vindictive rather than redemptive.

> More fierce, Archilochos! thy vengeful flame;
> Fools read and died: for blockheads then had shame.[28]

The passions that stimulate writers like Archilochos or Marston or Hall are so personal, so fired by indignation toward human discord, alienation, and failure, that the fury often darkens affirmation, no matter what they may protest otherwise.

But whether an image of satire's nihilism is advanced by the critics or the satirists themselves, the reproach has survived the

---

27. A. M. Clark, *Studies in Literary Modes* (Edinburgh and London: Folcroft, 1946), pp. 31–49; Jean de la Bruyère, "Of Polite Learning," *The Continental Model: Selected French Critical Essays of the Seventeenth Century*, ed. Scott Elledge and Daniel Schier (Ithaca, N.Y.: Cornell University Press, 1970), p. 338. In a related way, Elkin (p. 2) borrows the dubious generalization that seventeenth- and eighteenth-century satirists were merely self-interested, writing either defensively or maliciously.

28. Walter Harte, *An Essay on Satire* (1730), p. 14.

passage of centuries. After two hundred years, a critic-in-fiction like Wolfe continues to see Swift as an executioner mercilessly flaying man "with the scorpion lash of the most savage allegory ever written." Nabokov projects an even more extravagant version of the satirist's demon powers. With parodic vigor, as if he had borrowed Alecto to enforce the language and energy of retaliation, he depicts the stereotypical satirist as an avenger: "But how dangerous he was in his prime, what venom he squirted, with what whips he lashed when provoked! The tornado of his passing satire left a barren waste where felled oaks lay in a row, and the dust still twisted, and the unfortunate author of some adverse review, howling with pain, spun like a top in the dust." In a calmer mood, Charles Kinbote, the commentator of *Pale Fire,* admits to "a whiff of Swift in some of my notes. I too am a desponder in my nature, an uneasy, peevish, and suspicious man, although I have my moments of volatility and *fou rire.*" Still, Nabokov's persona implies, this "volatility and *fou rire*" serve only as antic interludes that offer no likelihood of lasting benevolence.[29]

Denial of regenerative satire would not have surprised readers in other centuries, paradoxically least of all those who lived in England's "Age of Satire." Certainly, it would have been familiar to one like Defoe, who himself had railed against the misuse of satire in the cause of malice and vituperation. Dismayed by the substitution of animosity and spite for wit and benevolence, he scolded because satire in his day had "no fancy, no brightness; there's nothing to keep the stench out of our noses; a man cannot say it is done clean." Such writing as Defoe described, and sometimes practiced for party hire, cast a shadow over legitimate satire and evoked indictments like that of Philip Yorke, who complained privately to Thomas Birch about "this idle age, which cares for nothing but a party pamphlet, a broadbottom journal, or a satire filled with spleen and ill nature." Charges considerably more bitter than this appear in writings intended for public consumption. Invective, it was repeatedly contended,

29. Thomas Wolfe, "Gulliver," *From Death to Morning* (New York: Grosset and Dunlap, 1948); Vladimir Nabokov, "Spring in Fialta," *Nabokov's Dozen* (Garden City, N.Y.: Doubleday, 1958); and *Pale Fire* (Harmondsworth, England: Penguin, 1973), p. 139.

had become the *lingua franca* of personal enmity, and success was as much dependent on the receptivity of nasty-minded readers as on the spleen of those who wrote for them. The disaffection of one early eighteenth-century pamphleteer becomes a howl of despair: "So corrupt and ungenerous are the hearts of a great part of mankind, that satire from the writer is apprehended to be in some measure panegyric upon the reader, and panegyric, satire."[30]

Protests of this sort had indeed become commonplace. Thus many years later, Charles Churchill, who could himself be guilty of "spleen and ill nature," self-righteously condemned Hogarth for "rancor" and vengefulness.[31] Aware that his mordant wit and vulgarisms made him readily vulnerable, Smollett anticipated attack from whatever quarter it might come, trying to set up his defenses in the perhaps ironic dedication to *Ferdinand Count Fathom* (1753). There he represented himself as a man of benevolent, instructive interests; an enemy of fraud, treachery, ignorance, and folly, to be sure, but one who in flaying human imperfection did so only to recall for his readers the virtues of humor, compassion, and indignation. It may be difficult to take Smollett seriously when he holds Fathom "up as a beacon for the benefit of the unexperienced and unwary." Nevertheless he does make the familiar gesture of treating a satiric subject—and such Fathom is in part—as a deterrent to "the practice of vice." If Smollett appears to indulge in lofty rationalization, he upholds literary tradition that insists upon pleading moral intention.

The essence of satire, we have suggested, is generally the symbol of an author's disappointment in, or even annoyance with, his world and its inhabitants. As though pulled between the tensions of love and hate, he needs to wound those for whom he harbors a coalition of sympathy and antagonism. Like the despairing parent who applies the verbal lash or the jeer as

---

30. Defoe, *Review*, 28 March 1713; Yorke to Birch, B. M. Add. MS 35,396, f. 173. Cf. *Some Considerations Humbly Offer'd, Relating to the Peerage of Great Britain* (1719), p. 35: "And as satire has ever been esteemed the easiest, as well as the lowest way of wit, so it becomes universally contemptible, when used upon subjects and persons that merit different treatment." See also *A Discourse on Ridicule* (1730).

31. "An Epistle to William Hogarth" [1763], Churchill, *Poetical Works*, pp. 213-30.

therapeutic instruments, he hopes that they will in time bring about a wholesomeness to compensate for the ache. What make the cruel accents of satire supportable are their echoes—however muffled—of authorial humaneness. Despite its surface lamentation, bitterness, or mockery, it attracts as a powerful vehicle of good-natured hope; not good-natured in the modern sense of easy-going compliance or mere kindliness, but in that defined by such men as Shaftesbury and Hutcheson.

While emphasizing the risible impulse identified with raillery, Shaftesbury noted: " 'Tis in reality a serious study to learn to temper and regulate that humor which nature has given us as a more lenitive remedy against vice, and a kind of specific against superstition and melancholy delusion. There is a great difference between seeking how to raise a laugh from everything, and seeking in everything what justly may be laughed at." He was attempting to lay down a moral basis for laughter as an antidote to human waywardness. There is nothing radical in that prescription. Many a satirist, indeed, for whom Horace was a congenial tutor could have accepted it without qualm. And yet no matter how benevolent, Shaftesbury was opposing a well-established tradition—philosophical as well as satirical—that jesting about grave matters is the devil's work. Raillery, as La Rochefoucauld had pithily remarked in the previous century, "is an injury disguised full of malice and ill nature." Shaftesbury persisted against such representative long-standing authority: "For nothing is ridiculous," he insisted, "except what is deformed; nor is anything proof against raillery except what is handsome and just. And therefore 'tis the hardest thing in the world to deny fair honesty the use of this weapon, which can never bear an edge against itself, and bears against everything contrary."[32] This, then, was Shaftesbury's license for the moral use of laughter and raillery.

We must recognize the limits of his influence on satire. At the

32. *Characteristics,* 1:85; "Mixed Thoughts, LXXV," *Moral Maxims and Reflections . . . by the Duke of Rochefoucault. Now made English* (1694), p. 191. See also Francis Hutcheson, *Reflections upon Laughter, and Remarks upon the Fable of the Bees* (Glasgow, 1750), p. 36. For the need to qualify or limit Shaftesbury's influence on satire, see Stuart M. Tave, *The Amiable Humorist: A Study in the Comic Theory and Criticism of the Eighteenth and Early Nineteenth Centuries* (Chicago: University of Chicago Press, 1960), p. 36.

same time, however, we should consider the tacitly sympathetic identification of the satirist's premises with his. Not all satirists, obviously, were responsive to the ever-widening atmosphere of sensibility. Nevertheless, a great many discovered, as had Shaftes-bury, outlets for good nature in matrices of wit and ridicule that still allowed a connection between charity and moral re-proach. In a parallel although more explicitly critical mood, numerous eighteenth-century satirists hoped that a smile would serve improvement faster than a snarl. Such satirists, moved by the affirmative possibilities of their calling, saw themselves as men of moral sentiment or compassion.

In this respect, satire is one of the literary "modes of feeling" (along with elegy and idyll) described by Schiller as being at-tuned to the contrariety between imperfect reality—*die Wirklichkeit als Mangel*—and the ideal, when considered the highest reality. That ideal should exercise man's spiritual dispo-sition; and the satirist must therefore evoke ridicule and indig-nation for what is corrupt and corruptive, veneration for what is suprasensuous and immutable. This aspiration to re-create the highest reality becomes the province of the tragic satirist—and to Schiller's examples of Juvenal, Swift, and Young we can add that of Johnson. But this same aspiration lies also within the sphere of the comic satirist, say, Cervantes, Fielding, Sterne. If the one weeps in sorrow and anger because of man's wickedness, the other laughs in wry compassion at his absurdities. Both, how-ever, are committed to a belief in man's fulfilling his talents as God bestowed them.

According to Schiller's thesis, satire is an inspiriting mode of discourse. But equally important, it belongs to a tradition of rhetoric, for one of the satirist's chief objectives, as we have already observed, must be persuasion. Specifically, he wishes to convince his audience that he correctly identifies the follies and vices that engage him as violations of ethical and social propri-ety. Too often, we know, the tone of disillusion is so close to that of unregulated contempt that it seems almost futile to distin-guish between the two. The cynicism of Rochester's attack upon man's false pride in rationality (*A Satire against Reason and Man-kind*) builds layer by layer until the shame of being human transcends any possibility of change. Becoming increasingly hostile, he challenges the notion that a humble or pious man can be found in his age and concludes with the misanthropic statement: "Man differs more from man, than man from beast."[33] Rochester has a powerful theme to convey, but he fails to make it more than superficially moving, for his rhetoric overpowers rather than supports conviction.

Refusing to effect a reconciliation between human potentiality and its abuse, he so emphasizes the latter as to tax belief. We miss the peripheral vision of a poem like *The Vanity of Human Wishes,* in which Johnson seems no less disaffected than Rochester by man's self-betrayal. Yet he does not turn away in angry despair. Rather he has the rhetorician's need to convert reproach into use:

> Must dull suspence corrupt the stagnant mind?
> Must helpless man, in ignorance sedate,
> Roll darkling down the torrent of his fate?
> Must no dislike alarm, no wishes rise,
> No cries attempt the mercies of the skies?
>
> [344-48]

He has seen too much of vanity to assume that man can find temporal solutions. But other resources exist: "Enquirer, cease, petitions yet remain" (349). Johnson's ultimate hope is that of divine intercession, and as long as this way remains open man is not lost. Johnson wishes to assure his audience that a bad action, as demonstrated in satire, should be the incentive for a good counteraction. Ideally, the satirist establishes a distaste for error and in so doing creates among his readers a reaffirmation of their obligations to supernal will. With greater specificity than many satirists, Johnson liked to spell out both the importance and prevalence of the moral self, which is for him the corollary of the good will postulated in classical rhetoric and ethics.

But good will alone, the satirist understands, is not a substitute for moral action. Nor, further, need severity of judgment be

---

33. *The Complete Poems of John Wilmot, Earl of Rochester,* ed. David M. Vieth (New Haven and London: Yale University Press, 1968). The *Satire* appeared in 1675.

confused with ill nature. As in rhetorical debate, the satiric impulse is often generated by intense emotion like rage or indignation; then it may reflect the author's turbulence, as though he were a frenzied Xerxes lashing the waves and trying to humble the winds. But that impulse is also frequently charged with a calmer affectiveness, a sympathy that resolves itself in pity. The two feelings, Aristotle observed in his *Rhetoric*, are polarized; yet they may and, in fact, do work within a single framework of intention. Thus, far in anticipation of Hobbes, he declared: "Most directly opposed to pity is the feeling called indignation. Pain at unmerited good fortune is, in one sense, opposite to pain at unmerited bad fortune, and is due to the same moral qualities. Both feelings are associated with good moral character; it is our duty both to feel sympathy and pity for unmerited distress, and to feel indignation at unmerited prosperity; for whatever is undeserved is unjust, and that is why we ascribe indignation even to the gods."[34]

By this standard the portrait of the rich Orgilio in *London* (194–209) catches the satirist's outrage as a breach of human and, seemingly, divine justice:

> Should heaven's just bolts Orgilio's wealth confound,
> And spread his flaming palace on the ground . . .

His lackeys turn the event into one of "public mourning" and treat him as a victim of "persecuting fate." The ironic depiction transparently excoriates the ways in which the legions of powerful men like Orgilio convert even acts of God—or nature—into self-advantage. Unearned affluence such as his arouses Johnson to taut anger, as though he has obeyed Aristotle's stricture, "to feel indignation at" and speak out against "unmerited prosperity."

---

34. Aristotle, *Rhetoric*, II. ix. 9–16. See Cicero, *De Oratore*, II. xxiv. 99 ff.; Thomas Hobbes, *Human Nature* (1650): 9. ii. The satirist, T. S. Eliot remarks in his introduction to Johnson's two verse satires, "is in theory a stern moralist castigating the vices of his time or place; and Johnson has a better claim to this seriousness than either Pope or Dryden" (London: Haslewood Books, 1930), p. 15. Cf. W. Jackson Bate, "Johnson and Satire Manqué," *Eighteenth-Century Studies in Honor of Donald F. Hyde,* ed. W. H. Bond (New York: The Grolier Club, 1970), pp. 145–60.

> Orgilio sees the golden pile aspire,
> And hopes from angry heav'n another fire.

Opposed to this indignation, but flowing from the same source of humane responsibility, arises our pity for Thales. Though paradoxically unheeded, he rather than Orgilio "wars with persecuting fate." He likewise suffers "unmerited distress," humiliated by "hated poverty" and "the varied taunt."

Johnson advances sympathy for Thales with each angry contention of man's injustice to his fellows. Then, almost overshooting the mark, poet and mask indulge in self-pity as they ponder the rhetorical question:

> Has heav'n reserved, in pity to the poor,
> No pathless waste, or undiscover'd shore [?]

The answer is obvious both to the satirist and those who read his poem. Their emotions fuse; their compassion for Thales, a "virtuous and worthy man," is strengthened by indignation toward persecutors who will allow him no "peaceful desart," no urban haven. The futility of his condition is captured by the climactic funereal rhythm: "SLOW RISES WORTH, BY POVERTY DEPRESS'D."

As a persuasive art indebted to rhetoric, satire attempts to transmit the strong convictions of its creator to its readers and thus implicate them in a particular set of emotions. A cunning artificer who spins out a pattern of feelings, he is also a moralist in whose tapestry he hopes can be discerned conclusions at once utilitarian and generous. Hence, he manipulates both his aesthetic and his rhetoric to accommodate an active, even militant, benevolence. He allows a sense of good will to be implied, if not actually stated. The result, to borrow D. W. Harding's excellent phrase, may be one of "regulated hatred," as in *A Modest Proposal* or *Humphry Clinker* or *Mansfield Park;* it may be one of pity riding tandem with indignation, as in *London;* it may be one of laugh-provoking censure, as in *Holy Willie's Prayer.* But whatever emerges as its prevailing disposition, satire articulates a controlled agitation and a feeling intelligence.[35]

35. "Regulated Hatred: An Aspect of the Work of Jane Austen," *Scrutiny* 8 (1940): 346–62.

IV

Seeking to establish their motivation in good nature, poets like Lucilius and Horace called their work *sermones*—a familiar, witty discourse—as counterpoint to the rigor commonly associated with *saturae*. Lucilius, whose contemporaries distrusted him for writing satires that wounded, indulged in euphemisms like *schedia* (improvisations) and *ludi* (games, play, sports). Despite his usual tartness, in short, he wished to imply that he had somehow skirted ill temper. For Horace, Lucilius was the predecessor who had helped him to set his own sights on a loftier, more sophisticated achievement. The art of satire, Horace said, consists in jesting that "oft cuts hard knots more forcefully and effectively than gravity." Lucilius had wit, he conceded, but it was "muddy" and therefore conducive to verbose, sluggish writing of a kind that nullified his "native gifts." It "is not quite enough," in Horace's opinion, "to make your audience grin from ear to ear, though a fine thing."[36] The felicity of satire lies in its inseparable amalgam of thematic and aesthetic rightness, of finely pointed ideas and of versification and wit perfectly in accord with them. As the good-natured satirist, Horace felt that he could persuade his readers to share his social intention if he created a delicate harmony of meaning and poetry. And this he believed he had done.

The urbanity of Horatian satire pleased readers discomfited by more sharply honed criticism. The "truth-telling" connoted by some kinds of satire, as Virginia Woolf observed, "implies disagreeableness. It is part of the truth—the sting and edge of it." A writer like Heinsius, on the other hand, while also looking for the truth of satire, did not so readily accept the sting of it. He believed that it should be closer to comedy than tragedy, jeering at, not berating, vice; and he therefore elevated the Horatian above the Juvenalian, typifying a common urge to flinch away from, even to fear, one who will not "go gentle." But far from having it all his own way, Horace became a principal in a spirited

36. Horace, *Satires*, I. x and II. 1; *Satires and Epistles of Horace*, trans. Smith Palmer Bovie (Chicago: Phoenix Books, University of Chicago Press, 1959), p. 77.

critical contest flourishing from the Renaissance onward, to determine whether he or Juvenal could be declared preeminent. Nothing conclusive emerged from dispute over two rightly celebrated poets. The quarrel did however make for lively discussion, in which the "bravery of chastisement" was closely linked with decorum. Whatever scruples Holyday had about Juvenalian "license," he reconciled himself to uncommonly strong language and imagery as correctives of gross behavior. By being made to see our own inadequacies in the flaws of others, he argued, we often react with a sense of personal ignominy, and "are naturally driven from acts of shame."[37]

Thus viewed as a preacher in verse, Juvenal won the admiration of Rigaltius and the Scaligers. Although the tradition of comparing Juvenal with Horace was strong, English writers hesitated to make an absolute judgment. After much hedging, Dryden—who identified satire as a form of moral philosophy— finally gave higher marks to Juvenal. Horace, he said, may be the better instructor (being more general); but Juvenal demands our respect as a splendid teacher and a better poet as well: "The meat of Horace is more nourishing; but the cookery of Juvenal more exquisite." A severe youthful Addison, writing just a year before Dryden in 1692, likewise found both poets to be "perfect masters in their different ways." Before arriving at this conclusion, he implied reservations about Horace's personal conduct, which he contrasted with Juvenal's rigid virtue. On balance, nevertheless, Addison justified them equally as spokesmen who had "accommodated their writings to the manners of their respective ages." The court of Augustus, he understood, called forth Horatian emphasis upon the trivial and ludicrous. Only the laughable was at stake. Juvenal, contrarily, "complains of enormities" during the reign of Domitian "which one would be ashamed to mention; and nothing less than the highest resent-

---

37. Virginia Woolf, "Phases of Fiction," *Granite and Rainbow* (London: Hogarth Press, 1958), p. 102; Holyday, "The Preface to the Reader"; cf. Boileau, *A Discourse of Satires,* in Harte, pp. 39–46. The phrase "go gentle" is from the Dylan Thomas poem "Do not go gentle into that good night," *Collected Poems, 1934–1952* (London: J. M. Dent, 1952), p. 116.

ment of soul, ardency of expression, and sharpness of speech
could be an equal match to crimes so notorious."[38]
Almost certainly, Steele, in writing *Tatler* 242 nearly two decades later, recognized the truistic nature of Addison's remarks.
But he also subscribed to them. Similarly historical in his
perspective, he treated both Romans as indispensable friends of
mankind. The satire of each, he agreed—one easy-going, the
other deadly with fury—conveys a tone and sociomoral position
that characterize either a world marked by nothing more hein-
ous than "impertinent affectations" or one scarred by a degeneracy possible only under a soul-destroying tyranny. Ironically,
however, Steele was probably not aware at this point in their
relationship that Addison had been undergoing a change of
attitude about Juvenal's right to recriminate vileness in shock-
ingly explicit terminology and metaphor: Addison could no
longer condone "levelling satires" like the sixth, which "are of no
use to the world" (*Spectator* 209).

Although tartly moral, Addison was not recanting; rather, he
was setting new and more conservative limits on the range of his
tolerance for graphic statement and image. By comparison,
then, the judicious *Tatler* essay exemplified a reluctance to make
hard choices; as a fulcrum, it offered Steele's contemporaries a
beautifully balanced case for an active altruism in either poet.
*Tatler* 242 delineated the satirist as a large-hearted but fearsome
man, the scourge of impudent bullies, a chivalric figure "on fire
to succor the oppressed": in essence, Don Quixote with a clear
vision and a dangerous lance. Steele belongs to a numerous
company of satirists who find it useful to fortify the evidence of
their good will openly. While their overview of existence is serious, they laugh gladly; like Butler, for example, and the French
satiric writers whose practice he described, their *dent riant* barely
conceals the fine biting edge of their social criticism. They repre-

38. Dryden, *On Satire*, p. xxxviii; *Dissertatio de Insignioribus Romanorum Poetis,*
trans. Christopher Hayes, in *The Works of the Right Honourable Joseph Addison,* ed.
Richard Hurd, 6 vols. (London: Bohn's British Classics, 1854–56), 6:587–99. See
Isaac Watts, preface to *Horae Lyricae,* in which he attributes universal prophetic
understanding to Juvenal (*Eighteenth-Century Critical Essays,* ed. Scott Elledge, 2
vols. [Ithaca, N.Y.: Cornell University Press, 1961], 1:163).

sent a norm that in theory at least seeks to make censure tolerable by good-tempered wit and a gracious promise of hope.[39]
But, in the wrong hands, Horatian amiability could be reduced to a nonsensical *sauce blanche*. Carried away by excesses of misguided benevolence, certain eighteenth-century satirists oozed sentiment, though seldom in such rhapsodic phrases as these:

> Then let Good Nature every grace exert,
> And, while it mends it, win th' unfolding heart
> As in some stream the bank's projected force
> Not stops the current, but directs its course,
> So let Good Nature o'er our mirth preside,
> Divert, not check; without impelling guide.

Whitehead has here neutralized his concept of satire so that it becomes a list of *sententiae*. To be sure, even more explicitly than Pope he eulogizes the destructive-redemptive potentialities of satire. But underplaying the first and concentrating upon the second, he threatens to swaddle us in the goodness of "gen'rous satire" that with "trickling balm . . . heals the wound it makes."[40]

His sentimentality is as foreign to the aims of lasting satiric pleasure and benefit as unqualified vengeance or purposeless laughter. In any form of immoderation—feeling without reason, punishment without aesthetic or moral aim, sportiveness without elevation—the satirist reduces his calling to personal gratification shorn of an idealizing *raison d'être*. By comparison with Schiller, who noted these caveats, most readers were critical groundlings; but even they in their pursuit of enjoyment and edification shunned extremism that overrode reason and evidence. Few, perhaps, would have applied to satire as Schiller did Longinian solutions of sublimity and beauty. Pragmatically, nevertheless, they found most satisfying responsible balance— witty, sentient criticism moderated by common sense.

The popularity of theorizing on satire was such that by mid-

---

39. Cf. Butler's Spenserian image of the satirist as a questing "Knight Errant." *Characters and Passages from Note-Books*, ed. A. R. Waller (Cambridge: Cambridge University Press, 1908), pp. 469, 409, and ch. 4. See also *Letters of Laurence Sterne*, ed. L. P. Curtis (Oxford: Clarendon Press, 1935), pp. 231, 402–3.
40. William Whitehead, *An Essay on Ridicule* (1743), ll. 378–87.

century even Richardson found an excuse to introduce it into his fiction. Writing to her "satiric" friend Miss Howe on March 31, Clarissa Harlowe proves herself to be familiar with current jargonish metaphors:

The most admired of our moderns know nothing of this [satiric] art. Why? Because it must be founded in good-nature, and directed by a right heart. The *man*, not the *fault*, is generally the subject of *their* satire: And were it to be *just*, how should it be *useful?* How should it answer any good purpose? When every gash (for their weapon is a broad-sword, not a lancet) lets in the air of public ridicule, and exasperates where it should heal. Spare me not therefore, because I am your *friend*. For *that* very reason spare me not. I may *feel* your edge, fine as it is. I may be pained: You would lose your end if I were not: But after the first sensibility . . . I will love you the better, and my amended heart shall be all yours.

Her remarks, obviously cast to fit a modish genre, seem very much like a literary pose. Yet, symptomatically, they reflect a prevalent compromise between the buried altruism of Swift's *saeva indignatio* and the static goodness of Whitehead's "trickling balm."[41]

Clarissa's facile terminology reminds us that many literate Englishmen knew and approved this satiric middle ground. Most would have agreed with Persius' Stoic teacher Cornutus "in rubbing against the bloated skin of morality and pinning vice into the ground." They would also have qualified the severity of this synecdoche with wit and instructive dialogue. The preference for temperate satire was clear enough but by no means exclusive, as may be inferred from the extraordinary popularity of *Gulliver's Travels*. Although Swift doled out bitterness with a lavish hand, he also inspired generations of readers with the fertility of his creative imagination. Nor did he fail, in the words of Dryden, to enrich them additionally through "some one precept of moral

---

41. With apposite primness, Richardson was "scandalized" by tasteless abusiveness in Pope, Swift, and undoubtedly Fielding. For his allusions, see *Selected Letters of Samuel Richardson,* ed. John Carroll (Oxford: Clarendon Press, 1964 [that is, 1965]), pp. 57, 59, 60, 127. Privately Richardson expressed his pleasure at "the goodness of [Whitehead's] heart, so much preferable to that of the head alone" (p. 59).

virtue."[42] Even in the midst of a softening contemporary spirit, thus, the exceptional satirist could still tumble his readers about, as long as he allowed them some measure of dignity. No one knew better than Swift the need to posit stability, thereby offering a set of constant values to make human pain not merely endurable but worthwhile.

v

Eager to distinguish between right and wrong, stupidity and wisdom, satire has become associated with a number of catchwords that characterize the ends to be expected. The chief of these—*Justice, Truth, Reformation*—are so truistic as to be unexceptionable. Sometimes, indeed, the words appear with glib formality. When Harte protests, "'Tis justice and not anger makes us write," we understand that he pays homage to a formula. Although there is often reason to doubt the practicality of satire, in the abstract at least it has function: satire must not only search out wrongs and show them up, it must also—as Churchill piously observed in *The Apology* (321)—bring wrongdoing to trial with the "strictest justice."

Satire becomes a tribunal in which the satirist himself debates and judges issues. Like Cicero's multivoiced legalist, the writer of satires plays several roles in a quest for justice.[43] Behind appropriate masks, he simulates the vigorous prosecutor and the impartial judge (with intermittent appeal to the spectators). To complete this critical masquerade, he even takes the stand as a defendant who has been indicted for crimes that run the gamut

---

42. *The Satires of A. Persius Flaccus*, trans. John Conington, 3rd ed. (Oxford: Clarendon Press, 1893), p. xxxii and Sat. 5; Dryden, *On Satire*, pp. xxxiii, xlvii. In the eighteenth century, British editions and issues of *Gulliver's Travels* numbered about 40. These included two serial editions and at least one abridgment. In addition, the *Travels* inspired 60 or more imitations (satires, fantasies, and the like). See *Gulliveriana*, ed. Jeanne K. Welcher and George E. Bush, Jr. (Gainesville, Fla., and Delmar, N.Y.: Scholars' Facsimiles and Reprints, 1970–76). Juvenal likewise—in the seventeenth and eighteenth centuries—enjoyed exceptional attention (some of it, of course, among students for whom he was required reading): of the British editions, some 20 were in Latin, 7 in Latin and English, 13 in English.

43. *De Oratore*, II. xxiv. 102. For an elaboration of this technique, see ch. 2.

from folly to knavery and political chicanery. Justice, we are
asked to believe, will be served by satiric method and with distinction:

> Dare nobly then: But conscious of your trust,
> As ever warm and bold, be ever just.
>
> [Brown's Essay, 159–60]

That, at any rate, is the injunction given by such essayists as
Shaftesbury and Steele. They concede that accusations contained in satire may at times appear to be indiscriminate; yet
finally guilt will attach only to the culpable. Not because they
have been singled out by name, but because they cannot dis-
sociate themselves from generalized indictments. Satire, then, is
frequently treated as the prod of conscience "of him that hears,
and readeth guiltily." Condemnation, though assisted by the
satirist, is self-generating, its locus within the errant individual
who cannot deny truth that applies to himself. The words *truth*
and *justice* carry amuletic appeal, the inseparable reminders of a
divine overseer. When satire aspires to "holy" status, it is a "sacred weapon" and yet mysteriously operable on a human level.

Satire traditionally has asserted its function of transposing
these abstract ideals of justice and truth into the realities of
practical reform. "All truth," said Johnson in this connection, "is
valuable, and satirical criticism may be considered as useful when
it rectifies error and improves judgment: he that refines the
public taste is a public benefactor." The satiric impulse depends
upon a twofold assumption that men are morally delinquent and
that they must be alerted both to self-confession and a desire for
self-amendment. In part, at least, those objectives are inherent
in Addison's remark that satire "should expose nothing but what
is corrigible."[44] The possibilities of reform lie within the readers.
They are served by a provocative agent, the satirist, who must
rely more on hope than certitude that his satire will in fact fulfill
its appointed role.

Not all satirists seek to promote the same degree of change. In

<hr>

44. *English Poets*, 3:242; *Spectator* 209. Cf. discussion of the *Epilogue to the
Satires* (II): Patricia Meyer Spacks, *An Argument of Images: The Poetry of Alexander
Pope* (Cambridge, Mass.: Harvard University Press, 1971), p. 206.

*The Vanity of Human Wishes,* for example, Johnson predicates man's capacity for a rejuvenation that follows the purge of sinful desire and the subsequent submission of ego to divine fate. After detailing the means by which "decay pursues decay," he concludes on a note of trust that the man in rapport with God can begin to find his own redemption. But Swift, certainly not without hope, is less sanguine. It is true that on one mocking occasion he theorizes in a way that brings him close to Addison and Johnson:

> His satire points at no defect,
> But what all mortals may correct.
> [*Verses on the Death of Dr. Swift,* 467–68]

The auxiliary *may* protects him from suspicion of unrealistic optimism. Then, of course, the ironic context, while seemingly lighthearted, nonetheless underscores man's persistent foolishness. And its disarming cliché, typical of the century's bland satire, pokes at the fools and knaves, mocking them for their stupidity. Nevertheless, Swift saw himself duty-bound—for two reasons—to essay a redemptive role. In the *Intelligencer* 3 (25 May 1728), he conceded the propriety of satire designed for "the private satisfaction, and pleasure of the writer; but without any view towards personal malice." That he was enticed by this pleasure, he would not deny. After all, he had "as good a title to laugh, as men have to be ridiculous; and to expose vice, as another hath to be vicious." Yet the private motive did not satisfy him wholly. Indeed, he stressed that it was "less noble" than what we take to be his real purpose. The real end of socially responsible satire, as he described it, "is a public spirit, prompting men of genius and virtue, to mend the world as far as they are able."[45]

In part this may be a self-laudatory vindication of his own practice. But it is also a good deal more than that. Characteristically, he expects the "noble" satire to aspire toward achievement and excellence while avoiding the extravagant claim that grasp and reach come together. He hopes only "to mend the world *as far as [he is] able.*" Like Juvenal, he strives primarily to "hinder"

---

45. *Prose Works,* 12:34.

or "check" social ills: he has some confidence, thus, in his ability to arrest the disease, but less in his ability to induce good health. "Why," he demands to know as early as the "Apology" for *A Tale of a Tub,* "should any clergyman of our Church be angry to see the follies of fanaticism and superstition exposed, though in the most ridiculous manner? since that is perhaps the most probable way to cure them, or at least to hinder them from farther spreading." More optimistic commentators than he—Boileau, Dryden, Pope, Young—admit the possibility of regeneration but would also gladly settle for the recognition of error as a step toward amending it. Prevalent and unmistakable in all is an almost pat insistence that satire engenders respect for moral decisiveness.

VI

Most satirists enjoyed a self-conscious didacticism. The role of reformer—limited or absolute—which they affected carried with it the implication that they must also teach. Some strode forth as stern masters who, like Hall, acknowledged the connection between "rimes" and the "ferule." And while some in the eighteenth century felt as he did, far fewer brandished the rod or the heavier whip of Alecto; these argued instead for "instruction *and* delight" as nearly collateral goals. Later satirists grew mellow—like Fielding, Goldsmith, and Burns—making their appeals through wit and exempla of decency rather than through threats, trying to engage their readers in discourse, not deafen them with abuse. Even Churchill, for all his carping, advertised his purpose with an unexpected kindly voice:

> To please, improve, instruct, reform mankind;
> To make dejected virtue nobly rise
> Above the tow'ring pitch of splendid vice.
>
> [*The Apology*, 315-17]

In eighteenth-century satire, whatever tone the author adopts, he makes clear his expectation that the reader will leave his classroom a better man than when he entered, vision enlarged and insight deepened. He may have uncertainties about his satire as a powerful agent of reconstruction; but if so, he more often than not conceals or subordinates them to what is in effect a missionary zeal. Virtually he can be heard to say that he can gain nothing if he ventures nothing. For "misconduct will *certainly* be never chased out of the world by satire, if no satires are written."[46]

46. *The Complete Poems of the Rev. Edward Young,* 2 vols. (1854), 1:344. Cf. "On Reading Dr. Young's Satires, called the Universal Passion," in Swift's *Poems,* 2:390–92.

# CHAPTER 2

# SHAPE AND ORDER:
# "How a Modern Satire Should be Made"

"The truth is," said Cicero, "that the poet is a very near kinsman of the orator."[1] More specifically, had he chosen to draw out the comparison, Cicero's praise of the qualities contributing to the excellence of oratory (or rhetoric) could have been applied to satiric poetry. Versatility of idiom and tone emerges almost inevitably as a common denominator of two modes with a shared dialectic purpose. As empiric moralists, rhetoricians and satirists alike fulfill their functions ambivalently. Although they denounce failures of human obligation, they demand change in the hope that ethical norms of behavior and thought may be either confirmed or reestablished. Through denunciation, then, the rhetorician means to persuade a judge and jury or legislative body, and the satirist an audience of readers or auditors.

Some critics suspect that whatever correspondence exists between the orator and the poet owes little if anything to authorial control. So uninformed a suspicion, however, confuses generally conscious process with happy accident. The connection between rhetoric and satire was at one time nearly a vocational one. We need only recall that Juvenal himself practiced both: long before he began to write poetry he worked as a professional rhetorician. Subsequently, no doubt, he transmuted into satire the structural formality that had helped shape his oratory. Instances like this

1. *De Oratore*, I. xv. 70; xxviii. 128.

need not be binding. But even as circumstantial evidence, they stir curiosity, inviting serious consideration of possible relationships. What soon becomes inescapable is the realization that two kinds of links—conceptual and structural—create an affinity between rhetoric and satire. Even elementary analysis reveals that such coordination needs something more than serendipity. Aristotle's insight into the conceptual role of rhetoric readily applies to that of satire, Roman or English. "Rhetoric," he said, "is useful because things that are true and things that are just have a natural tendency to prevail over their opposites, so that if the decisions of judges are not what they ought to be, the defeat must be due to the speakers themselves, and they must be blamed accordingly." All satire, comparably utilitarian in avowed aim, undertakes to examine virtues; all satirists, whether credibly or not, speak out for truth and justice. The makeup of the *vir bonus* shapes the satiric as well as the oratorical role.[2] Every educated Englishman from the Renaissance on was familiar with the related ethical aims of rhetoric and satire; and so too did he recognize similarities of structure. As late as the eighteenth century, classical rhetoric still had its place in the grammar-school curriculum; in the universities attendance at lectures on rhetoric was mandatory. Coordinately, the study of classical satire was built into the young Englishman's education. To take a celebrated instance, during adolescence and early manhood Samuel Johnson mastered the sixteen satires of Juvenal even as he had the rhetoric of Cicero and Quintilian. And in mastering them he also learned about strategies of design that in time helped to form *London* and *The Vanity of Human Wishes*.[3] Precisely how or at what point insight and practice became indivisible is neither known nor, probably, relevant. Whether through inference or tutorial procedure, students like Johnson became aware of the compatibility of satire and rhetoric. Disciplined scholarly understanding substantiated the intuitions of poetic genius.

2. *Rhetoric,* I. i. 1355. For the *vir bonus,* see Quintilian, II. xv. 33; IV. i. See also ch. 1 above on intention.

3. See E. A. and L. D. Bloom, "Johnson's 'Mournful Narrative': The Rhetoric of 'London,'" in *Eighteenth-Century Studies in Honor of Donald F. Hyde,* pp. 107–44.

From the ancient rhetoricians, English satirists became accustomed to precepts often as adaptable to literary as to epideictic or deliberative discourse. The Roman satirists had tacitly accommodated their processes to available rhetorical patterns; and many English writers in their turn adapted satires to the Roman improvisations.[4] If this assumption is correct, then the design of much eighteenth-century satire may be understood against a background of rhetorical tradition. Consider the major rhetorical divisions of *inventio* and *elocutio,* the first being a "careful analysis and planning of typical speeches" and the second "the correlative problem . . . the stylistic technique by which the orator carries out his plans." If *inventio* works for the presentation of oratorical argument, then it also has comparable satiric utility. Through analysis of Juvenalian satire and with Quintilian's rules in mind, "we can see how well the satirist grasped the rhetorical principles of fitting elocutio to inventio. His style cannot be separated from his conscious poetic purposes."[5] That judicious conclusion applies to all satire, Menippean and formal.

The *oratio,* or structure, of classical debate is doubtless more closely patterned than satire's. Rhetoricians utilized a design—formal, virtually ritualistic—consisting of four parts. First, the *exordium,* or introductory matter intended to win favor from the audience and judge; it aimed ultimately to establish good will on behalf of the cause or virtue being promoted. After the *exordium* came the *narratio,* in theory a clear, convincing, and attractive statement of the case. Next the *confirmatio* and *reprehensio* undertook to prove the speaker's case and refute the opponent's. And finally, the *peroratio,* or summation. In acknowledging this multiple design, rhetoricians elaborated a tradition descended from the Greeks.[6] More succinctly, Aristotle had restricted the essential components of rhetoric to statement and argument. Never-

4. But cf. the influential article by Mary Claire Randolph, "The Structural Design of the Formal Verse Satire," *PQ* 21 (1942): 368–84.
5. William S. Anderson, "Juvenal and Quintilian," in *Yale Classical Studies* 17 (1961): 25, 86.
6. Quintilian, IV. i; Cicero, *De Partitione Oratoria,* trans. Harris Rackham (London and New York: Loeb Classical Library, 1942), translator's introduction. Cf. G. L. Hendrickson, "Satura tota nostra est," *Classical Philology* 22 (1927): 46–60.

theless, he conceded the propriety, under special circumstances, of two additional elements, an introduction and an epilogue (III. xiii. 1414).

And yet, despite the appearance of a closed rhetorical system, satirists were able to move about in it without undue restraint. The sequential logic of these categories, already mentioned, makes each appear nearly self-contained and yet dependent on the adjacent unit. Like chambers with connecting passageways, they permit each detail of argument or proof, as it is concluded, to connect readily with a new detail. This capacity for order is admirably suited to rhetoric in which contention, refutation, and summation proceed with mounting energy. The scheme is well suited also to the intellectual, fictional, and emotional progression of satiric art, without imposing upon it a visible pattern. Rhetoric, furthermore, encourages contrast and digression, strategies that are both necessary and congenial to satire. Finally, then, as the structural analysis of *Absalom and Achitophel* will show, rhetoric and satire reconcile their differences within a common design.

The prose essay "To the Reader" avowedly apologizes for or defends the poet's art. But it also explains the poem's conceptualism. Dryden thus argues in his own voice on behalf of Absalom as a potentially excellent young man who has been led astray by Achitophel's satanism. Here the ground is laid for the sacramental and typological details to follow: "'T is no more a wonder that he withstood not the temptations of Achitophel, than it was for Adam not to have resisted the two devils, the serpent and the woman." Preparatory to the poem's ethical meaning, Dryden comments: "Things were not brought to an extremity where I left the story; there seems yet to be room left for a composure; hereafter there may only be for pity." Like the compassion that informs much satire, Dryden's prefatory remarks convey a formal hope that Absalom may still achieve grace by rejecting the tempter and renewing filial loyalty. This, however, is a rather shaky optimism when Achitophel's evil nature is taken into account, as it must be. "I have not so much as an uncharitable wish against Achitophel, but am content to be accused of a good-natured error, and to hope with Origen, that the Devil himself may at last be saved. For which reason, in this poem, he is neither brought to set his house in order, nor to dispose of his person afterwards as he in wisdom shall think fit. God is infinitely merciful; and his viceregent is only not so, because he is not infinite." Although a sardonic note creeps in, Dryden nevertheless emphasizes his own Christian tolerance without surrendering to misgivings about whether Achitophel can be brought around or will ever release his hold on Absalom. Catching the reader between artistic suspense and Christian doctrine, Dryden prepares a situation worthy of an epic format.

The proem encompasses the first forty lines. Initially, the tone is calm, benevolent, tolerant; the terms suggest the scriptural, and David, visible but regally aloof, is eulogized. Tipping expedience with irony, Dryden rationalizes David's promiscuity, the glowing essence of which is the idealized but imperfect son Absalom. "And paradise was open'd in his face" (30) in order to make him appealing as the noble heir to all the Davidic virtues. True to the rhetorical tradition of imminent surprise and inverse expectation, the tranquillity that opens the poem contrasts radically with the treachery and disorder to follow. This opposition projects not only a dramatic irony but, philosophically, a portent of the concluding reassertion of order. The contrast is enhanced by the absence of any hierarchical threat, "While David, undisturb'd, in Sion reign'd" (42). The proem is thus contrived to obscure (at least momentarily) the dialectic aim. Typologically, it enacts through concealment the adversary situation: David's mildness and affection counterpoint the youth's as yet unrevealed corruptibility.

The transition from proem to narrative statement is brought about by an aphorism, a rhetorical device frequently used by Dryden when he wishes to forward his own ethical observations. Immediately after the final line of the proem, consequently, the poet declares:

> But life can never be sincerely blest:
> Heav'n punishes the bad, and proves the best.
>
> [43-44]

The idyllic spell is quickly broken, bright promise is darkened by a foreboding, sermonlike threat. Kingship—benevolent, steadfast, and responsible—has been defied; and the reader plunges into contrarieties of diabolism, seduction, and disloyalty. Again, as with the proem, the statement, or *narratio,* is brief. It proceeds from the brooding rhythmic tenor of

> The Jews, a headstrong, moody, murm'ring race,
> As ever tried th' extent and stretch of grace;
>
> [45-46]

to the dour militancy of

> ... but who can know
> How far the Devil and Jebusites may go?
>
> [133-34]

The argument within these verses supplies the widening outlines of dissident, seditious detail important to both reflective and emotive response. By reversing the expectations engendered in the proem, the statement expands the mood and implicates the reader. He is asked to deplore a conspiracy that threatens the order David had sought for a troubled land. The disruption, according to the poet, may be blamed upon the aspirations of a few evil men who arouse many to ingratitude:

> But when to sin our bias'd nature leans,
> The careful Devil is still at hand with means;
> And providently pimps for ill desires;
> The Good Old Cause reviv'd, a plot requires:
> Plots, true or false, are necessary things,
> To raise up commonwealths, and ruin kings.
>
> [79-84]

These lines convey a marked heightening of emotional pitch: the epithets begin to build toward a tension, the tone increasingly sardonic, personal, and bitter. The satirist carries his attack as far as he deems persuasive, nearly abandoning generality to effect an equation between sacramental treason and political treason, between rebellion accepted unthinkingly by the rabble and superstition—"swallow'd in the mass, unchew'd and crude" (113).

*Confirmatio* and *reprehensio,* the positive and negative requisites of rhetorical proof, are counterweighted by appeal to authority, which is not always distinct from prejudice. The argument is thus advanced as history submerged in scripture; vivid
recent events are fictionalized as biblical matters familiar to any
Christian reader. Dryden's aim, by transfiguring historical reality into scriptural narrative, was to elicit a distaste for political
treachery comparable to that associated with breaches of sanctity. The Titus Oates plot "fail'd for want of common sense," but
that abortive failure nonetheless promoted matters of "deep and
dangerous consequence."[7] Taking full advantage of his rhetorical opportunities, Dryden now began to unfold proofs of his
argument. This he did mainly through a delineation of actors in
an epic of treason whose "dangerous consequence" fell just short
of tragedy. Indeed, had he written the poem some four years
later, after the capture and execution of Monmouth, his sole
choice would have been a tragic motif. Lacking this prescience in
1681, however, he fictionalized a Christian solution, As he,
perhaps ironically, agreed with Origen, even "the Devil himself
may at last be saved."

Of rhetorical interest as well as satiric is Dryden's observance
of the Ciceronian stricture that, for most persuasive effect in any
argument or debate, the strongest points should come first. No
debater or satirist could have evoked a stronger introductory
focus than that on Achitophel, "A name to all succeeding ages
curst" (151).

---

7. On the Popish Plot, cf. Hume: "The whole texture of the plot contains such
low absurdity, that it is impossible to have been the invention of any man of sense
or education. It is true, the more monstrous and horrible the conspiracy, the
better was it fitted to terrify, and thence to convince, the populace: but this
effect, we may safely say, no one could beforehand have promised upon; and a
fool was in this case more likely to succeed than a wise man. Had Shaftesbury laid
the plan of a popish conspiracy, he had probably rendered it moderate, consistent, credible; and on that very account had never met with the prodigious
success with which Oates's tremendous fictions were attended." David Hume,
*The History of England from the Invasion of Julius Caesar to the Revolution in 1688,* 8
vols. (1773), 8:75. For valuable contemporary impressions of the plot, see *POAS,*
2 (1678–81).

A fiery soul, which, working out its way,
Fretted the pigmy body to decay,
And o'er-inform'd the tenement of clay.

[156–58]

As a coalesence of satanic and political disobedience, Achitophel radiates demonic energy. Yet dwarfed in his own person and the sire of "a shapeless lump, like anarchy" (172), the arch-villain emerges as the very emblem of perverted generation and behavior. Dryden's vilification is crucial to the image; his insinuating voice controls our emotions.[8]

The presentation of Absalom seduced by Achitophel becomes a profound arraignment of rebellion, particularly because of its Christianized implications: there is the fall from innocence; and the temptation causing the fall is abhorrent. The depiction of Absalom, like the overtly worded proem, argues for tolerance because no one so inexperienced could resist the smooth-tongued tempter. For Achitophel, in terms of this premise, Absalom is the vessel available for his own ambitions, huge and malevolent. The younger man was corruptible, a fact Dryden acknowledges despite the romanticized portrait:

What cannot praise effect in mighty minds,
When flattery soothes, and when ambition blinds!
Desire of pow'r, on earth a vicious weed,
Yet, sprung from high, is of celestial seed:
In God 't is glory; and when men aspire,
'T is but a spark too much of heavenly fire.
Th' ambitious youth, too covetous of fame,
Too full of angels' metal in his frame,
Unwarily was led from virtue's ways,
Made drunk with honor, and debauch'd with praise.

[303–12]

But the narrator takes account of the inner strain of warring

8. *De Oratore*, II. lxxxv. 307 ff. Writers before Dryden had turned the biblical story into an analogue for contemporary politics. Others also had conceived of Shaftesbury as the deformed minion of the Devil: see the crude verse pamphlet *The Badger in the Fox-Trap, or, a Satyr upon Satyrs* (9 July 1681?). For commentaries on *Absalom and Achitophel* (Nov. 1681), see *POAS*, 2:453–504; Bernard N. Schilling, *Dryden and the Conservative Myth: A Reading of* Absalom and Achitophel (New Haven and London: Yale University Press, 1961).

influences: a fatal love of fame debasing the goodness of his "angels' metal." In a quibble, thus, he softens the charge against the young rebel, treating him as victim rather than perpetrator. Even that, however, does not prevent Dryden from showing a transformed Absalom, his ambition fired by Achitophel. Then the disciple becomes as one with the master. Finally, as in the beginning, Achitophel's treason—dominant, unmistakable, unequivocal—is the force to which we must respond. He changes not at all, and—though we may regret his squandered talents—we look upon him with repugnance. Toward Absalom, however, we are left with ambivalent feelings: regret for his fall; anger or shame for the way in which he has succumbed.

Dryden's case against Achitophel, a cumulative one, impresses. He is the seismic origin of disquiet, the epicenter from whom all evil impulses are transmitted. Even Absalom's role, despite its importance, takes on a lesser consequence. And so too do the roles of those characters,

> The malcontents of all the Israelites;
> Whose differing parties he could wisely join,
> For several ends, to serve the same design.
>
> [492-94]

Relatively minor among those close to Absalom and Achitophel, they still serve well as corollary proofs of man's propensity to err. Whatever degrees of corruption they represent as individuals, in their totality they comprise the full scale of human failure. They range from "mistaken men . . . Not wicked, but seduc'd by impious arts" (497-98) to others who "'gainst form and order they their pow'r employ" (531). Like a skilled rhetorician, Dryden digresses in order to augment tension, interrupting the main course of the narrative long enough to place the secondary characters on show. Some he identifies through dominant traits: Zimri, "not one, but all mankind's epitome" (546); the miserly Shimei, who "lov'd his wicked neighbor as himself" (600); Corah, "this arch-attestor for the public good" (640). The name-calling of this quasi-epic roster helps to frame an ideological intention within an emotional design. The signified characters, by no means the exclusive instruments of treason, are supported by others so numerous that "titles and names 't were tedious to rehearse" (569).

Recruited by Achitophel, they become "deluded" Absalom's "friends of every sort" (682–83). Dryden's verbal scorn displays a gallery of men who, if not always villains, feed villainy. Thus, when the narrative returns to the blemished Absalom, we must judge him further by the company he keeps. By now the charge against him has been so firmly implanted as to set the falsity of his arguments beyond doubt. The full implications of his guilt depend upon a progressive narrative pace, upon specious thinking revealed by dramatic circumstance and emotional shock. The ideas could be transmitted within a wholly expository design, to be sure. But Dryden wished to engage his audience in more than ideology. The fall from grace, if assimilable at all, had to be driven into the reader's spiritual as well as intellectual sensibility. Hence the poet resorts to a rhetoric of feeling amplified by fiction.

The slippery language of David's favorite, the self-proclaimed martyr, the "banish'd man, for your dear cause," can no longer evoke our sympathy. His treachery is magnified by a pointedly described gesture of dissimulation: " 'Take then my tears,' " says Absalom, after which "(with that he wip'd his eyes)." The satirist assists us to see and judge the hypocrisy. For the moment, the sense of a failed Absalom dramatizes an irony, still concealed from the duped spectators within the poem. Thus Dryden makes his rhetorical voice audible only to the reader:

> Youth, beauty, graceful action seldom fail;
> But common interest always will prevail;
> And pity never ceases to be shown
> To him who makes the people's wrongs his own.
>
> [723–26]

In mockingly *ad captandum* idiom, the poet challenges the unthinking rabble, the idolatrous hordes who "with lifted hands their young Messiah bless" (728), while Absalom "glides unfelt into their secret hearts" (693).[9] To this extent Achitophel succeeds. He has formed his cabal well, "with intent / To sound the depths, and fathom, where it went" (741–42).

9. Cf. a similar metaphor as applied by Johnson in *London* to patron-hunters (ll. 152–55): "For arts like these preferr'd, admir'd, caress'd, / They first invade your table, then your breast; / Explore your secrets with insidious art, / Watch the weak hour, and ransack all the heart."

By now the odds appear heavily against the mild David. How can he possibly counteract the stealth and the plots of conspirators?

> How fatal 't is to be too good a king!
> Friends he has few, so high the madness grows:
> Who dare be such, must be the people's foes.          [812-14]

Rhetorically considered, however, this is a sound trick—a form of *meiosis*—because David's true strength has been deceptively understated. In this passage still another irony inheres: a pretense of helplessness contrary to the refutation about to begin. Quickly, by comparison with his elaborated roster of conspirators, Dryden parades the honorable men prepared to fight alongside David. Chief in "this short file" (817) appears Barzillai, a forthright, well-tried patriot and warrior. The list is indeed short, and Dryden, as though to compensate, shifts from the earlier dramatic, hortatory tone—from the charged words of blame—to one of inflated piety and praise that confirms the typological scheme. Not only does he look to heaven for comfort but he invokes his muse, "here cease thy painful flight" (854). Fortunately, David can muster his own compensatory strength: in addition to Barzillai's military determination, the "godlike" king has for support the judgment, eloquence, and political good will of others. These need not be so sharply individualized as the adversary group. By isolating and thus stressing the influence of evil men, Dryden makes their defeat by the Davidic legion more telling. Those in direct support of David are generalized as a body of good men, whether taken singly or as a whole, though none is so great as David. If the reader is prepared to accept this assumption, then he is also prepared to believe David's subsequent refutation of his enemies, and to praise the way in which he proposes to withstand the mischief inspired by Achitophel.

David sums up a position, Christian rather than Judaic, sacramental and ethical rather than overtly political. " 'Tis time," he nobly asserts, "to show I am not good by force" (950). Simultaneously David appeals to the emotions of home and of family:

How easy 't is for parents to forgive!
With how few tears a pardon might be won
From nature, pleading for a darling son!

[958-60]

The magnanimity of kingship competes with pity and pathos in this first full-scale view of David. Until now he has been given to us in sanctified silhouette: the epithet "Godlike David," often repeated, elevates the monarch beyond mortality. Now, momentarily and with credible sorrow, he ceases to be the deified hero and becomes instead the parent—as fond as, but wiser than, the betrayed Lear—and the just ruler. But his mildness also deceives, for David, no matter how much he tempers the wind, will not allow personal interest to obstruct the rule of law:

Must I at length the sword of justice draw?
O curst effects of necessary law!
How ill my fear they by my mercy scan!
Beware the fury of a patient man.

[1002-5]

The epilogue consequently unveils David as a fully responsible individual, and also as a king who stands larger even than life in the cause of justice. "For lawful pow'r," he solemnly declares, "is still superior found" (1024). And lest this be mistaken for mere verbiage,

... Th' Almighty, nodding, gave consent;
And peals of thunder shook the firmament.

[1026-27]

Thus David, powerfully assisted—even though mortal "friends he has few"—reasserts the preeminence of order and justice.

And thus also Dryden has constructed a satiric poem that, in brief outline, satisfies the classical assumptions of rhetorical debate. The construction is four-tiered, its aim persuasive and ethical, its narrative elements delicately balanced between confirmation and refutation. The Davidic theme is an epideictic one of praise; the poet in dealing with a contemporary institution, kingship, magnifies and sanctifies it. Still within the epideictic tradition, he blames Achitophel as the symbolic threat to monarchical stability. The typology, further, unites proofs with historical and invented parallels.[10] Although Dryden deals with history at two distinct levels, the biblical and the modern, the narrative texture of the poem may be seen apart from its historic sources. Nevertheless, for the fullest and most satisfying meaning (as in allegory), the two must finally unite.

Dryden's poem mixes in sophisticated fashion literal and rhetorical disputation. As imaginative satire, it draws upon all the resources of invention, meter, language, and tone available to the creative intelligence. As political argument, it schematizes the narration. Intricately, it blends disciplined order, organizational logic, history, and vision. A randomly dispersed argument never convinces as much as one that proceeds from credible cause to inexorable effect. Rhetoric with its shaping power can supply that order to the more fluid structure of satire; but the satirist himself must determine the degree to which he will be bound by rules and categories. Dryden creates a modified impression of rhetorical design, but always within the context of his satiric imagination.

## II

The components of a satire will be more visible to the analytical critic than to the general reader, but both respond to an entire effect. This totality must be enforced through the elements—cognitive and metaphoric, tonal and stylistic—that go into a coherent organism. Such is the accomplishment of *Absalom and Achitophel*—a poem demonstrating exceptional control—and such the intention implied by Dryden in his instructions on "how a modern satire should be made." He concerned himself more immediately with ends than means, not because the parts of the satire were unimportant to him but because he took them for granted in his own scheme and could concentrate on the sum of their meaning. For all of Dryden's

10. See Aristotle's *Rhetoric*, II. xx. 1393, for "historical and invented" proofs; also Quintilian, II. iv. 1-2. In *Dryden's Poetry* (Bloomington and London: Indiana University Press, 1967), Earl Miner treats *Absalom and Achitophel* as "metaphorical history," biblical and English (pp. 106-43). He prefers to describe it as "a historical poem" rather than as a satire, although he concedes that "some fifth of the poem is undoubtedly satiric in cast" (p. 141).

indebtedness to Casaubon, he placed Persius lower in the satiric scale than did the scholar, lower, that is, than Horace and Juvenal. And yet he did agree that Persius, the least dignified "of all the three," had hit upon an important discovery for the design "of a perfect satire." This was the realization "that it ought only to treat of one subject; to be confined to one particular theme; or, at least, to one principally."[11]

Reluctant to be too closely identified with Casaubon's judgment,[12] Dryden enlarged upon the significance of unity by citing as even more impressive authority the concern with design of both Juvenal and Boileau, who emulated Persius. One of the controlling principles of thematic unity for the perfection of design, in Dryden's scheme, was the obligation of the poet "to give his reader some one precept of moral virtue; and to caution him against some one particular vice or folly." In both satire and drama, as he knew practically, the artist must often juxtapose and combine seemingly diverse matter. By extension, Dryden insisted (doubtless looking back to the authority of both Aristotle and Horace), even the divided manner of tragicomedy compels attention to "but one main design"; it "may not seem a monster with two heads." His attention to drama here, purely analogical, becomes his way of evoking both the dignity and scope of satire. More important for us, the unity of thematic design that he attributes to drama is a satiric necessity. Indeed, the classical identification *lanx satura*, he reminded his readers, associates abundance with a reconciliation of varied qualities. Hence, a unity of effect.

Despite Dryden's insistence upon unique design, the random

11. *On Satire*, pp. xlvi-viii. For commentary and notes see *The Works of John Dryden* [1956-], ed. A. B. Chambers and William Frost (Berkeley, Los Angeles, London: University of California Press, 1974), 4:513-86; and *The Poems of John Dryden*, ed. James Kinsley, 4 vols. (Oxford: Clarendon Press, 1958), 4:2006-18. Howard D. Weinbrot has illuminated the structural influence of Dryden's discourse *On Satire* in *The Formal Strain: Studies in Augustan Imitation and Satire* (Chicago and London: University of Chicago Press, 1969), ch. 3. For a detailed examination of Dryden's control in *Absalom and Achitophel*, see Miner, *Dryden's Poetry*.

12. Isaac Casaubon, *De Satyrica Graecorum Poesi et Romanorum Satira Libri Duo* (Paris, 1605), and the introduction by Peter E. Medine to the facsimile reproduction (Delmar, N.Y.: Scholars' Facsimiles and Reprints, 1973), pp. 355-56.

quality hinted by *lanx satura* persisted in many minds as the identifying trait of the genre. Thus Edward Young mistakenly thought himself a revolutionary when he attributed to his own satiric *Love of Fame* (1725–1728) a composite intention. Just vague enough to make one look for deeper meanings, he stepped forth as the castigator of Vice and Folly: "What men aim at by them is, generally, public opinion and esteem; which truth is the subject of the following Satires, and join them together as several branches from the same root: an unity of design which has not, I think, in a set of satires, been attempted before." Deeper meanings do not emerge. Seemingly Horace and Juvenal have been denied as authors of schematic "set[s]" of satires, while as theorists dealing with the same proposition, Casaubon and Boileau, to say nothing of Dryden, have been jettisoned. But Young's self-esteem is unimportant for itself. The significance, rather, inheres in his belated recognition of a truism. Within the first quarter of the eighteenth century his critical mind has caught up with the poetic reality, namely, that the diverse elements of satire are indeed properly reconcilable. Thereafter, for some minor satirists at least, Young became a model of moral purpose, to be imitated as the exemplar of conscious design and elevation.[13] The results may be heavy with derivativeness and repetition, but they do reflect some kind of agreement about the desirability of building satires architectonically.

That suggests a paradox, however, for structural wholeness does not appear to be consistent with the exaggeration upon which satire thrives. And yet the satirist, despite a technique that on the surface often seems rationally askew, seeks to offer assurance of his credibility. He capitalizes on the assumption that his basic truths will be recognized, that this awareness will not be blunted by the absence of precise or literal statement. Such truths may be enhanced, indeed, by hyperbole that sharpens response to their existence. Satiric credibility, as Edward Bysshe

13. Preface, *Love of Fame, the Universal Passion.* One of the poets for whom Young was mentor and guide was his long-time friend Thomas Newcomb, *The Manners of the Age: In Thirteen Moral Satires: Written with a Design to Expose the Vicious and Irregular Conduct of Both Sexes, in the Various Pursuits of Life* (1733).

observed, requires that "some allowance must be given: For satire may be fine, and true satire, though it be not directly and according to the letter, true. 'Tis enough that it carry with it a probability or semblance of truth."[14] The reader must be made to agree—"I accept all this as true"—to balance fantasy against probability. The organic design of a satire must invite confidence in its creative responsibility. Not unlike the Jamesian "central intelligence," the narrator fixes a point of view from which he addresses the audience. He may be recognizable *in propria persona* as the poet. Alternatively, however, he may efface himself in favor of one or more other narrative presences. The way in which he shapes the point of view, whether through his own or a masked identity, gives him a managerial authority: the director of the play is also one of its actors. Consequently the skill with which he controls the voices of satire will determine the degree to which he can communicate the range and subtlety of his argument. So it is with the aloof narrator of *The Rape of the Lock*. Except for the opening and closing lines, the only voices heard in the poem are those of the characters. And yet, despite the poet's near invisibility, he lurks as the constant observer-manipulator.

Sometimes, to make the personal identification unmistakable, the satirist will indulge in apology, explaining—as does Pope, with a paradoxically energetic world-weariness—why he must write. *An Epistle to Dr. Arbuthnot* virtually bears Pope's signature in each couplet:

> Shut, shut the door, good *John!* fatigu'd I said,
> Tie up the knocker, say I'm sick, I'm dead.

The *lebensmüde* poet, happily, can brace himself for the task of another 417 lines, naming and justifying himself, but also expressing the inevitability of composition.

> Why did I write? what sin to me unknown
> Dipt me in ink, my parents', or my own?
> As yet a child, nor yet a fool to fame,
> I lisp'd in numbers, for the numbers came.

14. Preface, *A Collection of the most Natural, Agreeable & Noble Thoughts*, in *The Art of English Poetry* (1702). See also Rosenheim, fn. 36.

> I left no calling for this idle trade,
> No duty broke, no Father dis-obey'd.
> The Muse but serv'd to ease some friend, not wife,
> To help me thro' this long disease, my life,
> To second, ARBUTHNOT! thy art and care,
> And teach, the being you preserv'd, to bear.
>
> [125-34]

Half-jestingly, half-seriously, the poet sounds glad merely to be kept alive by his physician's skill. Yet somehow and by some unknown power, he—the least aggressive of all men—has been elected to fight for the good spurned by the many.

Again, in Boileau's *Satire IX,* the poet's voice is heard distinctly, but the distance between poet and audience increases, the mood far less compelling than in the *Epistle to Dr. Arbuthnot.* Boileau's apology, too self-deprecatory, strains credulity. He begins:

> C'est à vous, mon Esprit, à qui je veux parler.
> Vous avez des défauts que je ne puis celer.

Ostensibly the poet reveals himself as in a confession to his spirit, acknowledging the existence of faults charged against him by his enemies. According to the following note by Claude Brossette, his editor, Boileau intended to undermine what he professed literally. Far from considering himself blameworthy, he sought only the repudiation of his critics: "Il jugea donc qu'il n'avoit pas d'autre ton à prendre que celui de la plaisanterie, pour tourner ses ennemis en ridicule, sans leur donner aucune pris sur lui."[15] Unlike Pope's forceful opening lines with their realistic details, Boileau's conform to the tradition of formal address and so restrict the speaker's ability to force a commitment from the reader. Within the bounds set by the apology, however, Boileau is present as the creative entity.

In view of the critical, often militant, temper of satire, apology is usually a transparent fiction for modesty and restraint. "I myself," Persius remarks, am "half a clown" who writes without

---

15. *Oeuvres en Vers de Mr. Boileau Despreaux,* ed. Claude Brossette, 4 vols. (Amsterdam, 1717), 1:130n.

aspiring to the laurels of nobler poets.[16] The sympathetic reader accepts the fiction as an element of the satire, is amused by it, and sometimes even identifies with it. At the same time he plays a game with the satirist even as the satirist does with him. Thus while yielding to the fiction, the reader suspects that Pope embroiders when he represents himself as a lonely warrior, that Boileau in the address to his spirit simply answers hostile critics, that Persius probably never saw himself in antic dress. Each satirist may give an impression of his affinity with the speaker of the poem; he also draws a fine but firm line between the creator and his creation.

Satiric apology is ironic. Swift, for example, varies its use through his first-person narrators. Gulliver in the earlier part of his career modestly clothes himself in self-justification: he had, he said at the outset of his second voyage, "been condemned by nature and fortune to an active and restless life." Therefore he does what he must, never demanding anything or making claims for talents that he does not possess. But almost imperceptibly, by the end of the fourth voyage, the humility has vanished—with regard to his fellow Englishmen—and has been succeeded by strident pride. His voice has altered from apology to arrogant recrimination. But nothing is odd about this. Once we get beneath the surface of his manner, we can account for the shift to aggressiveness. Appearance changes, not reality. The "real" Gulliver is steadfastly the hypocrite, facile, impressionable, self-interested. In such ways he joins other Swiftian creations, the dissembler reminiscent of La Bruyère's *faux dévot.* "Nothing but a hypocrite . . . without any human weakness or inconsistency, constantly vigilant, constantly rational, [he] steadily pursues the . . . plan which goes with his part."[17]

16. "Prologue to the First Satyr," trans. Dryden in *The Satires of Juvenal and Persius* (1693), p. 3. On the tradition of apology, see Elliott, *The Power of Satire,* pp. 113–15, and passim; Lucius R. Shero, "The Satirist's *Apologia,*" *Classical Studies,* in University of Wisconsin Studies in Language and Literature, no. 15 (Madison, 1922); Carnochan, *Lemuel Gulliver's Mirror for Man,* ch. 3. Elkin summarizes contemporary attitudes in *The Augustan Defence of Satire.*

17. Erich Auerbach, *Mimesis: The Representation of Reality in Western Literature,* trans. Willard Trask (Garden City, N.Y.: Doubleday Anchor, 1957), p. 317.

Gulliver is an evolving though not altogether full-bodied character. By the end of the fourth voyage we are reasonably sure what he stands for. Perhaps we are even more sure that he is a persona playing an adversarial role assigned to him by the author; that he is therefore separable from the author. When, on the other hand, we look back at the narrator of *A Modest Proposal,* we do not see him except as a murky, disturbing presence. We cannot help wondering just who he is. Considered superficially, he appears to be a brutally insensitive outsider uttering statistical enormities. But this is too easy a revelation and the search leads us to suspect a Swift who deliberately shakes us up with his masked ironies. Fiction and reason make competing demands upon our response to the essay.

Even Swift's ironies must be approached with caution: we must be alert, that is, to distinguish between his hopes for a just Ireland and the objective, horrendous reality of an oppressive Ireland. At the very end, to illustrate the point, the narrator intermingles a concern for a solution to the Irish problem—which we take to be genuine on his part—with inhuman sophistry: "I profess, in the sincerity of my heart, that I have not the least personal interest, in endeavoring to promote this necessary work; having no other motive than the *public good of my country, by advancing our trade, providing for infants, relieving the poor, and giving some pleasure to the rich.* I have no children, by which I can propose to get a single penny; the youngest being nine years old, and my wife past child-bearing." Alternatively, if the speaker is not Swift, then it seems that he must be identified as the hypocrite, the last word almost in empty benevolence and humility. Whoever this elusive speaker is taken to be, he becomes indigenous to the ironic structure of *A Modest Proposal.* He moves with a semblance of genuine diffidence and good will. But the hesitant gait becomes the militant stride of an overbearing majority; the earlier humility swells into gross pride.[18]

The identity of the speaker, let us then admit, is ambiguous. Essentially a disembodied voice, he lacks the wholeness of a per-

18. *Prose Works,* 12:109–18.

sona who would cause us to shun him as a self-revealing bar-
barian, a bloodless materialist. Were straightforward exposition
attributable to him, he would be antithetical to the purpose of *A
Modest Proposal,* which—contrary to the formidable opinion of
Leavis—is corrective. A monster may horrify, but to what end if
he does so only sensationally, without inducing feelings other
than of revulsion or fear? What we look for here is an opportunity to convert the calmly stated horror into a credible set of
circumstances susceptible to affirmation. Confronted with an
ugly fantasy, we want somehow to fight our way back to a better
reality that will provide economic and social justice for the Irish
poor. We agree with Ewald, that "the real force of the essay is
moral; it defines for us once again how great is the difference
between the world as Swift wanted it and the world as he saw
it."[19]

Beyond that, however, we suggest that Swift's moral hopes
encompassed an even profounder vision, which should be associated with the shadowy speaker of *A Modest Proposal.* There is
a spiritual dimension—and we do not insist that Swift imposed it
consciously upon the essay—that extends the macabre imagery
beyond economic and social acceptability. Implicit in that imagery is an ironically perverse "idea of the Eucharist, in which the
worshiper becomes united with Christ by incorporating Him.
This renewal of a savage and infantile belief in the possibility of
acquiring the superior object by eating it is tied to the condition:
'Except ye be converted, and become as little children, ye shall
not enter into the kingdom of heaven.'"[20] The masked speaker
makes a radical demand on our attention by shocking us. The
immediate shock of Swift's argument, in other words, is verbal
and narrative. The metaphor fails, however, unless it opens the

19. F. R. Leavis, "The Irony of Swift," *Scrutiny* 2 (1933–34): 364–78; William
Bragg Ewald, Jr., *The Masks of Jonathan Swift* (Cambridge, Mass.: Harvard University Press, 1954), p. 174. For a persuasive discussion of the complex possibilities of Swift's "stable" irony, *A Modest Proposal,* see Wayne C. Booth, *A
Rhetoric of Irony* (Chicago and London: University of Chicago Press, 1974), pp.
105–20.
20. Theodore Reik, *Myth and Guilt: The Crime and Punishment of Mankind* (New
York: George Braziller, 1957), p. 175; Tuveson, pp. 66–68.

mind and conscience to the higher truths of Swift's intention, as we are able to infer it: we cannot turn our backs upon iniquities without risking the attrition of human worth. Without pressing for an exclusively Christian interpretation, we nevertheless find an intriguing correlation between the metaphor of the return to childhood and rebirth in the communion service and Swift's ironic literalization of that service when the bodies to be consumed are those of infant children: after the age of one, we recall, the flesh begins to lose its nourishing desirability. The parallel is in the innocence which—religious or secular—promises salvation. Swift compounds the irony by identifying as the most propitious time for the slaughter of the innocents the year following each Lenten season, for the fish consumed by the Catholic population is conducive to fertility. Hence, as the mask blandly observes, out of religious celebration they produce the most edible children. But barely concealed in the irony is the angry charge that the voracious English landlords are destroying the substance and future of the starving Irish community. Translated from the profane to the sacramental, Swift's metaphor can be seen for what it is: the realization that the unspeakable "solution" is in truth an ironic revelation of man's breach of divine obligation. The voice behind the mask is in an expository sense unreliable; but its ironic implications are not. The mask helps restore Swift as the author; it is a reminder of how close he is to being the reader's moral prompter. It also impresses upon him the fictional strategy by which Swift maintains full control of complex, controversial materials.

Apology cannot be taken at face value when the author pretends to be a disinterested or even friendly scribe, a listener who records someone else's *vituperatio*. He must listen and record because the someone else may be speaking truth. This stance of impartiality offends the poet-narrator of Juvenal's *Satire I:* "Semper ego auditor tantum?" Here the "I"—closely akin to the poet—is the palpable though unbodied presence who judges indifference to evil an evil itself. He therefore proposes to be an activist like Lucilius before him, to reveal to an invisible audience his own injuries, however degrading they may be, or the frustrations of his native Romans. The sympathy between Juvenal and his mask never abates, but a semblance of restraint permits the poet to control the anger and pity, the rage and indignation, of the "I" that moves his readers. Juvenal maintains the voice of the first person through most of his satires. In *Satire III*, however, he fictionalizes withdrawal of the "I" to an obscure listener's post after twenty lines of introduction and allows Umbricius to assume the central position of righteous anger.[21] In the tenth satire, where problems take on a universal dimension, the voice becomes that of an indeterminate "I" spilling forth exempla of cosmic and human woe. Like a prolonged monologue, the complaint is addressed to an equally indeterminate audience.

Samuel Johnson, who judged Juvenal to be the greatest of Roman satirists, was never a translator but an "imitator," free to strive for originality while cognizant of his model. In *The Vanity of Human Wishes*, an "imitation" of Juvenal's *Satire X,* he did not experiment with point of view: he had neither the flexibility nor the aesthetic need, as he saw the poem's intention. The Johnsonian narrator likewise remains unseen and unnamed; and the audience, again like Juvenal's, is merely a felt presence whenever a sounded "thou" or silent "you" is heard and intuited. Whereas Juvenal depended on his lamenting *alter ego* to move from one exemplum of frustration to another, Johnson enhanced his own pictures of vanity in an insinuatingly repetitive pattern of military images complemented by further reference to entrapment.[22] Both poets stress the brutality that belies man's claim to being civilized. But Johnson dramatizes his theme with less dependence upon the vehemence and near-bombast that sometimes characterize Juvenalian art.

So far we have been speaking only of the single point of view

---

21. Cf. Aristotle: "With regard to the element of moral character: there are assertions which, if made about yourself, may excite dislike, appear tedious, or expose you to the risk of contradictions; and other things which you cannot say about your opponent without seeming abusive or ill-bred. Put such remarks, therefore, into the mouth of some third person. This is what . . . Archilochos [does] in his satires." *Rhetoric,* III. xvii. 1418.

22. E. A. Bloom, "*The Vanity of Human Wishes: Reason's Images,*" *Essays in Criticism* 15 (Apr. 1965): 181–92.

in satire, which has the capacity to render an argument and its proofs without interruption. In this respect its solitary speaker, comparable to a dramatic monologist, invites concentration upon the words and moods of a central persona. In tragic satire such prolonged discourse stresses the magisterial and suggests the irrefutable. In fact, the same technique works as well in the mock-heroic. Throughout the droning harangue of Dryden's Flecknoe, for example, self-esteem is inverted into muffled innuendo designed by the poet to belittle and denigrate an already diminished versifier.

But different values accrue also in the freer dramatic framework provided by a dual or multiple point of view, generally through dialogue. From the tensions of conversational exchange emerges a public or literary identity that gives—or at least hints at—a greater sense of natural liberation than does univocal satire. Such liberation can be deceptive, for the dialogues of Persius, of Horace, of Pope in his imitations of Horace all maintain their own formal integrity of design.

In his *Satire I,* Persius as narrator vigorously repudiates an *adversarius* (185-279) who not only sneers at a literary plain style but praises arty images and rhymes like "Berecynthian Atys," or "The dolphin brave, that cut the liquid wave, / Or he who in his line, can chine the long-ribbed Apennine." Persius thinks his friend a fool who has been hoodwinked by words without meaning:

> Cou'd such rude lines a Roman mouth become,
> Were any manly greatness left in Rome?
> Maenas and Atys in the mouth were bred;
> And never hatch'd within the lab'ring head.
> No blood, from bitten nails, those poems drew:
> But churn'd, like spittle, from the lips they flew.
>
> [205-10]

As a second speaker, the friend supports Persius's dramatic intention. Even words of blame in the mouth of the *adversarius*— "Your satires, let me tell you, are too fierce." (213)—become tacit praise in the judgment of the reader sympathetic to Persius. Simultaneously the satirist evades the trap of overt self-praise.

Two personalities in confrontation supply freshness to an old topic; that we know the victor from the outset in no way diminishes the excitement of the repartee.

At various times, Persius adopts a guise similar to that of the "querulous objector" attributed to Chaucer. The role, as it bears on Persius, prepares us to believe that "the persona-poet" is always on guard against critics—both friendly and unfriendly—who mean to "pick on" him.[23] Once the "humility topos" is fixed, Persius can assume the demeanor of a compliant, self-defensive poet who also wishes to explain his art. Thus *Satire V,* concerned in part with the nature of the writer's craft, presents an *adversarius,* but this time not in conflict with the poet. Repelled by the vapid grand style of would-be epic poets, Cornutus sardonically warns the poet, once his pupil:

> And why wou'd'st thou these mighty morsels choose,
> Of words unchaw'd, and fit to choke the Muse?
> Let fustian poets with their stuff be gone,
> And suck the mists that hang o'er Helicon;
> When Progne's or Thyestes' feast they write,
> And, for the mouthing actor, verse indite.
>
> [7–12]

The poet immediately acknowledges the absurdity of using language to inflate impoverished ideas. Armed with his own mock-aeolean imagery, he reassures the teacher:

> 'Tis not, indeed, my talent to engage
> In lofty trifles, or to swell my page
> With wind and noise; but freely to impart,
> As to a friend, the secrets of my heart.
>
> [27–30]

The adversary role, adaptable to varied circumstances, may even be reversed upon need, as in these two satires of Persius. The first depicts an opponent questioning the literary premises of the satirist; consequently the answer rises in angry intensity. With Lucilius and Horace as his models, he will not be stifled:

23. Morton W. Bloomfield, "The Gloomy Chaucer," *Veins of Humor,* ed. Harry Levin, in Harvard English Studies 3 (Cambridge, Mass.: Harvard University Press, 1972), pp. 64–65.

> and is my Muse controll'd
> By servile awe? Born free, and not be bold?
> At least, I'll dig a hole within the ground;
> And to the trusty earth commit the sound:
> The reeds shall tell you what the poet fears,
> King Midas has a snout, and asses' ears.
> This mean conceit, this darling mystery,
> Which thou think'st nothing, friend, thou shalt not buy.
> Nor will I change, for all the flashy wit,
> That flatt'ring Labeo in his Iliads writ.

[239–48]

The fifth satire, on the other hand, finds Cornutus asserting an artistic wisdom to which the poet-narrator can only accede:

> For this a hundred voices I desire,
> To tell thee what an hundred tongues wou'd tire;
> Yet never cou'd be worthily exprest,
> How deeply thou art seated in my breast.

[36–39]

The narrator, meeting each situation, shows himself to be flexible; he can be truculent but he can also love. This is so because, thanks to two insistent opponents and their colliding values, the poet has been obliged to reaffirm his faith—and ours—in the truth of his creative vision.

As mindful of his contemporary audience as of the classical past, Pope borrowed from Horace the *sermones* tradition of colloquy on controversial issues. In his first imitation (*Sat.* II. i), Pope with consummate skill concentrates much of his animosity toward the Walpole ministry. The *adversarius,* though secondary to the self-identified poet, is given the crucial task of posing issues that prompt the main speaker (*P.*) to confirm his values and test his moral perseverance. The choice of William Fortescue as the counterpart of Trebatius for the *adversarius* (*F.*) is a particularly happy one. A friend of both Walpole and Pope, Fortescue had already mediated between them, albeit without lasting effects. It was the lawyer who had introduced Pope to the first minister, attempting to bring them into some kind of social if not political harmony. Yet the poet obviously experienced no conflict or sense of threat in trusting this member of Walpole's court party. Contrarily, Pope praised him for his likeness to

"Trebatius, who was yet one of the most considerable lawyers of his time, and a particular friend of a poet."[24] Out of this analogy, the legalistic temperament of the *adversarius*—a kind of trial lawyer—is extracted and refined more deliberately than is that of the trusted intimate. Interspersed among the 156 lines of the poem are a half-dozen or so of the Friend's brief comments, each a reminder of the realistic obstacles that the Poet must expect to confront as a consequence of his stubborn idealism. Each time he retorts, the reader understands that another opening has been created for congratulation and esteem. The impression forwarded by the adversarial Friend is a shifting one—cynic, ironic trimmer, cautioner, prudent legalist, and courtroom virtuoso. Above all, he is the clever foil whose job is not so much to establish his own moral or political attitudes as it is to elicit from the Poet statements expressive of resolution, indignation, virtue, and friendship. The Poet, metaphorically, is testifying at his own trial.

With the pretended naiveté of apology, like Persius's to *his* friend, the Poet complains that the temper of his poetry has been misunderstood:

> There are (I scarce can think it, but am told)
> There are to whom my satire seems too bold.

The Friend sardonically recommends that he "write no more." And when the Poet protests that he cannot sleep at night, that "Fools rush into my head, and so I write," his adversary facetiously proposes that he avoid conflict, that he consider marriage or wine as alternative to public controversy. A nerve has been touched by the witticism (in these lines, as Pope once told Swift, lay the chief reason for the imitation). Even more rankling is the sly repetition of an option half-seriously recommended by Trebatius: "write Caesar's praise." All of this ironic nudging and

24. "Imitation of Horace," bk. II, Sat. I, in the *Twickenham Pope*, 4:5n. See pp. 4n.-5n. and 358 for identification of Fortescue. For political details, see Maynard Mack, *The Garden and the City: Retirement and Politics in the Later Poetry of Pope 1731-1743* (Toronto: University of Toronto Press, 1969). See also John M. Aden, "The Satiric Adversary," *Something Like Horace: Studies in the Art and Allusion of Pope's Horatian Satires* (Nashville, Tenn.: Vanderbilt University Press, 1969), pp. 3-26.

prodding moves the Poet through a register of moods, each contained (he announces in his own ironic voice) as though by the "honest mean" of "good Erasmus." "Satire's my weapon," he forthrightly declares at the midpoint of the poem, to be used against all corrupt and dissolute individuals—"hectors, thieves, supercargoes, sharpers, and directors."

The Great Man is there but subsumed in the crowd. The Poet's long speech (45–100), contrary to the claim of moderation, implies vengeful retaliation. It also invites the Friend's expedient warning that enemies will destroy him. Loftily indignant, the Poet immediately responds with another long balancing speech (105–42) that becomes a noble statement of virtue and friendship surmounting all odds and expediencies. The *adversarius*, seemingly moved but still cautious, reminds the Poet that the laws have never been kind to authors of "libels and satires." Thereupon the Poet identifies his art with the "grave epistles" whose "morality" (as Pope said elsewhere) is distinguishable from mere "wit":

> Such as a king might read, a bishop write,
> Such as Sir Robert would approve.

Convinced beyond doubt, the *adversarius* gives all the laurels to the Poet: "The case is altered" (a playful borrowing, perhaps, from the title of Ben Jonson's play)—

> In such a cause the plaintiff will be hissed,
> My Lords the Judges laugh, and you're dismissed.

The case is indeed the Poet's, but the *adversarius*—in the carefully measured counterpoint of the dialogue—makes precisely the right comments. His sometimes mocking, opportunistic hints bring forth the best in the Poet.

Even if invisible as an identified character—whether as an individual or collectively as society—the *adversarius* is present. When Boileau, for instance, appeals to "son Esprit" for support, the reader assumes that the poet is *the* creative force spinning out the web that will ensnare his enemies. No adversary as such can be seen or heard. Nevertheless, the very occasion of the poem suggests an undercurrent of conflict, and Boileau's monologue implies that he tilts against a concealed but formida-

ble army bent upon his destruction. In *London*, Thales speaks to
a sympathetic narrator, but his complaint also predicates the
unrecorded, composite voice of an unfeeling society that drove
him from the city. If, then, one allows oneself a stretch of imagination, a satiric adversary, even though not always consciously
audible, is fundamental.

The adversarial role may also be enacted by men of good will
like those Swift adumbrated as opponents of spiritual inadequacy. Mere nuances, they represent obligations unfulfilled just
as the visible dissemblers represent obligations violated. Like an
old-fashioned morality play in which forces of good and evil
contend for the individual's soul, *An Argument against Abolishing
Christianity* seeks to command the reader's latent probity. Addressing himself to the sense of guilt presumably within each of
us, Swift created a masterful impersonation of the Christian
apologist who pleads with mock sincerity that "it may perhaps be
neither safe nor prudent to argue against the abolishing of
Christianity, at a juncture when all parties appear so unani-
mously determined upon the point."[25] Through ironic distortion of conventional observances, the satirist causes the narrator
to elaborate the dangers besetting the Church of England. As he
unfolds his argument, he unconsciously proves his reliability
suspect, his propositions specious, and his religious motives re-
ducible to hypocritical self-seeking. With outrageous assurance
he holds that "the system of the Gospel, after the fate of other
systems, is generally antiquated." Primitive Christianity is dead,
so "nominal" Christianity—all that remains—is better than none
at all; certainly it is better than deism, nonconformity, and all
those chameleonlike forms of schism so upsetting to economic
and political order, to the Tory party with with its High-Flying
inclinations. Take away nominal Christianity and you take away
clerical employment from pleasure-loving young gentlemen,
and you deny the wits a popular source of ridicule.

The tone of the nominalistic argument, satanically mild and

25. "An Argument to Prove, that the Abolishing of Christianity in England,
may, as Things now Stand, be attended with some Inconveniencies, and perhaps,
not produce those many good effects proposed thereby," *Prose Works*, 2:26–39.
Cf. Tuveson, pp. 62–63, 65.

reasonable, makes Christianity appear fatuous. Less heroic than Milton's archenemy, Swift's clever speaker nonetheless descends from that same destructive tradition. He is represented as "the idol of true prudence," a master of disguise, and his model "the archetype of fraud." The fallen enemy of *Paradise Lost* had been careful to announce his strategy to followers who had necessarily to recognize their loss:

> our better part remains
> To work in close design, by fraud or guile
> What force effected not.
>
> [I. 645-47]

Swift's mask of course never announces his intention; he merely insinuates his "fraud or guile," cloaking his design in good manners and modish sophistry. Both characters, however, emphasize the invidious. And Milton's Satan being "the Father of lies," Swift's speaker is at the very least a son worthy of the parent.[26]

His particular mode of deception takes the form of ironic nuance opposed to which verbal rebuttal is futile. But the cumulative force of his sly words, if we understand Swiftian technique, exposes the self within the skin. No reasonable Christian, we may infer, will endorse these diabolistic insinuations. Contrarily we hope that Christian values will again come to be respected. These—on another expository occasion—Swift identified as "piety, truth, good sense, and good nature, affability and charity." Now, however, in the *Argument* he need not provide such bald explanation, for he has the advantage even over the Devil in the pulpit. A latter-day Jack the Giant-Killer, the satirist is protected by his own mask of invisibility. In addition, the absence of his identifiable voice is more eloquent than crafty rhetoric. Thus, unseen and unheard in his own person, Swift confidently allows sin to argue convincingly the cause of Christian virtue. That is his ultimate irony.[27]

26. John M. Steadman, *Milton and the Renaissance Hero* (Oxford: Clarendon Press, 1967), pp. 45-48; Swift's *Prose Works*, 1:152; 3:8-9; 5:116.

27. "A Project for the Advancement of Religion, and the Reformation of Manners," *Prose Works*, 2:43. Aristotle had this advice for the rhetorician: "Bring yourself on the stage from the first in the right character, that people may regard you in that light; and the same with your adversary; but do not let them see what you are about [i.e., hide your art]." *Rhetoric*, III. xvi. 1417.

The conflation of two satiric voices approximates the simplest organizational structure of debate. The public speech, Aristotle said, has "three elements . . . speaker, subject, and person addressed." We have seen in some satire two definable characters, the speaker and an *adversarius*, who may indeed be an antagonist or a teasing friend. In other satires, the speaker—even if we concede only a single audible one—assimilates at least two voices, his own and that of the *adversarius*. Both modes, rhetorical and satirical, have the common purpose of debating about things that may be proved. Satire, at its best, in other words, addresses itself to problems that have general implications and support conclusions. Now the auditor or reader, like Aristotle's hearer (I. iii. 1358), must be either spectator or judge, someone without immediate involvement but capable of being moved or prodded. The satirist has made a contract to reproach the bad or praise the good, to correct or reconcile the inequilibrium between flaws and virtues. He must persuade a third party, the reader, that a case for justice or against injustice has been made beyond all doubt.

When there is in fact not a debate but a friendly discussion leading to mutual understanding, the third party obviously has no external decisions to make. A colloquy between Persius and Cornutus, or between Horace and Trebatius, or Pope and Fortescue, as an instructive conversation, should bring salient, perhaps misunderstood, issues into the open. Such exchanges free the reader from a need to make a judgment in favor of this or that speaker. His role then becomes solely one of self-judgment, to test his own values in relation to those brought forth in dialogue. But when, as more frequently happens, the discourse is argumentative, the likelihood of a concession by either disputant diminishes. Then the reader finds himself in a mediating role, for before reassessing his own values—if he has doubts—he must decide which satiric position persuades him. Rhetoric provides a useful analogy for the satirist who turns to *De Oratore*. There Cicero describes a third, judicial voice expected to resolve the dispute appropriately. Speaking as the counsel, but with the same disposition toward right and justice as the satirist, M. Antonius describes how he weighs the pros and cons of an issue. First he thrashes out the case in dialogue with his client: "Then, when he has departed, in my own person and with perfect impartiality I play three characters, myself, my opponent, and the arbitrator." Admittedly a distinction exists between the satirist maneuvering his readers into compliance and the legalist preparing a brief to convince a jury and judge. But even though the satirist may never step inside a courtroom, he has a compatible need to argue, plead, and convince. The Ciceronian concept of three voices is analogous to vocal multiplicity in satire. M. Antonius's claim of "impartiality" must in the first place be questioned. He collects and examines all the evidence, but like any debater—or shrewd satirist—he may exclude anything disadvantageous to his argument: "Whatever consideration is likely to prove more helpful than embarrassing I decide to discuss; wherever I find more harm than good I entirely reject and discard the topic concerned." Moreover, we should recall the further link between the courtroom rhetorician and the satirist through the Ciceronian three-in-one: *meam, adversarii, iudicis.*[28] Not only is there a correspondence of the satiric persona and adversary with the first two roles enacted by the legalist, but the audience interacts with the satirist as *iudicis.* For him as for Cicero, the triptych consolidates indictment and trial and sentence.

The argumentative, accusatory tenor typifying much satire relates it almost inevitably to a design that resembles judicial process. But it will not do to forget that while the satirist has assumed the part of mankind's avenging conscience, he works at the same time as an artist. His often elaborate *elocutio* of style and character—especially as it affects persona and adversary— indicates a moral aesthetic. And it also signals commitment to a fictional understructure. Characters—the contending agents of satire—symbolize not only fools and knaves but their opposites as well, wise and honest men. Furthermore, human behavior, lest it evaporate in the clouded unreality of Mount Helicon, must

---

28. "Itaque cum ille discessit, tres personas unus sustineo summa animi aequitate, meam, adversarii, iudicis." *De Oratore,* II. xxiv. 102. Cf. Maynard Mack, "The Muse of Satire," *Yale Review* 41 (Autumn 1951): 80–92, for another concept of the three voices in one: *naif, vir bonus, hero.* Anderson, *Anger in Juvenal and Seneca,* p. 25, qualifies the legal implications of satiric argument.

occur within an appropriate environment. Formal satire, certainly, provides locations, perhaps "a moving panoramic background—a street, a royal court, another journey to Brundisium—some setting wherein people pass by and thus provide a steady stream of type-figures on whom the Satirist can comment to the Adversarius." Containing the narrative-dramatic circumstance is an outer frame, a composite of external details, which include the setting.[29]

The satiric design incorporates *topoi,* for—regardless of general applicability—social infractions are as a rule fixed within a place and a time. Juvenal, for example, equated a corrupt Roman civilization with a city in collapse, its natives threatened by falling houses or fires, and its visitors perverted by "Italian" behavior. Symbolically, the people of Rome "inhabit a weak city . . . which buttresses and props but scarcely bear" (*Sat. III,* 314-15). In order to emphasize the harsh exigency of Roman life, Juvenal introduces an edenic contrast into his satire. Momentarily the wistful, idealizing landscapist, he hints the purity of vaguely seen, distant places that escaped urban debasement. But that remote perspective is a fitful solace for most city-dwellers, as is his futile warning:

> Fly foreign youths from our polluted streets,
> And, ere unman'd, regain your native seats;
> Lest, while for traffic here too long you stay,
> You learn at last to trade th' Italian way;
> And, with curs'd merchandise returning home,
> Stock all your country with the figs of Rome.
>
> [*Satire II,* 240-45]

These sordid infestations, repeated seemingly without end, can occur in any city and at any time.

When Boileau (in 1660) composed his sixth satire, the malaise lamented by Juvenal in his third satire—with all the physical and spiritual decadence described there—was as vividly appropriate to seventeenth-century Paris as it had been to ancient Rome.

---

29. Randolph, "Structural Design," p. 372. See also Alvin B. Kernan, *The Cankered Muse: Satire of the English Renaissance* (New Haven: Yale University Press, 1959), pp. 7-14, for comments on scenes of disorder and crowding in such diverse artists as Bosch, Hogarth, and Nathanael West.

The affective quality of Boileau's lines transcends mere literary imitation or translation:

> Des filous effrontéz, d'un coup de pistolet,
> Ébranlent ma fenêtre, et percent mon volet.
> J'entens crier partout, au meurtre, on m'assassine;
> Ou, le feu vient de prendre à la maison voisine.
> Tremblant, et demi-mort, je me lève à ce bruit,
> Et souvent sans pourpoint je cours toute la nuit.
> Car le feu, dont la flâme en ondes se déploie,
> Fait de notre quartier une seconde Troie,
> Où maint Grec affamé, maint avide Argien,
> Au travers des charbons va piller le Troïen.
> Enfin sous mille crocs la maison abîmée,
> Entraîne aussi le feu qui se perd en fumée.

[101-12]

And when some forty years later John Tutchin launched a vitriolic attack upon King James, the city persisted as the central symbol of moral ruin. Now it was London, the scene of persecution and tyranny, that was in flames, its burning houses and temples the metaphors of hellfire zealotry. With the passage of still another forty years, Johnson could count on the continuing popularity of the city imaged as an inferno of the spirit. Under criminal siege, its hallmarks were murder, arson, and felony.[30] For him, as for Tutchin, Boileau, and countless others who utilized urban symbols of degeneration, the painfully pragmatic realities were the "here and now."

By extension, the specific functions as a symbolic truth pertinent to all places and times.[31] Occasionally a satirist wishing to stress the universality of locale leaves it unidentifiable. For *The*

---

30. *Oeuvres en Vers*, 1:93–94; John Tutchin, *The British Muse: or Tyranny Expos'd. A Satyr Occasion'd by all the Fulsom and Lying Poems and Elegies, that have been Written on the Death of the Late King James* (printed by Eliz. Mallet, and sold by the Williamite Book-Sellers of London and Dublin, who are Haters of Tyranny and Slavery [1701]); Johnson's *London,* passim.

31. T. S. Eliot, insistent on satiric specificity, is unduly restrictive—if we understand his argument—on the possibilities of fiction and fantasy. Of Jonson's drama, for instance, he writes that it is "only incidentally satire, because it is only incidentally a criticism of the actual world." "Ben Jonson," *Selected Essays, 1917–1932* (London: Faber and Faber, 1932), p. 151.

*Vanity of Human Wishes* Johnson selected a series of natural settings—mostly unnamed—that are bleak and threatening, a physical parallel for everything base, cruel, and disillusioned in the human state. Thus thieves who hide in "the rustling brake . . . and quiv'ring shade" harass the traveler; the hardships of winter and the isolation of a "barren strand" paralyze the soldier; valleys entomb dead enemies; summits (ironically stripped of poetic exaltation) become heights of inaccessible ambition. Johnson kept pictorial details of setting deliberately vague: they must in no way overshadow the imagery of conflict that dominates the poem; yet they must enhance and even give earthly substance to the poem's tragic irony.

Whereas Johnson symbolized locale as abstraction, Swift specified the grossness of reality: his grimly circumscribed vision of London in *A Description of a City Shower* includes physical and spiritual degradation, moral filth and smells, the detritus of wasted lives and hopes:

> Sweepings from butchers' stalls, dung, guts, and blood,
> Drown'd puppies, stinking sprats, all drench'd in mud,
> Dead cats and turnip-tops come tumbling down the flood.
>
> [61–63]

His Smithfield and Snow Hill and Holborn Bridge were as tangible as anyone living in 1710 could have wished. One of the most familiar regions to be used for local color, Grub Street persisted as a topographical fact in such poems as *The Dunciad, Trivia,* and *London.* In *The Beggar's Opera,* similarly, allusions to stock names neatly fix the location: Newgate, Hockley-in-the-Hole, St. Giles, Lewkner's Lane. But Gay did not always succeed when he attempted to give metaphoric distinction to Grub Street *topoi.* An air in *The Beggar's Opera* (I. vii), for example, likens virgins to the ambiguously *scented-sent* "fair flower in its lustre":

> But, when once pluck'd, 'tis no longer alluring,
>   To Covent-Garden 'tis sent, (as yet sweet,)
> There fades, and shrinks, and grows past all enduring,
>   Rots, stinks, and dies, and is trod under feet.

The wit was doubtless appreciated by contemporary London

audiences to whom Covent Garden was as notorious for its pros-
titutes as it was for its flowerstalls.[32] As with an extended pun—
and that is what these lines become—the joke ceases and we are
left with a seamy description that does not differ conspicuously
from seamy actuality. The satire has been abraded by the passing of so many years.

Still, along with many of his fellow satirists, Gay could stretch
the metaphoric from everyday vulgar usage into mocking
sophistication. In *Trivia* (II. 123–26), thus:

> Now had the watchman walk'd his second round;
> When *Cloacina* hears the rumbling sound
> Of her brown lover's cart, for well she knows
> That pleasing thunder.

The feigned delicacy reminds us of the rhetorician's *urbanitas,*
which "denotes language with a smack of the city in its words,
accent and idiom, and further suggests a certain tincture of
learning derived from associating with well-educated men."
Quintilian here (VI. iii. 17) describes wit linked to objects more
prim or more refined than those marked out by Gay. The latter's
earthiness nevertheless accommodates itself within the frame of
*urbanitas,* for it is contrived both in nuance and image as the
product of a city-bred imagination. Despite its broad intention,
Gay's circumlocution affects a gentility well suited to mannered
urban tastes. If only indirectly and by extension, Quintilian had
made available to the English poet a fiat for scatology comically
heightened, for the translation of street usage into drawing-
room polish. So too Pope played his literary game when in the
second book of *The Dunciad* he created pseudodecency out of
the generally unmentionable. There—though with prolonged,
more glittering panache than Gay's—he dressed excremental
details in classical allusion. Through a fantasy created by often
mythic language, Pope's derision enfolds the dehumanization of
city people. His allusions are elegant and learned, but they have
to do with slime, noise, and stink. The word-plays are both

---

32. For the importance of topological reference in satire, see Pat Rogers, *Grub
Street: Studies in a Subculture* (London: Methuen, 1972).

urban and urbane, and the realities of city existence are as ugly
to Gay and Pope as to Swift and Juvenal.

Grub Street is responsible for much city satire; in its squalor
hacks languished and knaves and debtors hid. Still, in an ironic
sense, another city always existed beyond the pestilential limits
of Grub Street, a decorous, sophisticated city as hospitable to
well-dressed sharpers and rascals as Grub Street to their less
fortunate kin. If the learned professions, for instance, dis-
claimed affinity with cheats, felons, and demireps, they did so
contrary to opinions like Peachum's. "A lawyer," he said, "is an
honest employment, so is mine. Like me too he acts in a double
capacity, both against rogues and for 'em; for 'tis but fitting we
should protect and encourage cheats, since we live by 'em" (I. i).
Polly likes to think of herself as a fine lady (I. vii) and to assume
the complacency of a young married woman (II. xiii). The wit
emanates from the obvious fact that Peachum is not honestly
employed and Polly is neither fine nor married. By virtue of
these comparisons, whatever else the case, Gay leveled social
distinctions to show that high and low are all one, that gentility
differs not at all from mock gentility.[33]

And Pope, when he turns his back on Grub Street to draw his
timeless sketches of Belinda at her dressing table, at ombre, at
coquettish sex play, implies conclusions not far removed from
Gay's: the *ton* supports vanities and follies no less deceitful than
the shady maneuvers of the Peachum substratum. Goldsmith,
making his Chinese traveler privy to the inanities of a later Belinda, saw no more reason than Pope or Gay to accept the tin-
seled absurdity of London high life.[34]

For all its ribaldry and horse laughter, city satire is so cynical

---

33. For other views of the high-low analogy, see Martin Price, *To the Palace of
Wisdom: Studies in Order and Energy from Dryden to Blake* (Garden City, N.Y.:
Doubleday, 1964), pp. 305–12; Ronald Paulson, *Satire and the Novel in
Eighteenth-Century England* (New Haven and London: Yale University Press,
1967), pp. 73 ff. Bertrand H. Bronson discusses certain "revolutionary" implications in "The Beggar's Opera," *Facets of the Enlightenment: Studies in English Literature and its Contexts* (Berkeley and Los Angeles: University of California Press,
1968), pp. 86–88.

34. See *Citizen of the World*, Letter 39. Cf. Hogarth's plates, *Marriage à la Mode*.

that it flattens the consequences of material fortune: well-bred affluence does not assure the exercise of human worth any more than do the filth and pathos of Grub Street. City satire is thus both realistic and innately gloomy enough to suggest only dim hope, its promise of commonsensical reform distant. Nevertheless it calls attention to human dignity, if only through myriad examples of obtuseness or villainy. The city as *topos,* generating anger as well as near-despair, creates a fertile environment for satire.

III

Actions that represent the polarities of human failure and triumph become indispensable agents of satiric thought and structure. Taken in sum, they may constitute a plot. Yet much satiric writing is centered in isolated incidents or events without dependence upon that complexity of sequential actions generally assumed to be plot. Sermons or political pamphlets and essays frequently incorporate scriptural, historical, or fictional analogues in simple narrative form. No one mistakes the paradigm for the whole or expects it to have the function of a plot that will supersede and even subsume a larger ethical statement. Further, when that complexity does take place in narratively disposed satire, the customary Aristotelian imperatives of plot may simply not be there. But why need they be? If we cannot require that all tragedy observe a "direct, linear progression" of action, then we would be unreasonable to insist upon straightforward, sequential movement in satire, which often tends toward fragmentation: "collections of loosely related scenes and busyness which curls back on itself."[35]

In satiric plot, further, we seldom if ever *see* change. The visible satiric structure need not bring before the reader's eyes mutations akin to the theatrical ones of dramatic discovery or recognition leading to a reversal in action and a resolution. Nevertheless, a process of change emerges even though we do not expect it to take place within the structure itself or in the

35. Kernan, *The Plot of Satire* (New Haven and London: Yale University Press, 1965), pp. 100–101, answers the critics of satiric plot.

objects, things and people, satirized. The kinetic phenomenon becomes rather one of vision, initially the disapproving vision of the author and—he hopes—ultimately that of the reader. The author, representing his own critical dissatisfaction with the world, shares the results not as a continuum but only as an *a posteriori* conclusion. If a narrative movement is shown or related within the satire, it seldom insists openly on an ethical choice. Belinda has learned nothing from her misadventure. Lemuel Gulliver undergoes superficial metamorphoses—regressive at that—but by the end of the fourth voyage he remains pretty much the same as he was at the start of the first: he is no better equipped to make discriminating judgments. The truth of inner reality may be clarified by experience, but not reversed. Similarly in satire, this inner truth may be sharpened, but not reconstituted as a different kind of truth. No longer the magician or miracle-worker of primitive times, the satirist may, by looking at the real with epistemological wonder, induce in his readers thereafter an attitude toward the real similar to his own.

The satirist's plot reconstructs a quicksand reality. Somewhere, he knows, there is substance, but disaster is more likely than fulfillment to reward the search for it. Reality is disguised by treachery made absurd, by illusion and corruption enacted with Chaplinesque pathos. Whatever the disguise, the victim remains. Because this vision of reality tends to be kaleidoscopic and fragmented rather than disciplined by successive events, it does probably translate itself into an appearance of "disjunctiveness." When action does not visibly follow action, when parts give no sensible notion of relationships to a whole, then random dispersal may become more apparent than causality. Satiric discontinuity may offend many readers as being somehow a failure in narrative logic. We cling to the myth that life flows along contiguously and rationally; but the perceptive satirist understands that human affairs are frequently governed by caprice or self-interest that subverts moral order. Indeed, the semblance of logic in satire may even be distrusted when, as in *A Modest Proposal,* the causality we see is ironic make-believe, a deliberate reversal of cherished but self-delusive norms. What passes for order is the lie, what the satirist fabricates is the truth.

As we have seen and shall see, various kinds of satiric plots exist but none lends itself more readily to satiric art than the episodic. Here in a series of actions or events or scenes, though each serves as a more-or-less complete narrative unit, it is not often linked obviously to the one preceding or following it. Multiple episodes in *The Dunciad* or *The Vanity of Human Wishes*, for instance, violate sequence. The violation is real because their authors have chosen to omit physical links. They have, rather, secured the episodes one to another through implication and the thematic weight of accumulated evidence.

Satiric plots, then, may proceed by means of unlinked episodes, or by fits and starts—digressively, erratically, enigmatically—as in *A Tale of A Tub* and *Tristram Shandy*. Or they may employ an ironic logic and so *seem* to achieve a mathematical—though specious—beginning, middle, and end. A favorite of Swiftian satire, the technique of delusion plays tricks, compelling the reader to differentiate between order and disorder, between genuine and debased values. But we need not assume that all satiric plots are disjunctive, pieced together out of chaotic bits, or even logically illogical. Satiric plot can also be reasonably straightforward. Certainly this is true of *Absalom and Achitophel* and the separate voyages of *Gulliver's Travels*. And what can be ordered more tidily than *The Rape of the Lock,* which begins with the rising of Belinda's sun and ends with its setting? What we must conclude is that satiric plot never satisfies a single or dogmatic definition. It shows up in many structural shapes but in good satire the plot contributes always to wholeness.

Two qualities may be insisted upon as the essence of satire. One is ethical, the confirmation of human "norms, systematic values, and meanings." The other is aesthetic, "an appreciable degree of fictionality." These qualities intertwine, although the ethical often appears to be the more pronounced.[36] The satirist "makes" fables and myths and fantasies. His stuff encompasses

36. Mack, "The Muse of Satire," pp. 84, 92; Aristotle, *Rhetoric*, III. xvi. 8. Although, according to Rosenheim, the satirist is not obliged in the work itself to be affirmative, he does assume an obligation to deal with "truth" (pp. 180–81). See his chapter "The Satiric Truth" (pp. 179–238) in *Swift and the Satirist's Art.*

the absurdity of a chivalric Quixote and of Swift's Aeolistic Enthusiasts, the merdamantean heroics of Pope's demiworld hacks
and of Fielding's conniving clergy, as well as the grotesques of
Smollett. Symbolic distortion often becomes the indelible mark
of satire, as vivid and timeless as the creations of Bosch or
Hogarth. Grotesquerie collides with experience in Ezra Pound's
rendering of the begrimed moneylender and in Nathanael
West's surrealistically mutilated Lemuel Pitkin.[37] But the distor-
tions simply emphasize the illogicality and brutality of experience; they convey a sense of residual truth beneath the buckled
surface. Such fictions thrive on greed, stupidity, and injustice,
on fools and knaves and their victims, for all of whom are invented traits commensurate with whatever is pathetic, laughable,
contemptible, or with whatever causes indignation in the
satirist's ethic. These fictions sort out people, electing through
character and personae those who must be brought to public
notice for blame as well as for praise. These fictions, with the aid
of exaggeration or diminution, burlesque or parody, are meant
not only to entertain but also to put audiences on guard against
folly and sin. Fuguelike, the satiric composition can be
polyphonic, but its very diversity induces at last a singleness of
temper and meaning.

37. Cf. Elliott, pp. 20, 59-61, 91, 129, 260, 271-72; Northrop Frye, "Mythos
of Winter," *The Anatomy of Criticism* (Princeton: Princeton University Press,
1957), pp. 223-39; Rosenheim, p. 133; Paulson, *The Fictions of Satire* (Baltimore:
Johns Hopkins Press, 1967), pp. 9, 13; Nathanael West, *A Cool Million: The
Dismantling of Lemuel Pitkin*, in *Complete Works* (New York: Farrar, Straus and
Cudahy, 1957); *The Cantos of Ezra Pound* (New York: New Directions, [1934-]
1948), 6th printing, cantos XIV, XV, pp. 61-67. Pound comments: "Satire reminds one that certain things are not worth while. It draws one to consider time
wasted." See "The Serious Artist," in *Literary Essays of Ezra Pound*, ed. T. S. Eliot
(Norfolk, Conn.: New Directions, 1954), p. 45. According to Auden, Nathanael
West's failure to relate fantasy and unreality to voluntary acts of conscience
removes him from the orbit of satiric concern. See "Interlude: West's Disease," p.
240.

CHAPTER 3

# APOTROPAIC VISIONS:
## Satiric Tone and Meaning

One of the most empiric of all literary methods, satire
schematically challenges pretense and error, opening them to
common review as though they were items like Fielding's "bill of
fare to the feast." Such, typically, is the promise on the title page
of an anonymous novel (1775), *The Adventures of a Cork-Screw: in
which under the pleasing method of a romance, the vices, follies and
manners of the present age are exhibited and satirically delineated. Interspersed with striking anecdotes, characters and actions of persons in
real life; all drawn to promote virtue, expose vice, and laugh folly out of
countenance.* Whatever the dubious worth of this novel, its function is plainly demotic. Because satire preoccupies itself with
received morality, one of the most damning charges against it is
undue obscurity; one of the most telling arguments in its favor is
that it projects a credible image of human nature.

The language and style, consequently, and the tone in which
they are conveyed become measures of persuasion. In satire a
degree of subtlety enhances the fiction. But a danger always
lurks that in his zeal to create an aesthetically palatable vehicle
the satirist will blur his didactic intention and thus diminish its
applicability. Granted, there is generally little rational taste for
the hacking, dismembering technique that once made the satirist
synonymous with the state executioner: "Our poets, the John
Ketches of the nation, / Have seem'd to lash ye, ev'n to excoriation." A neater touch than Mrs. Ketch—with questionable
accuracy—claimed for her husband is wanted of the satirist.

What "a vast difference," Dryden memorably remarked, "betwixt the slovenly butchering of a man, and the fineness of a stroke that separates the head from the body, and leaves it standing in its place."[1] But the stroke must not be so fine that the victim remains unaware of his beheading. Most spectators, hence, relish the startled recognition of James Thurber's decapitated fencer as a jubilant opponent cries out "Touché!" The best satire makes its way somewhere between rarefied irony and crude imprecation, and always within the range of verifiable experience. And the best satirist, to change metaphors, proves himself an expertly practical marksman who knows how to

> shoot Folly as it flies,
> And catch the Manners living as they rise.
> [*An Essay on Man*, I. 13-14]

Johnson would have subscribed to such a sentiment. He too, like Pope in numerous satires, scrutinized man's "living," that is, his *real* state, to discover where he had fallen short of his promise. Satire, Johnson therefore insisted, has no relevance if it fixes too much attention on the unfamiliar and the eccentric. *The Memoirs of Martinus Scriblerus* is faulty by this test because it "cures diseases that were never felt." *The Rape of the Lock,* on the other hand, juxtaposes the commonplace and the new. In the poem "nothing real is introduced that is not seen so often as to be no longer regarded, yet the whole detail of a female-day is here brought before us invested with so much art of decoration that, though nothing is disguised, every thing is striking, and we feel all the appetite of curiosity for that from which we have a thousand times turned fastidiously away."[2] *The Rape* continues unabatedly a triumph, in Johnson's opinion, because it renders a brilliantly evocative statement of experience that never stales.

Admonitory in spirit and attitude, satire thrives upon realistic or topical matter. This assumption presupposes clear, well-defined subjects; but the clarity that informs a work in the age

---

1. Dryden, prologue to *Albion and Albanius,* ll. 3–4; *On Satire,* p. xlii. See the macabre half-sheet broadside: *The Apologie of John Ketch Esq; the Executioner of London, in Vindication of Himself as to the Execution of the Late Lord Russell, on July 21, 1683.*

2. *English Poets,* 3:182, 233–34; cf. Boswell's *Life,* 4:17.

for which it was written may become murky in another. And indeed, sometimes with the satirist's caution or malice aforethought, the references may be hidden even in his own time. In many instances allusions to persons and events are not intelligible unless they are annotated. And this need in turn often provokes complaints of obscurity. The reproach may not be wholly without basis. According to classical fiat the satirist can justify topicality only if it leads to generalized conclusions. Otherwise the satire of passing events is marred by receding time and thus nullifies itself.

For reasons like these, Johnson's approach to Butler combines the ambivalence of pleasure and distrust. Despite an addiction to oddities, Butler "had watched with great diligence the operations of human nature and traced the effects of opinion, humor, interest, and passion." Nevertheless, his sense of the peculiar and the temporal had limited his vision, giving to *Hudibras* the appeal of singularity, which—no matter how engaging—was attuned only to current mores. "Such manners," wrote Johnson, "as depend upon standing relations and general passions are co-extended with the race of man; but those modifications of life and peculiarities of practice which are the progeny of error and perverseness, or at best of some accidental influence or transient persuasion, must perish with their parents." Although Johnson admired Butler for being involved in the world about him, he felt that his allusions were so bound to a particular time that they became "every day less intelligible and less striking."[3]

If satire is to be applicable for all times, then its occasional or historical allusions may have to be annotated for later generations. Codes—anagrams, initials, asterisks, and allied cryptogrammic tricks—are entertaining *and* useful when their shorthand can be understood. Yet sometimes the utility of a code eludes recognition, as often happens in Sterne's contrived chaos of nuance and sign. Then the reader has the choice between a floundering search after hidden epistemological truths and floating with the pleasant tides of absurdity that are Sterne's

3. *English Poets*, 1:213–14; cf. Trapp, *Lectures on Poetry*, p. 232.

truths. He knew how to orchestrate his materials for their best effects—comic, bawdy, provocative—through a mix of alogical and nonverbal symbols: "'Tis a point settled,—and I mention it for the comfort of *Confucius*, who is apt to get entangled in telling a plain story—." The narrator carefully explains: "*Mr. Shandy* is supposed to mean **** *** ***, Esq; member for ******,—and not the *Chinese* Legislator" (V, 25). The satire of this passage is no more than inferential, parody being hinted in the asterisks and self-mimicry in the comment about confused storytelling. Beyond these fragile thrusts at order, meaning— that is, the signification to be deduced from material things and persons—seems less essential than the comic spirit that pervades *Tristram Shandy*.

Certainly nothing material has been cloaked in this witty obfuscation. More rigorously minded authors than Sterne, however, faced the sometimes awkward task of composing satires that could be understood despite their outward masking. Attacks on important individuals and institutions were risky enough to justify camouflage, which had necessarily to be penetrable. Some prominent subjects could of course be deciphered without undue difficulty, especially by select audiences. For larger circulation, however, layers of disguise might have been self-defeating, had not many an editor busied himself with explications. Without editorial assistance what are the uninitiated to make of Churchill's elaborate dissection of the participants in the Cock Lane affair? Who were "Trifle" and "Whiffle"? Having been informed, we may not be especially enlightened. And yet we are reassured for knowing that these and many others were real men behind masks. And to compensate for a lack of distinction, we are given the powerful identifiable presence of someone like "Pomposo"—Johnson himself, about whom we do care.[4] Notes then help to perpetuate the satiric bite and warrant the use of literary indirection.

4. "The Ghost," in Churchill's *Poetical Works*, bk. II, ll. 361–90, bk. IV, ll. 485–568, and pp. 491, 503. Churchill's degenerate "Whiffle" suggests the effeminate captain of that same name in Smollett's *Roderick Random* (ch. 34). For "Pomposo," see bk. II, ll. 335–36, 653–88. Dryden (*On Satire*, p. xxxi) discredited Persius's addiction to obscurity.

Swift believed that even contemporary readers could not be trusted to understand subleties. Consequently, he warned Pope (16 July 1728) that the notes for *The Dunciad* should

> be very large, in what relates to the persons concerned; for I have long observed that twenty miles from London no body understands hints, initial letters, or town-facts and passages; and in a few years not even those who live in London. I would have the names of those scribblers printed indexically at the beginning or end of the poem, with an account of their works, for the reader to refer to. I would have all the parodies ... referred to the authors they imitate—When I began this long paper, I thought I should have filled it with setting down the several passages I had marked in the edition I had, but I find it unnecessary, so many of them falling under the same rule.... How it passes in Dublin I know not yet; but I am sure it will be a great disadvantage to the poem, that the persons and facts will not be understood, till an explanation comes out, and a very full one.... Again I insist, you must have your asterisks filled up with some real names of real Dunces.[5]

Apparently Swift was not satisfied with Pope's assumption that the quasi anonymity of his duns did not matter. And Pope obviously changed his mind before bringing out the variorum *Dunciad* in 1729 replete with notes and names. But originally he "would not have the reader too much troubled or anxious, if he cannot decipher them; since when he shall have found them, he will probably know no more of the persons than before."

Swift had never accepted this calculated indifference, certainly not in *A Tale of a Tub* and *The Battle of the Books*, which mockingly identify principals or allusions. In an introductory note to *A Tale,* for instance, he wastes no subtleties: "Here the author seems to personate L'Estrange, Dryden, and some others, who after having passed their lives in vices, faction and falsehood, have the impudence to talk of merit and innocence and sufferings." And if Swift is parodic in "A Digression concerning Critics," he carefully insures exposure of his victims. "Every true critic," he writes, "is a hero born, descending in a direct line from a celestial stem, by Momus and Hybris, who begat Zoilus, who begat Tigellius, who begat Etcaetera the Elder, who begat

5. Swift, *Correspondence*, 3:290–91, 293. Swift's "long paper" is his response to Pope's request, 28 June, for criticism. For the history, texts, and editorial apparatus, see *The Dunciad* in the *Twickenham Pope*, vol. 5.

Bentley, and Rymer, and Wotton, and Perrault, and Dennis, who begat Etcaetera the Younger."[6] Whatever happy malice had moved Swift to make his recommendations to Pope is balanced for later readers by sound critical perception: once the identification has been fixed the pleasure-giving qualities of satire take a new turn for the informed reader. These include the intellectual satisfaction of telescoping the past into the now, and of restoring remote or elusive truths. As fully as they had for Pope's contemporaries, his wit and irony—intensified by the perspective of time—today remain killingly honed. With a poet as enigmatic as Pope, the joy of reading beneath the ciphers is quickened by notes that lead to discovery and surprise. A master of transparent deception, he makes his inventiveness particularly apt in *The Dunciad,* where he not only creates labyrinths but also charts them, ultimately as Swift would have wished. At every turn he fortifies the poem with editorial apparatus—his own and that of other commentators.

But although the notes and explanations become aesthetic accessions, most of them must serve meaning if names, places, events, and mythic allusions are to emerge. The attack on John Henley is one instance of what, without the poet's explication, might have remained pretentiously obscure insult:

> "But, where each Science lifts its modern type,
> Hist'ry her pot, Divinity his pipe,
> While proud Philosophy repines to show
> Dishonest sight! his breeches rent below;
> Imbrown'd with native bronze, lo Henley stands,
> Tuning his voice, and balancing his hands.
> How fluent nonsense trickles from his tongue!"
>                                        [III. 191–97]

As it is, however, the orator finds himself placed in the stocks for all to see not once but twice. First he is besmirched in the text by

6. *A Tale of a Tub,* pp. 42n., 57, and *The Battle of the Books,* pp. 159–65, in Swift's *Prose Works,* vol. 1. In *Gulliver's Travels,* however, only two years before publication of *The Dunciad,* Swift did without "very large" notes and commentary. Presumably he was satisfied that great men and events had revealed themselves even through a fictional disguise. Anyway, it was safer to avoid being too explicit about state affairs.

excremental imagery. The obvious scatology of line 195 is slyly complemented in line 197, where "trickles" becomes the mark not only of garrulity but of senile incontinence. And then Henley is subjected to Pope's explicit diminution in the notes, accused of slander, pulpit chicanery, philosophical buffoonery, and "unintelligible nonsense." Pope chose to be doubly offensive, making the low mockery of the verses even lower by feigning their dependence upon the overt explanation of the notes. He makes a game of obscurity that is in fact outrageously decipherable.

His gamesmanship was perhaps most apparent—most tauntingly deliberate—when he wished to allay any suspicion of faintheartedness. At any rate he liked to swagger a bit, prepared to complement the indirection of satiric wit with arrogant statement. For instance, "as the only certain way to avoid misconstruction, to lessen offence, and not to multiply ill-natured applications, I may probably in my next [that is, following the *Epistle to Burlington*] make use of real names and not of fictitious ones."[7] Pope here expressed a commonly held notion that satire must not be unduly subtle. "Gentlemen," Defoe had urged in the *Review* (20 January 1708), "back your satires with some names, or at least speak so plainly, that things and people might be guessed at." Satire, even when less personal than *The Dunciad*, must find its targets in identifiable experience. Defoe, to his subsequent grief, discovered this truism when in December 1702 he rashly flung himself into England's turbulent politico-religious squabbles. Ostensibly, his pamphlet *The Shortest Way with the Dissenters* was an "ironical satire" on the Occasional Conformity controversy. The main purpose of its ridicule, however, strained not so much against the tensions provoked by Occasional Conformity as it did against the absurdity of the unbending Anglican attitude toward Dissent. Behind the too real masks of the persona enunciating the Church Party accents of Sacheverell, or of Defoe's one-time schoolmate Samuel Wesley (the elder), and of other enemies of nonconformity was an ironist

---

7. *The Dunciad, Twickenham Pope,* 5:172–74; Pope to Burlington (Jan. 1731/32): *Correspondence,* 3:266.

whose irony ricocheted upon himself. Reproachfully, he remarked soon after the appearance of *The Shortest Way,* "When
the persecution and destruction of the Dissenters, the very thing
[the High Flyers] drive at, is put into plain English, the whole
nation will start at the notion, and condemn the author to be
hanged for his impudence." A decade later, Defoe was still insisting that he meant only to transcribe "the persecution and
destruction of the Dissenters . . . into plain English."[8] The plain-
ness was to be a semantic trap for the Church Party, designed to
trick its members into cheering their own intolerance and to
stand self-accused.

By mimicking much that was offensively doctrinaire to him,
Defoe seems initially to have assumed that the irony of his trans-
posed reasoning would be obvious. When High Flyers seriously
attacked the "swarm of sectarists" and the "conventicles" in
which they were "nursed," he attacked conventicle insurrection
even more boldly; and he called for retribution against the Dissenters not by mere "mulcts" and "fines" but by exile and even
execution. Unfortunately for Defoe, the irony misfired because
it had been accepted at face value by the Anglican enemy. In
what they had taken to be a literal context, they were delighted
to see the dissenting rascals served so well by enthusiastic assaults
*ad captandum, baculum, ignorantiam, populam,* and *conflandam invidiam.*[9] Defoe soon realized that his whimsy was likely to get him
into trouble, and he decided to clear up the joke in *A Brief
Explanation.* Frankly, he wrote, "It seems impossible to imagine

8. *The Shortest-Way with the Dissenters; or, Proposals for the Establishment of the
Church* (1702); *A Brief Explanation of a Late Pamphlet, Entitul'd, The Shortest Way
with the Dissenters,* p. 18 (appended to an edition of the offending essay 28 Feb.
1703); *The Present State of the Parties in Great Britain: Particularly an Enquiry into the
State of the Dissenters in England, and the Presbyterians in Scotland* (1712), fols. A2ᵛ–
A3, p. 24. See also James Sutherland, *Daniel Defoe: A Critical Study* (Cambridge,
Mass.: Harvard University Press, 1971), pp. 43–48; Maximillian E. Novak, "De-
foe's *Shortest Way with the Dissenters:* Hoax, Parody, Paradox, Fiction, Irony, and
Satire," *MLQ* 27 (1966): 402–17, and "Defoe's Use of Irony," William Andrews
Clark Memorial Library Seminar (Los Angeles, 1966).

9. For an ironical treatise on the *argumentum baculinum,* see Fielding's *Champion,* 5 Jan. 1739/40; on *argumentum ad conflandam invidiam,* Addison's *Old Whig*
1, 19 Mar. 1718/19, and Steele's *Plebeian* 2, 23 Mar. 1718/19. See also *Tristram
Shandy,* I, 21; and ch. 5, fn. 30, below.

[*The Shortest Way*] should pass for any thing but a banter upon the high-flying Churchmen." Not so. Rather than allaying consternation and anger, *A Brief Explanation* had the opposite effect: it outraged the duped High Flyers and deepened the suspicions of the Nonconformists. Consider, for instance, the author of *The Fox with his Fire-Brand*, a pamphleteer who saw only impudence and malice in Defoe's irony, and who consequently accused him of treason and feigned fanaticism. If the purpose of *The Shortest Way*, he argued,

> had not been purely malice and a seditious design to do mischief, why did he take all these pains, to strike this ironical terror, and fear of a mock-persecution, into the very hearts of the Dissenters? He professes himself to have no apprehensions of it from the *Occasional Bill*, but he knew most others had; and that therefore, this was the best time to give the alarm, to cry out first, *The* Philistines *were upon them;* and then the next cry is, *The Sword of the Lord and of* Gideon. These are a sort of ironies that have cost us too dear in *England.*

Defoe had set off an inflammatory paper war that—leaping from his ironic intention to the malevolent abuse of those who thought themselves injured—engulfed him. For all parties, his ridicule was uncomfortably close to being a home truth, it worked for none, and it earned him the humiliation of the pillory.[10]

His very smartness threatened to defeat the satire, for it erased the distinction between appearance and reality; when the fictional illusion fails, there is a danger that the satire also will fail. *The Shortest Way* must be admired as an ingenious literary spoof and as the almost too clever manipulation of a persona. Even in the afterglow of history, its topicality gives the essay an important local (that is, biographical and social) interest but not that universality expected of enduring satire.

Making satire evocative and durable, apart from its artistry and its historical associations, is its continuing pertinence, cul-

---

10. *The Fox with his Fire-Brand Unkennel'd and Insnar'd: or, a Short Answer to Mr. Daniel Foe's* Shortest Way with the Dissenters. *As also to his Brief Explanation of the same* (1703), p. 21. Cf. also *Reflections upon a Late Scandalous and Malicious Pamphlet Entitul'd,* The Shortest Way with the Dissenters; ... *With its Author's Brief Explication Consider'd, his Name Expos'd, his Practices Detected, and his Hellish Designs Set in a True Light* (1703).

tural or ethical. Satirists may take pleasure in their combined aesthetic and educative roles, but they also take pains to disclose themselves finally as men of the world, as observers attuned to life, which changes only superficially with the passage of generations and centuries. A writer like Horace is a paradox of sophisticated simplicity or of simplified contrivance. A self-conscious artist, he nonetheless harbors social impulses that demand as much of him as do his literary goals. In the aristocratic "public school" tradition subscribed to by many later satirists, Horace protests that he writes not for the crowds but for the select few.[11] And yet he also modestly insists that his satires—compounded of daily Roman customs that give him substance for judgment and censure—should not be regarded as poetry but as conversations, one-to-one dialogues that recall his practical involvement with an individual and a community they happen to share. Although Horace takes great pride in literary achievement, he does so as an intelligent social creature who can wed seemingly diverse concerns. Both imagination and mind, as he observed of all poetry in *De Arte Poetica,* contribute to the creative faculty: "Of good writing the source and fount is wisdom." *Scribendi recte sapere est et principium et fons* (309). Although the writer of satire is an artist, he stresses his duty to record a flawed experience. But also, precisely because he is an artist, he transfigures the immediate and mundane, giving their topical lessons a continuing, creative appeal.

As the satirist makes his rounds in the market place of human idiocies, weaknesses, and tragic shortcomings, he gathers the evidence that will enable him to report emotions and judgments stimulated by his offended conscience. The task he has set himself, with its built-in difficulties, requires the reconciliation of the hortatory with the literary. In the rhetorical tradition previously considered, the satirist must be at the very least the forthright judge who will induce others to sit on the bench with him and share his rulings on matters of truth and justice. And he must also be the attorney whose brief will effect a favorable outcome. Ultimately he must translate his criticism into literature.

11. Horace, *Sat.* I. x. 72–77; Dryden, *On Satire,* p. xxxii; Stephen Spender, *The Destructive Element,* p. 216.

II

Significant to satiric art, therefore, is its tone, the persuasive verbal pitch. To assure a sympathetic hearing, the tone must appeal to the imaginative as well as to the intellectual faculties. Both, it must be insisted, are connected by emotional demands. Because every satire is built upon some form of reproach, the satirist generally accommodates that reproach by ringing changes on the basic emotions of derision or anger. The laughter elicited by a satiric situation rarely if ever provides joy. The root cause of the satire, in other words, may be serious and yet, because of its treatment, antithetical to sober reaction. The ensuing laughter, Francis Hutcheson speculated, arises from a conjunction "of images which have contrary additional ideas, as well as some resemblance in the principal idea: this contrast between ideas of grandeur, dignity, sanctity, perfection, and the ideas of meanness, baseness, profanity, seems to be the very spirit of burlesque; and the greatest part of our raillery and jest is founded upon it."[12] Hutcheson's notional view of contrarieties as a source of laughter, well taken, bears upon familiar arguments linking wit and judgment.

But he moves too quickly—at least for the ends of satire—to reject the Hobbesian theory of laughter as a passion of "sudden glory" erupting from an abrupt assumption of individual superiority, of the egoistic awareness that derives from unexpected insight. This is what happens with "the sudden imagination of our own odds and eminence; for what is else the recommending ourselves to our own good opinion, by comparison with another man's infirmities or absurdity?"[13] Laughter, according to Addison, who subscribed to Hobbes's thesis (*Spectator* 47), is a serious business: "Every one laughs at some body that is in an inferior state of folly to himself."

The psychology of laughter does not lend itself to easy resolu-

12. *Reflections upon Laughter,* pp. 7, 18–19. Cf. *Spectator* 62, and the discussion of wit below.
13. Thomas Hobbes, *The Elements of Law, Natural & Politic,* ed. Ferdinand Tönnies (Cambridge: Cambridge University Press, 1928), pt. I, ch. 9, sec. 13, pp. 31–32; *Leviathan, or the Matter, Form & Power of a Commonwealth, Ecclesiastical and Civil* (Cambridge: Cambridge University Press, 1904), pt. I, ch. 6, p. 34.

tion, and nothing can be gained here from enlarging upon the dispute over whether a laugh betokens merriment or pride. Doubtless a strong case could be established for either. The satirist remains our concern, however, and clearly he often laughs to reassure himself about his own eminence as well as to disguise punitive intention. Concurrently he proposes in effect that any reader or auditor capable of sympathizing with the complaint—be it against an institution or a person—stands superior to fools and knaves. The satirist's appeal is psychological, but it is also physical. His audience may previously have had no more than a dormant awareness of a certain object of reproach. But when the satirist brings it to the surface, makes it conscious, the hitherto inactive revulsion explodes into derisive laughter, and the unsuspected scapegoat becomes a reality. The cruelty of laughter recurs as a truth of western myth and culture. Bergson argues that the function of laughter "is to intimidate by humiliating. Now, it would not succeed in doing this, had not nature implanted for that very purpose, even in the best of men, a spark of spitefulness or, at all events, of mischief.... [Laughter,] also, is a froth with a saline base. Like froth, it sparkles. It is gaiety itself. But the philosopher who gathers a handful to taste may find that the substance is scanty, and the after-taste bitter."[14]

When Pope in *An Epistle to Dr. Arbuthnot* racks Lord Hervey as Sporus, "That thing of silk, / . . . that mere white curd of ass's milk," the laughter he evokes is reminiscent of *Schadenfreude*: prompted by misfortune, it explodes out of malicious pleasure, which seeks to enlist as many readers as possible in the satirist's vendetta.[15] Even as Pope's enemies cruelly derided his physical deformities, he turned his wit on their crippled ethical values.

14. Henri Bergson, *Laughter: An Essay on the Meaning of the Comic*, trans. Cloudesley Brereton and Fred Rothwell (New York: Macmillan, 1914), pp. 198–200. In another fanciful metaphor, Arthur Koestler describes "the bacillus of laughter [as] a bug difficult to isolate" in *The Act of Creation*, p. 32.
15. "An Epistle from Mr. Pope to Dr. Arbuthnot," *Twickenham Pope*, 4:91–127; Erich Segal, "Marlowe's *Schadenfreude*: Barabas as Comic Hero," *Veins of Humor*, pp. 69–91.

Satiric laughter, although its immediate source or object may be private, is a form of release that takes effect only as a shared activity. Laughter invites others to share the reason for the laughter. Throughout *An Epistle to Dr. Arbuthnot,* numerous details draw us into a liaison of scorn. And yet, despite a prevalence of ridicule and detraction, the poem as a total experience is neither comic nor unconcerned with redemptive meaning. An oscillating design of light and somber, of trivial and serious, of irresponsible and moral, results in a remarkably controlled diversity of tone.

That tonality orders the reflexive quality of the poem: an emotionally exhausted poet, thinking back upon his career, tries to seclude himself from importunate petitioners who "rave, recite, and madden round the land." From a position of privileged intimacy, the reader listens to the (at first) gently complaining voice. The tone, however, is not one of self-indulgent petulance, for the poet—so often accused by his enemies of ingratitude—celebrates the benign influence of Arbuthnot, "Friend to my life." Pope identifies himself metaphorically as well as physically with the virtuous, moderate healer: the idealized counselor, model for his own virtue, refraction of that other, blood father, "The good man [who] walk'd innoxious thro' his age." The self-portrait of the poet highlights the attributes to be admired—for instance, his capacity for respect and friendship, his devotion to parents. But it also reaches out for compassion toward the harassed and victimized poet, disillusioned and justly fretful.

The egocentric tone is consciously moderated by the quasi modesty, the reluctant admission of a divine gift, the wryly adumbrated comparison with Horace, Alexander the Great, Ovid, Virgil, Homer. Deferring to the author's genius, we join in the rhythm of his contempt for the countless mediocrities and worse who "fly to Twit'nam," uninvited, for his patronage and advice. By destiny he serves as a magnetic force, the consummately rational man who attracts to himself all those boring, clutching hacks in whom are epitomized incompetence and irrationality. Madness, frequently mentioned in *An Epistle to Dr. Arbuthnot,* has little to do with clinical behavior. Rather—somewhat like Erasmus's Folly or Pope's Dullness—it becomes a comprehensive epithet suggestive of every kind of unreliability, from the economic and cultural to the literary. It can be a group malady, as we have seen when Pope's hacks "rave" as they "madden round the land." Whether applied to the mob or the vindictive individual, literary madness equals the desperation of inadequate and unwanted authors. For Pope, as for Locke, such irrationality symptomizes confused, silly men. "There are degrees of madness, as of folly," the philosopher wrote; "the disorderly jumbling ideas together, is in some more, and some less."[16]

The greatest folly, hence madness, of all is pride, which supplies Pope with ammunition for use against his enemies and gives special definition to the three famous portraits—Atticus, Bufo, and Sporus—at the center of the poem. In each instance, further, the pride feeds itself on vanity, hypocrisy, and love of flattery. The intensity of Pope's disdain, as he moves from fragmentary or mob-absorbed figures to three perceptible individuals, can be judged by the changing pitch of his tone. The movement is sharply downward, from the pathos of Atticus's fallen greatness, to the comic detestability of the swollen Bufo, to the utterly loathsome satanism of the perfumed Sporus. Everything that passed before, to use Pope's image, is like "dirt, or grubs, or worms" preserved "in amber." But now, after nearly 200 lines, the time for the encapsulated trifle is past, and Pope must get down to the darker and larger task that has been preying on him. With one sweeping gesture he dismisses such as "slashing Bentley" and the "pidling Tibbalds," venal Gildon, raving Dennis, and the others.

"Peace to all such!" the poet ironically declares, and begins the well-known repudiation of Addison. The tone at first is laudatory, but the praise is muted by nostalgia and regret. Atticus, "born to write, converse, and live with ease," has sacrificed his "True Genius" to pride and expedience. Pope's language is measured, as line by sardonically balanced line he builds the case

16. Johnson quotes Locke in his definition of "madness": *An Essay concerning Human Understanding, In Four Books* [II. xi. 13] in *The Works of John Locke, Esq.*, 3 vols. (1714), 1:60. For some modern comments on this theme, see J. Paul Hunter, "Satiric Apology as Satiric Instance: Pope's *Arbuthnot,*" *JEGP* 68 (Oct. 1969): 632–33; Spacks, *An Argument of Images,* p. 168.

against a secretive, reticent man accused of arrogance and self-esteem; powerful yet never quite willing to be a forthright leader or, for that matter, enemy. He would "damn with faint praise . . . Willing to wound, and yet afraid to strike." The timbre of Pope's voice, as he unfolds an account of Addison's sin of pride, steadily erodes the positive initial impression. The lost genius is irrecoverable, the Addisonian "leer" magnified by the Popean "sneer"—the sneer his one-time friend could teach but would not practice. The bill of charges—only about twenty lines—becomes a miracle of compressed effectiveness. Controlled and precise, Pope advances his argument by stages from reserved compliment to intensifying scorn, to the pitying conclusion, "Who would not weep, if Atticus were he!" Neither vehement nor theatrical, Pope succeeds in diminishing him; but if he allows him finally a vestige of nobility for what he might have been, the luster is really too badly tarnished for Atticus to be of tragic stature.

The transition to "full-blown Bufo"—literally, a swollen toad—strips away any possible claim upon our sympathy. A hybrid of Bubb Dodington and the Earl of Halifax, Bufo is the advertised patron, "puff'd by ev'ry quill; / Fed with soft Dedication all day long." Bloated and duplicitous, he conveys a hint of the demonic. Pope's tone, however, consistently demands a response weighted by scorn rather than fear or overwhelming revulsion. Like Atticus, Bufo is scarred by pride and love of praise. And also, more overtly than in the previous portrait, Pope very neatly crystallizes the patron's treachery when he converts the double peaks of Parnassus to a "forked hill" on which Bufo sits, incongruously "proud, as Apollo." Still, he falls short of absolute evil, for he is too much the sensualist, too much the self-server to achieve the outwardly directed energy associated with satanism. To a far greater extent than Atticus, for instance, Bufo is the devotee of easeful living. Finally, after all, he is ludicrous, a corpulent clown; and for all his proprietary demands upon starving writers, we can laugh at him.

But some fifty lines later, when the portrait of Sporus is unveiled, the risibility has virtually ceased to exist and the laughter has become a snarl of hatred. In a matter of fewer than 150 lines, from Atticus's corrupted genius to Sporus's reptilian venom, Pope has traced the outlines of degeneration from fallen eminence to bestiality. His tone, comparably, follows the line of descent: from the serious, often regretful accents toward Atticus to the ridicule of a conceited, worthless Bufo to the aggressive revulsion accorded an evil Sporus. The language of negation becomes progressively less abstract as Pope's horror becomes progressively more intense. The affective distance between Pope and Atticus, proportionately, is greater than that between him and Bufo, and even more so than that between him and Sporus. The movement of feeling, in short, becomes increasingly personal and spiteful. Pope has calculated the verbal tone of each characterization with a precision we would expect of the caricaturist whose pencil or brush emphasizes blemishes and oddities while subordinating the normal or unremarkable. In *An Epistle to Dr. Arbuthnot,* the painter and poet are in harmonious agreement. The same calculation is responsible for the sequence of portraits. With Atticus, we have observed, the satire operates on a fallen Adam, now beyond any possibility of restored grandeur. The personal motive cannot be discounted; but Pope chose also to create a satiric exemplum about what happens when pride dominates all other passion. The result is this carefully graded chain of imperfection, which begins where rational order leaves off and which concludes in evil.

The final degenerative link, then, is Sporus, whose evocation cannot but disgust. Pope spits out his lines with a contempt that barely hides something more sinister than personal antipathy. The connotations of the opening couplet—cited earlier—warn against a disintegration that is potentially destructive of an entire society. Whether extracted from Suetonius or Dion Cassius, the very name "Sporus" sets up pejorative associations. A reminder of the boy who became Nero's ceremonial bride, Sporus is the male *manqué,* a violation of normal or at least rational expectation.[17] In a physical sense, Pope's punning allusion to ass's milk

17. Butt, *Twickenham Pope* (4:177n.), traces Sporus to Suetonius. Hunter argues for Dion Cassius as Pope's source (p. 645), and also seems to prefer Nero's consul as the prototype of Atticus over Cicero's friend (p. 641).

and silk extends his attack to implications of asininity, debility, and effeminacy. "Curd" in this context is unpleasant-sounding. Closely followed by terms for filth, insects, and dogs, the word stirs up a "cur-curd-turd" pun and buried rhyme. "Curd" also intimates sourness that is none the more palatable in its utilitarian sense of a medicine for consumptives. And imbedded in the entire description is a cosmetic image, ass's milk having long been affected by women as a luxurious bathing substance. The extended epithet is packed with hints of bisexuality, mincing frailty, foppishness, and bitchery. Curd, according to one interpretation, is an indeterminate property between the malleable and the shapeless. Metaphorically, that is, it complements the moral elusiveness of Sporus who, "one vile Antithesis. / Amphibious Thing," can be anything and everything. By extension, the curd's whiteness—colorless and neutral—is the ideal cover, as noncommittal as Sporus himself.[18]

Naming and describing Sporus as he did, Pope unburdened himself in a fashion typical of personal satirists from the time of Archilochos and earlier. But Pope, despite the patent specificity of his assault, has moved beyond the privately abusive to a larger symbolic concern with the nature of evil, from the human culpability of Atticus and Bufo to a diabolical Sporus who "at the ear of Eve, familiar toad, / Half froth, half venom, spits himself abroad." Pope's tone allows for no equivocation. Sporus is a low copy of Milton's Grand Deceiver:

> Eve's tempter thus the Rabbins have exprest,
> A Cherub's face, a reptile all the rest;
> Beauty that shocks you, parts that none will trust,
> Wit that can creep, and pride that licks the dust.

To conclude here, however, is to overlook another meaning of the poem, its celebration of the virtuous poet. In triumphant counterpoint, he periodically interrupts the catalogue of pride-driven sinners and offers himself as a contrary example. We

18. For Pope's use of ass's milk and its presumed therapeutic benefits, see Marjorie Nicolson and G. S. Rousseau, *"This Long Disease, My Life": Alexander Pope and the Sciences* (Princeton: Princeton University Press, 1968), pp. 37–44. Hunter (p. 638) treats the curd as one aspect of Pope's self-mockery and as a symbol of Sporus's variability.

observed earlier that he emerges as the writer who must suffer
fools and vicious men. He is defiantly righteous, even in the face
of his friend's warning that he deals "in dang'rous things" when
he speaks truth about monarchs and their ministers. Although
Atticus and Bufo are besieged by seekers of their benefactions,
Pope reminds the rest of us that *he* at least "sought no homage."
Before introducing Sporus, he declares the fearless integrity of
his aim: "A lash like mine no honest man shall dread." The
struggle for ethical wholeness, he implies, is difficult but not
futile. Although he nears bitterness in the excoriation of everything unworthy, he wishes us to believe that he is no misan-
thrope. Essentially affirmative, he exhorts discrimination between the good and the bad, a determined resistance to the
surrender of hope.[19]

The ludicrous, we know, often serves the tone of satire. Yet
what the satirist considers necessary, his critics may draw back
from with abhorrence. This is especially true when a reader,
missing the point of satiric laughter, believes that the apparent
mirth cannot be reconciled with the gravity of the satirized subject. Then the satirist may expect to be condemned for violating
decorum. "A man who laughs at folly or vice," one anonymous
writer typically objected, "gives us as bad a sample of his morals
as of his understanding."[20] This pamphleteer literalizes satire by
failing to distinguish between the satirist and his persona, between technique and meaning. He misconstrues the reversible
effect of satiric laughter because he cannot disentangle moral
assumptions from sober statement. Such insensitivity to tone
reinforces Barten Holyday's declaration that "a perpetual grin
does rather anger than mend." Similarly, Isaac Watts wanted to
dismiss satire that deals with "the grinning and the growling
muses" where, rather, a "manly invitation to virtue and a
friendly smile may be successfully employed."[21]

19. For a Christianized reading, see Thomas E. Maresca, *Pope's Horatian
Poems* (Columbus: Ohio State University Press, 1966), pp. 73–116.
20. *An Essay on Ridicule* (1753), p. 69.
21. Holyday, "Preface to the Reader;" Watts, "Preface," *Horae Lyricae* [1709],
in *Eighteenth-Century Critical Essays,* ed. Elledge, 1:159–60.

Horace had a sensible answer to cavils such as these. While denying that it is "enough to make your hearer grin with laughter," he argued for a wise diversity that by no means precludes lightness. A terse sobriety may at times be useful, but gravity has less strength than the jest cuttingly meant for an unsuspecting fool or villain. As has been demonstrated frequently, satire does not require the drooping posture of a Jaques who "can suck melancholy out of a song, as a weasel sucks eggs." The practitioners of satire's missionary art frequently deride affectations and inanities in order "to laugh mankind out of their favorite follies and vices."[22]

Such a commonplace may give a misleading impression of authorial distance that does not square with the proximate effects of satire. Neither innocent nor disinterested, the satirist expresses himself as one who knows he is vulnerable to those actions in others at which he has pointed his own accusing finger. Pope's audience may join in waspish laughter at Hervey's expense, but they—like the poet himself—cannot feel completely exonerated until they are satisfied that a victim (other than themselves) has been poetically mauled. This, they would argue, affirms rather than denies humanity, for they have been persuaded that the object under attack has been a threat to *humanitas,* and that its reprehension becomes socially and morally beneficent.

For many satirists, then, laughter is analogous to propitiatory sacrifice: a form of discovery and released emotion through which a scapegoat makes it possible for a community fragmented by shame and guilt to reintegrate itself. Society has always needed *pharmakoi,* ceremonial victims, upon whom man's aggregate sins are publicly and symbolically discharged. The scapegoat becomes the agent in whom is concentrated whatever threatens totemic well-being. Comparably, the butt of satire may be a convenient surrogate for expelling communal vice or folly. His availability perhaps betokens man's sadistic instincts, but it also provides an illusory source of healing transference. Very

22. Dedication of *Tom Jones;* cf. "Preface," *Joseph Andrews,* and *Covent-Garden Journal* 24. For Horace, see *Satires,* I. x. 5 ff.

much as the patient is said to benefit from an apotropaic relationship with his analyst—the tendency of the doctor to share
the patient's suffering—the reader transfers his assumed inadequacy to a nearby satiric target. Then he feels better about himself for having found a scapegoat on whom to unload his own
faults: in judging others guilty, he can pretend that virtue ac-
crues to him. Instead of being whipped, he places himself in the
role of the superior, aggressive whipper.[23]

By extension, satiric laughter may become a source of both
catharsis and redemption for satirist and reader alike. When
Addison alludes to man as "the merriest species of the creation,"
something of this wholesomeness is intuited. To be sure, the
essayist tolerated only that "talent of ridicule employed to laugh
men out of vice and folly"—ridicule aligned with spite he would
not abide. Metaphorically, however, he thought of benevolent
laughter as inducing serenity, comparable to the calm engendered by nature during its most vital seasons. Laughter thus
conceived, like flowering fields and trees, produces the tranquillity that accompanies the amiable and the beautiful. Addison
thought of laughter as an instinct that counteracted ill temper
and thus wrought a sense of well-being, the displacement of
gloom "with transient and unexpected gleams of joy" (*Spectator*
249).

Steele (in *Tatler* 76) touched upon the cathartic principle more
explicitly when he observed that "whilst we laugh at, or detest
the uncertain subject of the satire, we often find something in
the error a parallel to ourselves; and being insensibly drawn to
the comparison we would get rid of, we plunge deeper into the
mire, and shame produces that which advice has been too weak
for; and you, sir, get converts you never thought of." In a like
vein Edward Young concluded: "Laughing at the misconduct of

23. See Sir James G. Frazer, selected ed. *The Golden Bough: A Study in Magic and Religion* (New York: Macmillan, 1940), pp. 540 ff., esp. 562–87; C. G. Jung, *The Practice of Psychotherapy*, trans. R. F. C. Hull, in *Collected Works*, 17 vols. (New York: Pantheon Books, 1954, 1966), 16:167–201. See also Elliott, *The Power of Satire*, pp. 135, 138–39. Cf. W. H. Auden's concept of himself as the healing psychoanalyst, the "spiritual diagnostician": Monroe K. Spears, "Late Auden: The Satirist as Lunatic Clergyman," and "The Dominant Symbols of Auden's Poetry," *Sewanee Review* 69 (1951): 50–74, 392–425.

the world will, in a great measure, ease us of any more disagreeable passion about it." There may be truth in his assumption that merry teachers are more attractive to their pupils than unsmiling ones—and often, consequently, more adept at their task.[24]
Satiric laughter, though it need not be sweet-tempered, must be rational if it is to affirm, and it must point up corrigible human failings. Many militant satirists would find Shaftesbury's groping for "a sober kind of cheerfulness" too temperate. Yet they would probably reject offensively derisive laughter. To maintain so fine a distinction, the satirist can learn from Hobbes, who declaimed against the dangers of laughing "at mischances and indecencies, wherein there lieth no wit nor jest at all."[25] Reason and judicious selection must be part of the satirist's performance. If, like Democritus, he finally laughs at everything and everyone, he runs the risk of self-diminution, of being derided as one who does not know when or how to be serious.

Man is such a foolish creature, as Laurence Sterne broadly hints, that he often fails to recognize his own absurdity. And such failure contributes to occasions for laughter. Rhetorically, the narrator in *Tristram Shandy* asks: "Did you think the world itself, sir, had contained such a number of jack asses?" (VI, 1). Gently insidious, then, he reminds the reader-listener that while the travelers are inspecting the jackasses, they—mankind—are being inspected in turn by the animals. We may smile tolerantly, even with a nod of superiority. But how do we help feeling a little uneasy also when the target is so comprehensive that we ourselves may be in the bullseye? Like the muddled master constable of *Much Ado About Nothing*, we may achieve the climactic state of incriminating truthfulness, not knowing that truth itself can destroy. The hilariously literal Dogberry officiously asserts, "Remember that I am an ass." And ass he is, of course, not only by virtue of ingenuous admission, but by being unable to distin-

---

24. Young's *Complete Poems*, 1:344. Cf. *De Oratore*, II. lviii. 236; Quintilian, VI. iii. 7; *English Poets*, 2:144: ". . . we love better to be pleased than to be taught."
25. Shaftesbury, "A Letter concerning Enthusiasm," 1:12, in *Characteristics*. For Hobbes, see fn. 13. As Hutcheson observed: "Ridicule, like other edged tools, may do good in a wise man's hands, though fools may cut their fingers with it, or be injurious to an unwary bystander." *Reflections upon Laughter*, pp. 34-35.

guish his own qualities. What is true of him and what is not, all come together in his own mind:

> I am a wise fellow; and which is more, an officer; and which is more, a house-holder; and which is more, as pretty a piece of flesh as any is in Messina, and one that knows the law, go to! and a rich fellow enough, go to! and a fellow that hath had losses; and one that hath two gowns and every thing handsome about him.
>
> [IV. ii. 66–78]

Bound absolutely to the letter, he records the black and the white of himself with unalloyed imperception. Although more comic than Gulliver, Dogberry resembles him in descending to a comparable level of ignorance about himself and everyone else.

Ridicule of this nature, long an entertaining staple of satire, is basic to an "apology" (sometimes attributed to Fielding) that reduces the Cibbers, father and son, to arrant fools. The satire is two-pronged, for it mimics the elder Cibber's autobiography while quoting from it; and it turns the son Theophilus into a self-admitted "coxcomb" who enjoys the "sweet liberty" of talking about himself. The absurdity, palpable to the reader, becomes the "apologist's" parodic confession of inadequacy. As his own slanderer, Theophilus writes at one point:

> No man can be obliged to accuse himself: I write to put a gloss upon my acts and deeds, not place them in the most odious light, and erect myself in an historical pillory. It would also be an endless work to vindicate all the simple accusations which have been brought against me, and which no persons have any business to trouble their heads about. Should men say, for instance, I used my first dear and well-beloved wife, of ever blessed memory, *J-n-y C——*, with ill usage: Should they affirm, that when her all pale and breathless corpse was in the coffin laid, and I, with sobs and tears and interjected sighs, had moaned to many a witness, my too unhappy fate, yet that same night had a brace of *Drurian* doxies vile in the same house.—Again, should base Defamation whisper in my ear I sold and bartered away my present most virtuous spouse, and that I was a voluntary cuckold on record: Should Scandal with her hundred-tongued cursed mouth rumor it up and down, that neither *common honor* nor *common honesty* were lodged within the centre of my soul. —Should even all this be said, calm and unruffled would I contemn all, and look on such reports in the cool light of mild philosophy.

Everywhere in this *Apology,* the author turns the authority of Colley Cibber's inflated, digressive language and style into an irony on imperception. The tone, a sly mix of Cibber's text and complementary satire, descends to comic scurrility. The "factuality" (like Sterne's "naiveté") is just evident enough to make candor a mimicry of protesting innocence.[26] The laughter provoked by such as the Cibbers and Dogberry has satiric substance because it aims at specific targets. Were it otherwise, it could stir only aimless amusement, bewilderment, or even contempt for the satirist. Satiric attack works only if the writer and his audience agree that the focal object deserves to be diminished or repudiated. Since intensity of feeling will rise or fall in proportion to the distaste generated for the object, the level of laughter is subject to the artist's manipulation. Consequently, critics attempted to name and explain gradations of tone, although—except perhaps to a remarkably disciplined ear and eye—definition makes some of them appear so closely contiguous as to obscure their alleged results. One of the best eighteenth-century commentaries on the laughable comes from Corbyn Morris, and yet the shortcomings of his categorizing approach are evident, as in his conclusion that

the aim of raillery is to please you by some little embarrassment of a person; of satire, to scourge vice, and to deliver it up to your just detestation; and of ridicule, to set an object in a mean ludicrous light, so as to expose it to your derision and contempt.... Raillery is used only upon slight subjects, where no real abilities or merits are questioned, in order to avoid degrading the person you attack, or rendering him contemptible; whereas ridicule observes no such decency, but endeavors really to degrade the person attacked, and to render him contemptible.[27]

26. *An Apology for the Life of Mr. T[heophilus] C[ibber], Comedian. Being a Proper Sequel to the Apology for the Life of Mr. Colley Cibber, Comedian. With an Historical View of the Stage to the Present Year* (1740), pp. 11, 100. Cf. *An Apology for the Life of Mr. Colley Cibber . . . Late Patentee of the Theatre Royal. . . .* (1740). For the questionable attribution, see Wilbur L. Cross, *The History of Henry Fielding*, 3 vols. (New Haven: Yale University Press, 1918), 1:188, 282–84; 3:337. Even more doubtful about Fielding's authorship is Bertrand A. Goldgar, *Walpole and the Wits: The Relation of Politics to Literature, 1722–1742* (Lincoln and London: University of Nebraska Press, 1976).

27. *An Essay towards Fixing the True Standards of Wit, Humor, Raillery, Satire, and Ridicule* (1744), p. 37. *N. B.* Shaftesbury's casual use of such terminology in "Sensus Communis, an Essay on the Freedom of Wit and Humor" (1709), *Characteristics*, 1:43 ff. Cf. Charlotte Lennox, *The Female Quixote; or, the Adventures of Arabella*, 2 vols. (1752), 2:143–45: "Which contains some excellent rules for raillery."

Refinements of definition, like the distinction between raillery and ridicule, tend to underscore the inherently subjective nature of this critical problem. Even his examples depend upon individual preference, of course, but Morris made a useful attempt to methodize principles. Modern commentators may be forgiven if they enlarge on a few of his explications to discriminate further among what might be called the working tones of satire. The point is demonstrated in a few passages from Oliver Goldsmith's *Retaliation:*

> Here lies the good Dean re-united to earth,
> Who mixt reason with pleasure, and wisdom with mirth;
> If he had any faults, he has left us in doubt,
> At least, in six weeks, I could not find 'em out;
> Yet some have declar'd, and it can't be denied 'em,
> That sly-boots was cursedly cunning to hide 'em.
>
> [23-28]

True of the poem generally, the tenor of these lines expresses good humor. If Goldsmith has some fun at the expense of Dr. Thomas Barnard, a recent acquaintance, he gives no sign of wishing to cause hurt. On the contrary, even in the last two lines, which strongly hint that the Dean did indeed have faults, what emerges is pleasant raillery of the sort that Morris writes about, a *jeu d'esprit.* Nothing, in short, makes us suspect that Goldsmith's motive is more deeply rooted than some harmless "little embarrassment of a person."

But later, in the same poem (95-108), he has this to say about David Garrick:

> As an actor, confest without rival to shine,
> As a wit, if not first, in the very first line,
> Yet with talents like these, and an excellent heart,
> The man had his failings, a dupe to his art;
> Like an ill judging beauty, his colors he spread,
> And beplastered, with rouge, his own natural red.
> On the stage he was natural, simple, affecting,
> 'Twas only that, when he was off, he was acting:
> With no reason on earth to go out of his way,
> He turn'd and he varied full ten times a day;
> Tho' secure of our hearts, yet confoundedly sick,
> If they were not his own by finessing and trick,
> He cast off his friends, as a huntsman his pack;
> For he knew when he pleas'd he could whistle them back.

Here Goldsmith no longer teases. Although not cruelly severe, he is nevertheless far less generous than in the profile of the Dean. He presents virtues and immediately overshadows them with faults that he insists upon detailing. Then we remember that Garrick had made fun of him, as in this extempore couplet:

Here lies Nolly Goldsmith, for shortness call'd Noll,
Who wrote like an angel but talk'd like poor Poll.[28]

We realize that Goldsmith's retaliation takes the form of ridicule in which he derides Garrick lightly but with patent annoyance. He hopes—and with determination—"to degrade the person attacked, and to render him contemptible." The humor here is spicy and tart, whereas in the sketch of the Dean it is mild and friendly. The texture of the first passage suggests the neutrally bland; that of the second verges on the prickly.

As Steele intimated (in *Spectator* 422), the line between raillery and ridicule wants precise marking, but it does exist. Although both possess purposive tonality, ridicule comes closer to conscious satiric need. Raillery will impress many as being too relaxed and discreet to be convincing. Ridicule, on the other hand, generates a tension. As a complement of rhetoric, ridicule is argumentative and—in intention, at least—persuasive. Addison (in *Tatler* 257) chose this manner of discourse as one means of discrediting non-Anglican religious values and practices. To accomplish his purpose he fabricated a traveling waxwork, a raree show populated by seven dolls representing various religions and sects. These waxen figures symbolize praise for Anglicanism mainly through derision of other faiths. The doll that represents the Church of England "was formed like a matron, dressed in the habit of an elderly woman of quality in Queen Elizabeth's days": she is cheerful, scrubbed, dignified. But her chief adversary, Catholicism, is cheaply ludicrous by comparison. She is a superannuated strumpet, a "tawdry composition of ribbons, silks, and jewels." Hardly more companionable is Presbytery, tight-lipped, frigidly disapproving. There the Puritan doll glow-

28. Charles N. Fifer, ed., *The Correspondence of James Boswell with certain Members of the Club* (New York and Toronto: McGraw-Hill, 1976), p. xxxii; Boswell's *Life*, 1:413n.

ers, "a peevish figure, soured with discontent, and over-cast with melancholy.... plain, homely, dowdy." Addison's ridicule diminishes the offending sect without troublesome ambiguity, yet suavely and convincingly. His essay is a rhetorical triumph managed with fictional politeness.

*Tatler* 257 follows by about six years Swift's vigorous treatment of a comparable subject in *A Tale of a Tub* (1704). Therein, through the character of Martin, Swift forwards an argument for moderate Christianity. He is seemingly impatient at first with the ritualized excesses of his church but judicious enough to realize that radical change is neither necessary nor satisfactory. Allegorically, "where [Martin] observed the embroidery to be worked so close, as not to be got away without damaging the cloth, or where it served to hide or strengthen any flaw in the body of the coat . . . he concluded the wisest course was to let it remain, resolving in no case whatsoever, that the substance of the stuff should suffer injury." The portrait of Martin, in other words, lures any good Christian with comfort and empathy to join Swift in a celebration of "the Church of England as the most perfect of all others in discipline and doctrine."

Contrarily, neither restraint nor tolerance reveals itself in *A Tale*'s version of Calvinism. Virtually maddened by zeal, Jack importunes: "Ah, good brother Martin . . . do as I do, for the love of God; strip, tear, pull, rent, flay off all, that we may appear as unlike the rogue Peter as it is possible: I would not for a hundred pounds carry the least mark about me, that might give occasion to the neighbors of suspecting I was related to such a rascal." Jack's "love of God" becomes an outrageous irony, underscoring Swift's detestation of zeal. But just as abhorrent to him appeared the doctrinaire absolutism of Peter, which capitalized on superstitious fear of hell and damnation. Through penances, indulgences, confessions, papal bulls, and the like, "Peter grew so scandalous, that all the neighborhood began in plain words to say, he was no better than a knave." Throughout his provocative treatise Swift satirizes religious excess, waging war against Dissent and Catholicism. Nevertheless, many Anglican clergymen misread the *Tale* as an assault upon orthodox Protantism. For one thing, they confused Swift's tone with a failure in reverence and accused him of having created "one of the profanest banters upon the religion of Jesus Christ, as such, that ever yet appeared." For another, they were unprepared to assess Martin's role: they did not know what to make of his alteration from cooling violence to moderation, and they attributed his assumption—"there yet remained a great deal more to be done"—to the charge that Anglicanism had either grown "lukewarm" or dissipated the purity of primitive Christianity.[29]

Belatedly, Swift addressed his mock "Apology" to any obtuse "clergyman of our church" unable to recognize that he was disclosing "the follies of fanaticism and superstition ... though in the most ridiculous manner." Then, in a credibly sober tone, he confirmed that he denigrated not religion but abuses of it: "Religion they tell us ought not to be ridiculed, and they tell us truth, yet surely the corruptions in it may; for we are taught by the tritest maxim in the world that religion being the best of things, its corruptions are likely to be the worst." Anglicanism such as Martin's, in Swift's opinion, was the proper, rational source of Christian teaching; it adjusted itself to historical truth and changes dictated by time; it escaped the nonsensical subjectivity of Jack and the nonthinking ritual of Peter.

By contrast with Addison, Swift in the allegory of the three brothers resorts to vivid particularity. His tone is almost too good in fact, so realistic in its multiform narrative frame that the ridicule may be difficult to assimilate. Addison steps delicately around his subject; Swift advances upon it with the zest of feigned specificity. A dazzling virtuoso, he conceals his identity behind numerous masks as he moves between narration and digression. *A Tale of a Tub,* Johnson observed, "exhibits a vehemence and rapidity of mind, a copiousness of images, and vivacity of diction such as [Swift] afterwards never possessed or never exerted. It is of a mode so distinct and peculiar that it must be considered by itself."[30] Whereas the mildly disdainful Addison pursues a single strand of ridicule, Swift maintains an acid contempt underlying a rich diversity of burlesque, parody,

29. *A Tale of a Tub,* secs. iv and vi, pp. 75 and 87.
30. *English Poets,* 3:51.

impersonation, even puns. *A Tale* is a satire on religious abuses, but it is also a work of great comic imagination. Ridicule, Swift demonstrates, provides a source for belittling laughter, but it is a laughter evocative of both ire and thoughtfulness.

Because of its characteristic pungency, satire of all kinds has frequently been suspected of malice. And it would of course be foolish to deny that all too often satire has been a cover for personal baiting, for revenge and blood-letting, despite stated high-flown intentions. But of more immediate concern is the view of satire as corrective running from Quintilian to Shaftesbury and Johnson. The Roman had insisted that, ideally, jests should never wound—and he appears to have had in mind the concept of the jest told in earnest, that is, the didactically intended satire.[31] Shaftesbury would certainly have agreed with Quintilian, even while acknowledging that in fact ridicule sometimes is misdirected, thus a source of distress to someone undeserving of diminution. On the whole he did not regard this as a serious possibility, arguing that in a free society, where reason and justice prevail, there is little danger that ridicule will not find its proper target. Ridicule in his opinion leads to the discovery of truth and any misdirection will soon be corrected.

Even Johnson, who doubted such confidence, told Boswell that the "sense of ridicule is given us, and may be lawfully used." In a spirit somewhat more cynical than Shaftesbury's, he noted that "the great use of delineating absurdities is, that we may know how far human folly can go." All of these speculations, however—from Quintilian to Johnson—would have seemed both short of the mark and too soft for an aggressive critic like Dennis. Dissatisfied with merely nominal solutions, he applied his pragmatic tests of ridicule to English comedy. Hence, he contradicted the philosophical basis of Steele's genteel sentimentality. More specifically—with Etherege's *Man of Mode* as the critical center—he argued that the boundaries of ridicule be reexamined. Invoking Aristotle and Horace, Dennis flatly asserted that "corrupt and degenerate nature" may be ridiculed. And with equal aggressiveness he held that the proper business of comedy is "to expose persons to our view, whose views we may

31. Quintilian, VI. iii; XII. ix. 9.

shun, and whose follies we may despise; and by showing us what is done upon the comic stage, to show us what ought never to be done upon the stage of the world.... As 'tis the business of a comic poet to cure his spectators of vice and folly, by the apprehension of being laughed at, 'tis plain that his business must be with the reigning follies and vices."[32]

Dennis's appeal to decorum may seem heavy, but he has also made a significant if conventional declaration concerning the responsible uses of ridicule. Fundamentally, however deep their mutual dislike, the declaration should have satisfied a professional satirist like Pope, who also vigorously promoted satire as the voice of truth unearthing error. With stress upon the impossibility of escaping one's own guilt, he insisted that "nothing . . . moves strongly but satire, and those who are ashamed of nothing else, are so of being ridiculous." Contrarily, La Rochefoucauld decried belittlement as moral distortion, as an evil in excess of reality itself: "The exposing of a man and making him ridiculous, dishonours him more than a real dishonour." A confident Pope could, nevertheless, critically assess the effective limits of his or anyone else's satire. Even he, that is to say, seemed to have dark moments when he conjectured that intended victims of satire—through a perverse force of rationalization—turn ridicule away from themselves in order to negate its purpose. Most individuals, he implied, try to barricade themselves against the humiliation of stinging truths. The same frustration is enunciated by Swift, who within a traditional metaphor describes satire as "a sort of glass wherein beholders do generally discover every body's face but their own; which is the chief reason for that kind of reception it meets in the world, and that so very few are offended with it."[33]

32. Boswell's *Life,* 3:379–80; 4:17; "A Defence of Sir Fopling Flutter," in *The Critical Works of John Dennis,* ed. Edward Niles Hooker, 2 vols. (Baltimore: Johns Hopkins Press, 1943), 2:241–50. Only evil, said Socrates (*The Republic,* bk. V), should be the subject of ridicule.

33. Pope, *Correspondence,* 3:276; also 2:419–20, La Rochefoucauld, *Moral Reflections* (CCCXXVI), p. 83; Swift, "Preface," *The Battle of the Books.* The speculum was a familiar metaphor for self-revelation or self-deception in medieval and Renaissance writing. See M. H. Abrams, *The Mirror and the Lamp: Romantic Theory and the Critical Tradition* (New York: Oxford University Press, 1953), pp. viii, 32. George Gascoigne, "The Steel Glass" (1576): "And every wight will have a looking-glass / To see himself, yet so he seeth not" (ll. 176–77).

Pope, by and large, was less inclined than Swift to worry that his art might not be suitable for the task he set himself. At times, thus, it is true that he seems to be humble and unaffected, at other times disillusioned. Always, however, and especially when he gives the impression of being straightforward, the ironic trap is a distinct possibility. Beneath the camouflage of a sometimes diffident or quixotic posture lies the Popean assurance that truth—with his digging and prodding—will out, for conscience can be reached. On occasion he could be moved to state that "bad men were grown so shameless and so powerful, that ridicule was become as unsafe as it was ineffectual." And on occasion he doubtless felt that way. But he had a deep reservoir of ego that helped him to resist any lasting notion of his ineffectuality: his mockery would gall the most insensitive hides. He fought, he argued, against "insuperable corruption and depravity of manners," but without tilting at windmills and wineskins. After all the ambiguities were consolidated, the poet finally had "reason to be satisfied with the approbation of good men, and the testimony of his own conscience."[34]

Satirists in theory and in practice, we have observed, like to insist that there is nothing improper about wounding their quarry as long as the ultimate intention is curative. And so we know it often is. But many times we would be able to believe this only if we were blessed with more trust than those countless generations of pupils whose schoolmasters, rod in hand, sighed: *Castigo te non quod odio habeam, sed quod amem* ("I chastise thee not out of hatred, but out of love"). Such deception had formulaic credibility, and only that. Swift's interpretation of the analogy moves to the point: "I have observed some satirists to use the public much at the rate that pedants do a naughty boy ready horsed for discipline: first expostulate the case, then plead the necessity of the rod, from great provocations, and conclude every period with a lash." Butler's earlier doggerel leers, but it also adapts the familiar metaphor to satiric purpose:

> For one man, out of his own skin,
> To firk and whip another's sin:

---

34. Note at the end of "Dialogue II, Epilogue to the Satires." For Pope and the tradition of the "fearless satirist," see Mack, *The Garden and the City*, pp. 170–71.

> As pedants out of school-boys' breeches
> Do claw and curry their own itches.

The writhing schoolboy may be terrified by the whip and the fool humiliated by abusive satire, but none of the rest of us are obliged to equate their pain with cure.[35]

For strictly punitive purposes the Iron Maiden had a certain efficacy once upon a time, but no one pressed into it has ever left a record of his gratitude. Retributive satire has always existed and often with more popularity than it deserves. Even Steele, an exponent of *humanitas,* sometimes lapsed into petulance when driven by political necessity. In the second number of his Opposition journal *The Plebeian,* he rudely punned on the dying Addison's *Old Whig,* the journal written on behalf of the Stanhope ministry: "I am afraid he is so old a Whig, that he has quite forgot his principles." But breaches of civility like this were out of character for Steele, who habitually observed the premise that satire should "gain the good will of those with whom you converse." Supporting this theme of restoration, he argues for censure that generalizes rather than specifies. And he argues further for delicacy of touch. Unabashedly indebted to Dryden's metaphor, he takes exception to those who "do not thrust with the skill of fencers, but cut up with the barbarity of butchers" (*Spectator* 422).

Intrinsic to this well-known comparison is the satirist's fondness for the clever play on word and image, the teasing manipulation of the reader's reason and imagination. His exercise of the deliberate evasion called "wit" can be deployed over a wide field of satiric need. The cleverness generally attributed to wit has imbued the concept with an often uneasy ambiguity, so that we may be torn between two considerations of the satirist, as clown and as pundit. The comedian competes with the wise man as though the two are necessarily incompatible; and if the commen-

---

35. For the flogging line, see *Tom Jones,* III, 6; "Preface," *A Tale of a Tub;* *Hudibras,* II. ii. 463–66; also II. i. 811 ff., II. ii. 439–40; Congreve, *Amendments of Mr. Collier's False and Imperfect Citations* (1698). Quoted as an exercise for schoolboys by William Lyly [Lily], *Propria Quae Maribus Quae Genus,* as in *Praesenti, Syntaxis, Qui Mihi, Construed* [ca. 1513] (1761), p. 72. Byron's satiric contribution on flogging the young ("It mends their morals, never mind the pain") occurs in *Don Juan,* II. i.

tator on wit happens to be a disapproving Sir Richard Blackmore, the wise man as a rule vanishes before his myopic gaze while the clown cavorts foolishly in a bid for public approval. Addison, in rebuttal, proposed that wit be reappraised for its ethical instrumentality. "The good or prudent man," he wrote, may through the means of wit "be diverted without prejudice to his discretion or morality."[36] Like the classical notion of *facetus*, wit does not restrict itself to what is merely droll or laughable. Rather it may extend outward to embrace other connotations, among them, the elegance or charm of *lepos*, the sharpness of *acumen*, the synthesizing power of *ingenium*.[37]

Such a concept of wit leaps beyond Locke's sparse definition, which excludes the judgmental and analytical. The philosopher nevertheless contributes to the role of wit in satire, especially when he emphasizes its capacity for integration. With "quickness and variety" wit puts together ideas "wherein can be found any resemblance or congruity" appealing predominantly to the fancy or the pictorial imagination—if not to the mind. Locke's probing of the term and its patterns was influential throughout much of the century. Corbyn Morris, for example, takes his text from Locke and similarly proscribes intellectual activity in "the province of wit."[38] In its satirical frame, however, wit is something more than a screen on which flash pairs of associated

36. Note, for instance, the translator's dilemma in dealing with German *Witz:* is it to be "wit" or "joke"? See Sigmund Freud, *Jokes and their Relation to the Unconscious,* trans. James Strachey et al. (London: Hogarth Press, 1960), p. 7*n.* We say "as a rule" because Blackmore (*An Essay upon Wit,* in *Essays upon Several Subjects,* 2d ed., 2 vols [1716–17]) is not consistent. Ideally "Wit is . . . the accomplishment of a warm, sprightly, and fertile imagination . . . under the direction of a regular judgment, that takes care of the choice of just and suitable materials" (1:191–92). (Blackmore had in 1700 produced a poetic *Satyr against Wit*); Addison, *Freeholder* 45.

37. The classical gradations of wit were: *ingenium, acumen, lepos, facetiae, sal, dicacitas.* Quintilian's terms (VI. iii. 17–21) also include *urbanitas, venustus, iocus.* These and related terms (such as *sel, acetum*) became current in the Renaissance. See the discussion of epigrams by J. C. Scaliger, *Poetices* (Lyons, 1561). We are indebted to Peter E. Medine for bringing this to our attention. Cf. Johnson's eight levels of wit in the *Dictionary;* and Pope, *Essay on Criticism.* For Sterne's Hobbesian concept of wit as being inseparable from judgment, see Henri Fluchère, *Laurence Sterne: From Tristram to Yorick,* trans. Barbara Bray (London, New York, Toronto: Oxford University Press, 1965), pp. 79–89.

38. *An Essay concerning Human Understanding* [II. xi. 2], in Locke's *Works,* 1:58; Morris, *True Standards of Wit,* p. 1.

objects or perceptions. As Addison and like-minded theorists have shown, these congruities do indeed stimulate evocation. But they also lead the intellect into depths of meaning, implication, and surprise. Wit can supply an architectonic frame, a textural bond, to help assure the satirist's control.[39] The often fragmented, disjunctive nature of satire requires a shaping attitude or set of attitudes to give it cohesion: that is, to make it consistent with the author's emotional and thematic aims. The opening lines of *Mac Flecknoe* serve as example:

> All human things are subject to decay,
> And when Fate summons, monarchs must obey.
> This Flecknoe found, who, like Augustus, young
> Was call'd to empire, and had govern'd long:
> In prose and verse, was own'd, without dispute,
> Thro' all the realms of *Nonsense,* absolute.

Here we see virtually all of the requirements for wit set forth by Locke and his successors. They are crystallized in the grand, pseudo-epic aphorisms followed quickly by the comparison of an inferior poet with a great emperor. The satirist fuses epithet and similitude to render harmonious a patent absurdity. The details that follow, consistent with a mock-heroic descent into "the realms of *Nonsense,*" encourage us to amplify Dryden's comparisons into other ideas of mediocrity and pretensions suggested by them. When wit operates effectively, as we believe it does here, it contributes significantly to the unity of design insisted upon by Dryden. Wit is therefore not synonymous with satire; it is instead a part of it, as essential to the totality as the proper integration of the warp and the woof to the completed fabric.

By long tradition wit has been identified with the laughable,

---

39. This unifying quality is usefully if cumbersomely literalized by the term *Ineinsbildung* and the related "esemplasy" of Coleridge. The relation of wit to satire and its corollaries is often mentioned but never—as far as we are aware—treated problematically. See: Quintilian, VI. iii. 7–16; William Congreve, "Concerning Humour in Comedy" [1695], in *Critical Essays of the Seventeenth Century,* ed. J. E. Spingarn, 3 vols. (Oxford: Clarendon Press, 1908), 3:243–44 (and Spingarn's introduction, I, lviii-lxiii); John Gay, *The Present State of Wit, in a Letter to a Friend in the Country* (1711); Blackmore, 1:190; Morris, passim; *Coleridge's Miscellaneous Criticism,* pp. 111–30, 440–46; Elliott, p. 264; Norman Knox, *The Word Irony and its Context, 1500–1755* (Durham, N.C.: Duke University Press, 1961), p. 220.

which to many critics is the same as the trivial and superficial. Blackmore, for instance, after a good deal of vacillating, concluded that wit should be applied only to "the ordinary customs and manners of life." It has "no place in the works where severe knowledge and judgment are chiefly exercised; those superior productions of the understanding [that is, history, philology, philosophy, great lyric and epic poetry] must be expressed in a clear and strong manner, without intervening strains of wit or facetious fancies, which, were they admitted, would appear incongruous and impertinent." Doubtless a measure of Blackmore's distaste for wit grew from what he construed as misuse, a complaint that he could have borrowed from ages past as well as his own.[40]

But in his eagerness to banish impertinences, Blackmore apparently forgot lessons that he should have learned as a schoolboy. Cicero, who had no qualms about "a witty saying," reminded his audience, "Whatever subjects I may touch upon, as being sources of laughing-matters, may equally well, as a rule, be sources of serious thought." And that certainly was the position of Addison responding to Blackmore. Witty statement—or raillery, as he calls it at this point—does not nullify sobriety. On the contrary, he asserts, wit sharpens by temporarily unbending "the mind from serious studies and severer contemplations, without throwing it off from its proper bias. It carries on the same design that is promoted by authors of a graver turn, and only does it in another manner." Wit may also induce self-awareness by causing a culpable individual to confront his faults even while he laughs at them. For Addison as for Cicero or Horace wit wins good will, creating a welcome relief from the dullness of too much exhortation.[41] The variability of wit in satire makes it as receptive to *ingenium* or *acumen* as to *facetiae, sal,* and *dicacitas.* Good sense and clever, pungent discourse are in fact often the indispensable companions of satiric wit.

The context that wit helps to shape almost always gives a sense of occasion, that is, of a probability that the subject is a specific

40. *Essay upon Wit,* 1:198–99. Cf. Ben Jonson's disgruntlement with the corruptive wit of his times: *Timber, or Discoveries made upon Men and Matter* (1641).
41. *De Oratore,* II. lxi. 249; *Freeholder* 45.

circumstance or person. In a very broad sense, therefore, we must recall the demand for wit as "propriety of thought and words," or remember the Horatian warning, "If the words you utter are ill suited, I shall laugh or fall asleep." Much effort goes into satiric tonality, but the work must reflect the temporal condition that bred the impulse to satirize. By extension, then, wit must likewise convey a semblance of spontaneity, the impression of being written or spoken to the moment, the retort apropos. And further, according to Quintilian, "Wit always appears to greater advantage in reply than in attack."[42]

Among the many gradations of satiric wit, repartee (*dicacitas*) engages especially, for it is cast to resemble natural banter. To cite Persius as an instance: in *Satire I* he cleverly simulates informality in a dialogue about the lamentable state of Roman letters and morality. The conversation (translated by Dryden) begins:

*Persius.*
> How anxious are our cares; and yet how vain
> The bent of our desires!

*Friend.*
> Thy spleen contain:
> For none will read thy satires.

*Persius.*
> This to me?

*Friend.*
> None; or what's next to none; but two or three.
> 'Tis hard, I grant.

*Persius.*
> 'Tis nothing; I can bear
> That paltry scribblers have the public ear:
> That this vast universal Fool, the Town,
> Shou'd cry up *Labeo*'s stuff, and cry me down.
> They damn themselves; nor will my Muse descend
> To clap with such, who fools and knaves commend:
> Their smiles and censures are to me the same:
> I care not what they praise, or what they blame.
>                                              [1-15]

---

42. *Essays of John Dryden*, ed. W. P. Ker (Oxford: Clarendon Press, 1926), passim; Horace, *De Arte Poetica*, ll. 104-5; Quintilian, VI. iii. 13. William Empson makes a comparable point about the relevance of situation to ambiguity in general: *Seven Types of Ambiguity* (New York: Meridian Books, 1958), pp. 265-66.

The combined presence of the poet and his friend brings the discourse down to a level of vigorous but reasonable and unpretentious exchange with which we feel comfortable. The tone assimilates a sharp, wry humor; it also conceals any affected strain of art in its forthright shrewdness.

From concept and practice, thus, wit emerges as a compound of intellectual and creative ingenuity: Swift's *jus divinum*. Its effect in satire, as in any art form, depends to a large extent upon subjective reaction. But we may also assume that survival over an extended period connotes acceptance by a variety of readers. The satirist, if this assumption be correct, has learned to gauge public taste for wit, one of whose most satisfying ingredients is surprise. Trying to explain surprise by the rules is a little like trying to explain a joke: neither stands up well to prescribed standards of execution, both being more notable for singularity than for regularization. To set forth a proposition, surprise in wit is the element of the unexpected evolving out of a connection of ideas that customarily would not be brought together. They should have some kind of congruity, of course, but not so close that the resemblance is obvious.[43] Had Pope, for example, limited his famous list of dressing-table items to puffs, powders, patches, and billet-doux, hardly an eyebrow would lift. But by intruding bibles into this ordered clutter, he brings us up short in delighted surprise. There is no reason why a single bible should not be on the table. More than one, however, is preten-

43. *Spectator* 62. For an unacknowledged borrowing from Addison, see *The Young Gentleman and Lady Instructed in such Principles of Politeness, Prudence, and Virtue, as will Lay a sure Foundation for Gaining Respect, Esteem, and Satisfaction in this Life, and Eternal Happiness in a Future State; Interspersed with Observations and Maxims, as Demonstrate the Danger and Folly of Vice, and the Advantage and Wisdom of Virtue,* 2 vols. (1747), 1:301 ff. Morris (p. xvii) asserts that "surprise is a necessary passport to wit" only "where the agreement is strained and defective ... but surprise is not necessary to wit, where the agreement between the two subjects is natural and splendid." Cf. Jean Paul Richter: "Wit is the disguised priest who unites every couple ... [it is] the skill to combine with surprising quickness many ideas foreign to one another." Quoted by Fred Mayne, *The Wit and Satire of Bernard Shaw* (New York: St. Martin's Press, 1967), p. x. Regarding the durability of certain examples of wit, Johnson observes: "About things on which the public thinks long it commonly attains to think right" (*English Poets*, 2:132). For Swift's wit as *jus divinum*, see Edward Young, *Conjectures on Original Composition* (1759), p. 97; on wit and humor, see "Apology," *A Tale of a Tub, Prose Works*, 1:10–11.

tious and just as undiscriminating as the multiplication of other items. Symptomatic of her infatuation with appearance, Belinda's religiosity serves her vanity as much as does her mirror. Her faith is unstable. A self-proclaimed Christian, to be sure ("On her white breast a sparkling cross she wore"), she is hospitable to the dogma of any creed that happens to be socially acceptable. Even "Jews" and "Infidels" may adore her without danger to their spiritual states. And, further, making the bibles coordinate in worth with cosmetic tools and love letters compounds the mockery of pride in so fragile a creature, of disorder in one so exquisite.

In a related way, Pope's Cloe of *Epistle II* [*To a Lady*] demonstrates the unreliability of her feelings and values:

> She, while her lover pants upon her breast,
> Can mark the figures on an Indian chest;
> And when she sees her friend in deep despair,
> Observes how much a chintz exceeds mohair.
>
> [167–70]

The wit turns on the surprisingly juxtaposed opposites, so that we may sympathize with the frustrated lover but find entertainment in the whimsy. There is nothing surprising about a liaison; nothing, that is, until natural emotions are balked by contrived indifference. Pope's wicked capacity for driving convention into unexpected reversals and shifts of direction also drives his wit forward. When, as is his custom, he spices normality with the lurking threat of humiliation, he does so calculatingly like a surgeon wielding his lancet. But sensitivity to language and nuance such, for example, as he and Addison admired was being swallowed up in newer, less attractive literary convention. Critics continued to write about the imperatives of delight and surprise. Nevertheless the esteemed "true wit" of satire was in actual practice losing out to a leveling overtness of tone and implication. Thanks probably to a combination of blunted reading tastes and shrinking poetic talents, wit was being reduced to a function mainly comic, exploiting puns or vulgarisms, turns of phrase or diction more likely to emphasize jocularity than *ingenium*.[44]

44. For an ironic attack on the deterioration of wit, attributed to Pope, see the broadside: *God's Revenge against Punning Shewing the Miserable Fate of Persons*

That leveling did nothing to alter the face of wit as a valuable quality—however imprecisely understood or articulated. Many satirists and their critics played out their ritualistic roles. They had created an interlocking stereotype of wit and satire to which they paid often fulsome tribute. As a result, when expressing dissatisfaction—real or pretended—with representations of satire, they protested not the genre but the deficiency of wit. Smollett, to single out an instance, objected that satire had become faulty in a time when "humor turns changeling, and slavers in an insipid grin." Even more damagingly, "wit is volatilized into a mere vapor." This wit-less atmosphere, as he sensed it, threatened the very presence of satire, which "dares not show her face." Earlier, Defoe had wrung his hands over the degeneration of wit into malice and animosity; justifiable satiric criticism, in other words, yielded its ground to backbiting. Similarly, a patently self-interested Blackmore was infuriated by *A Tale of a Tub,* which he recognized only as a "pernicious abuse of wit."[45] Plainly, he was not in a mood to enjoy the cleverness of Swift's derogatory allusions to his writing, which occur in both *A Tale* and *The Battle of the Books.*

Of course, even "proper" wit and a command of ridicule well directed do not guarantee critical acceptance. Johnson made that clear when he implied of Butler's *Hudibras* and Green's *The Spleen* that they needed something more than wit and humor for the elevation of true poetry. Wit, we have seen, is expected to help us relocate the familiar in human experience. But Butler, according to Johnson, had burlesqued and thus distorted reality: "All disproportion is unnatural; and from what is unnatural we can derive only the pleasure which novelty produces." Magisterially wrongheaded as he could be at times, Johnson declared: "Nothing odd will do long. 'Tristram Shandy' did not last." Al-

---

*Addicted to this Crying Sin, in Court and Town* (1716). Cf. *Spectator* 62 (1711) on false wit. A comparable regression of wit has been observed in the mid-seventeenth century. See William G. Crane, *Wit and Rhetoric in the Renaissance: The Formal Basis of Elizabethan Prose Style* (New York: Columbia University Press, 1937), p. 12.

45. Smollett, *Ferdinand Count Fathom,* ch. I; Defoe's *Review,* 20 Jan. 1705; Blackmore, 1:217. Cf. Pope's "Epistle to Dr. Arbuthnot": "It is the slaver kills, and not the bite" (l. 106).

most equally spectacular as an instance of erroneous judgment, Warton minimized Pope's satiric writing subsequent to *The Rape of the Lock*, "for wit and satire are transitory and perishable."[46] Such lapses in prophecy amuse but also cry out for caution, since the durability of wit can never be a subject for flat legislation. It is altogether too complex and circumstantial for consensus or universal reaction.

## III

Contrary to ridicule, indignation acts as an explicitly moral state of mind and feeling that denies laughter. An overspill of righteous anger, it is an instrument of man's elevated striving and measures a sense of both justice and personal worth. From Aristotle to Hobbes, indignation becomes a "grief which consisteth in the conception of good success happening to them whom they think unworthy thereof. Seeing therefore men think all those unworthy whom they hate, they think them not only unworthy of the good fortune they have, but also of their own virtues."[47] In a satiric context, indignation coalesces the same strains of ethical and private necessity that Aristotle and Hobbes talk about. The satirist when angered is moved by "the right things and . . . the right people." Furthermore, he can persuade us of his rightness only when he maintains control of his art as well as his passion. Like Aristotle's right-thinking man, he too reacts vigorously to injustice.

Reputable writers seem at times to express their feelings in what Addison (*Spectator* 256) called "some implicit kind of revenge," or in what Johnson (*Rambler* 22) related allegorically to malice. The difficulty surfaces when the anger has no clear moral focus. Yet, blatant partisanship aside, every serious satirist would have us believe that his art avoids the merely punitive. Lucilius, so declared Juvenal, "roars and rages as if with sword in hand." But this threatening energy swerves from brutal retaliation. "The hearer," we are told, "whose soul is cold with crime,

46. Boswell's *Life*, 3:38; 2:449; *English Poets*, 1:218; Joseph Warton, *An Essay on the Genius and Writings of Pope* (1756), p. 334.

47. Aristotle's *Rhetoric*, II. ix. Aristotle on indignation and pity, *Rhetoric*, II. viii. 1386–87; on anger, the *Nicomachean Ethics*, IV. v. 1126; Hobbes, *Elements of Law*, pt. I, sec. 11, p. 31.

grows red: he sweats with the secret consciousness of sin."[48] Lucilius, in other words, may experience vast anger, but he molds it for an end, both worthy and foreseeable. His declamatory rage achieves a victory in tropes, a reconstitution of real scorn or indignation arising out of a real situation that warrants the poet's response.

Paired with indignation—to pursue the Aristotelian theme—is pity as a source of sympathetic identification. When the satirist states his indignation he means also to call forth compassion: the closer we stand to the depiction of unwarranted misfortune or of its victims the more likely we are to identify with them. The satirist makes us feel pity because as moral social beings we abhor injustice and because at the same time we fear for ourselves in comparable situations. We are susceptible to a democracy of response that encourages sympathy for unjustifiable suffering and deprivation, for the afflictions of old age, isolation, and so on. Indeed, such response transcends station; it may also allow affinity with monarchs or heroes who have been destroyed by fate or their unruly passion.

Even at their most subtle, pity and indignation combined may signal a desire for the restoration of human esteem and justice and for the reawakening of affection and good taste. We would be hard pressed to judge the quantity or depth of tenderness stored in the satire of Juvenal or Swift. The indignation towers there to be countered, and the tendency to be put off by its vehemence can be virtually instinctive. Swift, conceding his own "sourness of . . . temper," thought of this indignation as a compulsive outlet for protesting injustice. He did not believe that it would "amend" rascals, only that it would "serve to vex" them—to discourage them from further depravity. Despairing because the laws of the land were ineffectual, and general complacency had made the moral atmosphere stagnant, he concluded that he had little recourse to anything but indignation. His satire, he

48. Loeb *Juvenal, Satire I*, ll. 165–67; cf. William Whitehead, *An Essay on Ridicule* (ll. 193–94): "Yet, if, crusaders-like, their zeal be rage, / They hurt the cause in which their arms engage." But also Churchill, "The Author" (ll. 215–16): "Lives there a man, who calmly can stand by, / And see his conscience ripp'd with steady eye?" The divided response to satiric anger is summed up in the apt title alluding to Swift, *Rage or Raillery*, by George P. Mayhew (San Marino, Calif.: Huntington Library, 1967).

asserted, had originated in frustration but not in capitulation. Better than no action at all, it aimed at "those whom neither religion, nor natural virtue, nor fear of punishment, were able to keep within the bounds of their duty." Such, he hoped, "might be with-held by the shame of having their crimes exposed to open view in the strongest colors, and themselves rendered odious to mankind."

Obviously less sanguine than other satirists that offenders could be cured of their weakness, Swift nevertheless sought to deter, not avenge. Certainly his personal feelings boiled over at times, but despite his passion he did not run amok. Rather he tried to exhibit errant men as examples for those who were still redeemable. In an age—any age—fouled by sin and cruelty, the average person shrugs and accepts his world. But the exceptional, indignant few think mankind entitled to something better and will take risks to guarantee that right. So Swift wanted to restore values without which he felt as endangered as his readers. He bitingly concluded in the *Examiner* that "next to taming or binding a savage-animal, the best service you can do the neighborhood, is to give them warning, either to arm themselves, or not to come in its way."[49]

Here, in explanatory statement even as in much of his actual satiric writing, Swift makes the intensity and limits of his indignation lucid beyond doubt. But on other occasions ironic ambiguity better suited his purpose than overt representation. The contrived, periodically complex banality of, say, the modest proposal for consuming infant flesh is a remarkable cover for wrath. Expressively flat—and that functions as a central irony—Swift's vision of a human abattoir horrifies because its ordered, mathematical conclusions support a grotesque premise as un-Christian and as outrageous as the persona's Christian protestations.[50] Again, there is Johnson's dysphoric portrait of the dying miser (*The Vanity of Human Wishes*, 261–90) surrounded by vulpine kin who

> Improve his heady rage with treach'rous skill,
> And mold his passions till they make his will.

49. *Examiner* 38 (26 Apr. 1711), *Prose Works*, 3:141; see also Swift to Charles Ford (5 Apr. 1733), *Correspondence*, 4:138.
50. See the discussion of *A Modest Proposal* in ch. 2.

APOTROPAIC VISIONS 151

This produces a shock of revulsion. Most of us probably recoil
from a *mise en scène* in which traditionally sanctified moments are
violated by the rapacity of "watchful guests" and by the unnatural greed of a "dotard" who

> views his coffers with suspicious eyes,
> Unlocks his gold, and counts it till he dies.

Life and death in this metaphoric configuration are equally
cheapened. And so also had Juvenal in his third satire deplored
a corrupt Rome whose futility he imaged in successive vignettes
and which he despairingly saluted in the mask's terse *Quid
Romae faciam* (41).

When well used in satire, indignation serves as moral cautery,
purifying while it burns. Thus conceived, it becomes a figurative
resource that embraces extremes of feeling without violating the
creative design. Heightened indignation implies an exceptional
overflow of emotion, which within the metaphoric frame may
nevertheless be contained: the outburst itself may be made to
approximate outraged sensibility and yet remain accessible to
rational judgment. A capacity for such disciplined turbulence,
according to Wycherley's eulogy, accounts for the strength of
Dryden, whose ". . . sense . . . humor, and satiric rage / At once
can teach, delight, and lash the age."[51] A favorite stereotype
enshrines indignation as though it had talismanic value. Often
described in this context as rage, it rises by association to "holiness" (an implication presumably of the poet's divine madness-
*cum*-genius as well as of his profound conscience). Rage is usually
"unbridled," "hot-blooded," "manly." Comparably, in the name
of high purpose variously attributed to "virtue," "truth," and
"conscience," Churchill beats a sanctified path upward from
scorn to the pious "rage of song."[52]

Controlled passion is dramatic, measured to enhance a moral
aesthetic far in excess of more temperate address. When control

51. "An Epistle to Mr. Dryden," in *The Complete Works of William Wycherley*, ed.
Montague Summers, 4 vols. (London: Nonesuch Press, 1924), 4:156.
52. "An Epistle to William Hogarth," ll. 209-12, and "The Author," ll. 215-26,
Churchill's *Poetical Works*. Cf. bk. I, Sat. I, and bk. IV, Sat. I, of *Virgidemiae*, in
Hall's *Poems; The Compositions in Prose and Verse of Mr. John Oldham*, 3 vols. (1770),
2:104; *The Works of Monsieur Boileau*, 3 vols. (1711-13), Sat. IX, 1:231-37; Hobbes, *Elements of Law*, pt. I, ch. 9, sec. 11, p. 31.

wavers, however, the stated violence of satiric feeling may be read as invective or irrational hyperbole. Not all satirists are able to make their work evolve as something other than diatribe. John Oldham's "pointed wit"—as he described his late seventeenth-century satire *Upon a Printer*—suggests a sadistic itch. Graphically, he describes how

> ... strait to thrusts I go,
> And pointed satire runs him through and through.
> ...................................................
> Torn, mangled, and exposed to scorn and shame,
> I mean to hang, and gibbet up thy name.
>
> [37–44]

In some distant age Archilochos similarly had exulted in his imprecations, their vehemence and deadliness. "Listen to me cuss," he had boasted. And he had warned:

> But for what he did
> To me,
> He won't get away
> Unstruck.[53]

What we miss in such verse is a hint at least of disinterested moral perspective.

Rhetoric like that of Archilochos and Oldham has frequently brought disrepute to satire because we cannot easily associate spite with the good in either intention or result. Doubts, once they occur, undermine confidence in satiric integrity, even darkening into suspicion of impropriety. Under the vague rubric of "obscenity," a satirist could be castigated at will for almost anything that displeased the reader. Although the noun *obscenitas* has always had sexual overtones, the adjective *obscenus* could be connotatively more flexible. Its primary significations were related to that which was "adverse," "unfavorable," "repulsive," "filthy," and to allied synonyms emphasizing the unattractive in human behavior. Indeed noxious, cloacal associations became commonplace even in judgments on satire, though seldom with

53. Oldham, *Compositions*, 2:104–6; *Carmina Archilochi: The Fragments of Archilochos*, trans. Guy Davenport (Berkeley and Los Angeles: University of California Press, 1964), pp. 4, 25.

the naked disgust of one early commentator, for whom satirists were "like beetles ... hatched in dung, or vermin bred out of ulcers, perpetually feeding upon the frailties and imperfections of human nature." Attacks milder than this filter through the eighteenth and nineteenth centuries and even into our own time. But as judgments they mislead. To depict ugly reality unvarnished and without circumlocution undoubtedly offends if the standards of representation are calculated by a facade of decorum that disregards the offensiveness of the reality itself. A distinction must be made between cheap excitation and a re-creation of being. When experience, in the seventeenth-century or eighteenth-century sense, is "obscene," then a satirist often feels that he must state his case in that verbal and substantive idiom. Even long before then, St. Augustine and other Church Fathers had sometimes argued for obscenity as a way to lay bare the maggotlike nature of immorality, its widening and convoluted disorder.[54]

Like any form of literary expression, satire is subjective even as are most of the criteria for determining decorum. Propriety thus becomes relative; and the satirist, without violating his critical obligation, may be allowed to press his thesis as far as he thinks necessary for persuasion. There is simply no clearcut way to conclude whether he has breached the line between acceptable realism, however sordid, and bad taste. As Anthony Collins observed to a would-be legislator of propriety:

When you draw up your law, you will find it so very difficult to settle the point of decency in writing ... that you will be ready to lay aside ... your project, and ... will be no more able to settle that point of decency, than you would be to settle by law, that cleanliness in clothes, and that politeness in dress, behavior, and conversation, which become men of quality, and fortune in the world, and should be habitual to them. [p. 26]

When the truth envisaged by a satirist nauseates with an undeniable grossness, he must risk falling out with those squeamish

54. Walter Charleton, *A Brief Discourse concerning the Different Wits of Men* (1669), p. 119. Cf. Anthony Collins, *A Discourse concerning Ridicule and Irony in Writing* [1729], ed. E. A. and L. D. Bloom (Los Angeles: Augustan Reprint Society, 1970), p. 26; Pierre Bayle, on St. Augustine and obscenity, in *An Historical and Critical Dictionary*, 4 vols. (1710), p. lxxxvii (end of vol. 4).

readers for whom, like Swift's fools, the comfort of self-deception is preferable to the medicinal bitterness of discovery.[55]

Seventeenth-century translators of Juvenal uneasily tried to compromise between rendering him truly and yet without offense to chaste English ears and eyes. That effort generally became an exercise in grundyism, as when Barten Holyday chose to correct rather than translate and exonerate Juvenal's candor. Several sections in the third satire, for example, define the poet's hostility to the Greeks in Rome. One line in particular contains a controversial reading: should it be *aulam* (home) or *aviam* (grandmother)? The controversy becomes more acute because Juvenal stresses that the Greeks in their systematic process of a Roman takeover will engage even in rape. The question then is, who or what is being raped by the Greeks: the Roman home—a safe enough bit of symbolism—or the grandmother—a repugnantly explicit allusion? Holyday chose safety, translating *horum si nihil est, aulam resupinat amici* (112) as "They'll ransack house and heart." A victim of his scrupulosity, Holyday made the wrong word choice, as modern Juvenalian scholarship has proved.

Yet he had sufficient scholarly integrity to admit in his notes that

the scholiast here reads *aviam*, very aptly and satirically; meaning, that if there were neither a young son nor daughter, nor a young master nor mistress in a house to be corrupted, the impudent and vile Greeks would comply even with their friend's grandame though never so aged and deformed, and by corrupting her, though themselves with her, to explore the secrets of a family. An acute exposition if warranted by copy, which therefore I rather propose than approve.

Of Holyday's rendition of Juvenal, we can only recognize the translator's dedication to a Miltonic premise inverted: "Better it is a book should be lost, than a man." Similar mannered tests of delicacy continued on into the eighteenth century, as in the words of the anonymous poet who wished to "Declare that

55. For a modern psychoanalytical revaluation, see Norman O. Brown, *Life against Death: The Psychoanalytical Meaning of History* (New York: Modern Library Paperbacks, 1959), pp. 179-201.

what's obscene shall give offence, / Let want of decency be want of sense."[56] The same kind of exhortation prevails about ten years later when we read in *An Essay on Criticism*, that "no pardon vile obscenity should find" (530). Pope's zest for the off-color situation or for the "merdamantean" quip of *The Dunciad* (as in Book II) is of course a familiar part of his poetry. The disclaimer in the *Essay* should therefore be taken no more seriously than a solemn joke, his obedience in spirit if not in fact to social propriety.

As a *pro forma* tenet of satire, decency animated authors as diverse as Defoe in England and Boileau in France. But frequently readers confused decency with reticence and indecency with wanton nastiness or titillation. In language of hackneyed disapproval, thus, James Beattie remarked that the

*Provoked Wife*, the *Old Bachelor*, the *Beggar's Opera* are dangerous plays no doubt, and scandalously immoral; but it is the wit and the humor, not the villainy, of Brute, Belmour, and Macheath, that makes the audience merry; and Vanbrugh, Congreve, and Gay are blamable, not because they have made beastliness, robbery, lying, and adultery ludicrous, (for that I believe was not in their power), but because they adorn their respective reprobates with engaging qualities to seduce others into imitation. . . . While the moral faculty is inactive or neuter, the ludicrous sentiment may operate; but to have a just sense of the enormity of a crime, and at the same time to laugh at it, seems impossible, or at least unnatural.[57]

Sterne quickly established himself as a scapegoat on these grounds, and the antipathy built. The Victorian critics were particularly hostile, allowing their cloistered imaginations to see indiscretions in *Tristram Shandy* that today are considered innocuous. The fault was compounded for them not only because they were inflamed by unmentionable sins but also because the fires were started and stoked by a parson. Even in the more tolerant atmosphere of the eighteenth century, Goldsmith's Chinese persona (Letter 53) obliquely repudiates Sterne for contravening

56. Holyday, pp. 39, 51. For a fuller commentary, see E. A. and L. D. Bloom, "Johnson's *London* and the Tools of Scholarship," *HLQ* 34 (1971): 136–38; *A Satyr Against Wit* (1700), pp. 12–13.

57. *Essays . . . on Laughter* [1764], *and Ludicrous Composition* (Edinburgh, 1776), pp. 660–64.

moral decorum, and he damns him for being an artist *manqué,* "a bawdy blockhead [who] often passes for a fellow of smart parts and pretensions." Goldsmith's critical perception, blurred here by his particular brand of sentimentality, cannot adequately come to terms with Sterne's impudence. Because the absurd indecencies that form the nucleus of the novel approach uncomfortably near to the truth of human conduct and misconduct, they must therefore be dismissed by the critic-traveler as offensive aberrations. The dilemma of morality-in-art fortunately can be looked at through the more objective vision of today's critics. They make us aware that Sterne's "obscenity" is a trap he springs on the unwary moralist dedicated with sufficient intensity to virtue that he fails to sight his own possible priggishness. Sterne may be flouting convention, to be sure, but that serves at best as a secondary concern. Actually there is a chance that he can return us to a sense of our wholeness. If he pokes into the dark, hidden corners of man's salacious life, he challenges no notion of perfection, only the notion of hiding what may be flawed. But the flawed is natural, Sterne tells us, and he shows us natural man as he exists, warts and all.[58]

If his purpose owes something to the salutary so also does the tonality of his so-called bedpan humor. We are still left to ponder why satire made dynamic by professedly holy rage often approaches the underground of indelicacy, why in literature intended ostensibly to correct or reform the satiric tone may approximate revulsion. Steele, as we have seen in the first chapter, understood the compulsion of candor and could comment upon it with perspective. Juvenal, he remarked in *Tatler* 242, lived under a tyrant-ruler in whose reign "the fall of empire, contempt of glory, and a general degeneracy of manners are before his eyes in all his writings. . . . Vice and corruption are attacked by Juvenal in a style which denotes, he fears he shall not be heard without he calls to them in their own language, with a barefaced mention of the villainies and obscenities of his contemporaries."

Whether obscenity operates as an appropriate idiom for conveying satiric meaning precisely and affectively has never ceased

58. See Fluchère, pp. 218 ff.

to be a critical concern. Consequently we experience little shock from twentieth-century arguments that for almost every major satirist the language of obscenity is inevitable. The business of the satirist causes him to reveal human beings in their public roles, and this means that some people are stripped of jealously guarded privacy, that they are exposed in actions generally withheld from polite observation. The satirist becomes a leveler with a prerogative to exploit even man's physiological needs—excretory or sexual—until he is reduced "to a bodily democracy paralleling the democracy of death in the *danse macabre*."[59] Obscenity in this context warns us that we often seem no better than our fellow naked apes, unclean, lecherous, brutal.

But obscenity differs from other keys in the satiric register only by its particularized intensity. Like any compartment of satire, it can serve as an impulse toward inner knowledge. The paradox of obscenity is that it compels while it repels. Appealing to man's most submerged feelings, it vicariously breaks through his inhibitions, and yet it fills him with detestation and shame toward what was hitherto unmentionable. Though blunt, obscenity can sharpen satiric meaning; though crude, it can refine meaning. In a discussion of the concealed recesses of truth, goodness, and meaning, Jung acknowledges that sometimes they must be sought out even in filth. *In stercore invenitur,* according to an axiom of alchemy, but worth in satire as in alchemy loses nothing because of its discovered hiding place.[60]

IV

Quintilian had urged that persuasion is undercut by transparent rancor. "For it is a dog's eloquence," he said, "to undertake the task of abusing one's opponent" (XII. ix. 9). Some satirists might have profited from the aphorism. Quintilian's influence notwithstanding, however, the lesson often went unheeded and abuse was long accepted as a byproduct of satire, especially when modified by wit and irony. Yet in seventeenth-century and eighteenth-century culture there flourished a verbal respect for the civility of restraint, even when it was no more than ironically

---

59. Frye, *Anatomy of Criticism,* p. 235; Brown, pp. 179-201.
60. Jung, *Practice of Psychotherapy,* p. 189.

polite masquerade. Boileau, for instance, wanted to be remembered—contrary to his own assertions of tempestuous rage—as "a poet of great moderation." More hawkish satirists also adopted the genteel fiction of forbearance. No matter how they strained credulity, they claimed moderation and in fact offered it as part of ceremonial expectation. Smollett, playing the game of propriety, assured the "delicate reader" that his assaults upon vice and folly would not deter him from exemplary self-control.[61] The mask of moderation could be made to serve in almost any satiric situation. Its range, consequently, moved from the excoriation of reprehensible moral and intellectual infractions to gentle wrist-slapping for mere breaches of social conduct.

Long before the explosion of seventeenth-century and eighteenty-century satire, George Wither had protested in one of his epigrams, "To the Satyromastix":

> Oh Lord, Sir, y'are deceiv'd. I'm none of those
> That write in anger, or malicious spleen,
> I have not taken pepper in the nose,
> Nor a base forger of false libels been:
> Such ones there be indeed, such I have seen.

The argument for benevolence did not change greatly with the advance of time, but its declaration is convincing when it comes from Fielding, that lifelong exponent of good nature. "Satire on vice or vicious men," he wrote, "though never so pointed, is no more a sign of ill-nature than it would be to crush a serpent, or destroy a wild beast." Then, sounding a popular medical analogy, he continued: "If the mind be only tainted with one particular vice, this is but a potion given to our disease; and though it may be attended with some pain in the operation, the satirist is to be regarded as our physician, not our enemy."[62]

61. Boileau, *A Discourse of Satires,* appended to *An Essay on Wit,* by Walter Harte, pp. 39–46; also Boileau's *Works,* Sat. VII, p. 205, and preface to Sat. X, p. 251; dedication to *Ferdinand Count Fathom.* Cf. Addison, *Spectator* 209; *Defoe's Review* (21 Feb. 1706); Whitehead, *Essay on Ridicule,* ll. 378–87.

62. "Epigram 4," *Abuses Stript and Whipt; or, Satirical Essays* (1613); Fielding, *Champion,* 22 Mar. 1739/40. Cf. *Champion,* 13 Mar., on good nature and the proper objects of satire (as an interesting complement of the preface to *Joseph Andrews,* distinguishing between the objects of pity and ridicule). See also Henry Knight Miller, *Essays on Fielding's Miscellanies: A Commentary on Volume One* (Princeton: Princeton University Press, 1961), pp. 54–88.

Although the process of satiric healing may cause nearly as much discomfort as the illness itself, we do not expect the healer's art to be more radical than the malady warrants. Nor, on the other hand, do we accept Robert Dodsley's expedient prescription of satire as a "sugar-plumb" tossed out to obviate "affronting the boxes." Much satire is like Ignatz Mouse's ambiguous brick: although it satisfies the thrower, he is too malevolent and the lovesick Krazy Kat too self-deluded for the weapon to be other than destructive.[63] But perversity like this defies the control even of an oppressive Offissa Pup. Inconclusively saccharine satire will of course change nothing beyond harmlessly endorsing the status quo. On the other side, those Ignatz-like satirists who insist upon throwing their purely personal bricks doubtless achieve release of spite. Momentarily, at least, they and their weapons often entertain the unstruck; but barren of *humanitas,* they invalidate that moral and aesthetic perception which should make satire bearable.

63. Letter from Robert Dodsley to William Shenstone, regarding an epilogue to the former's tragedy *Cleone* (1748): B. M. Add. MS 28,959, f. 227; E. E. Cummings, intro. to *Krazy Kat,* by George Herriman (New York: Henry Holt, 1946).

# CHAPTER 4

# SACRAMENTUM MILITIAE:
## Religious Satire

Among the records of any religious controversy are the satiric
statements promoted by it. Such controversies in the eighteenth
century were numerically formidable; and in a curiously an-
tipodal atmosphere Church of England men validated satire, but
so too did nonconformists and unbelievers. Whatever the specific opposition—Anglicans against Catholics and Dissenters,
Trinitarians against Socinians, Deists against those who accepted
the mysteries of faith, High Flyers against Low Churchmen—
one may count upon satire designed to whip up or maintain
theological partiality. Undeniably, many arguments in satiric
dress were bracing performances directed to both serious reflection and public diversion. Other debates, however, often threw
off more heat than reason. Especially after the return of Charles
II in 1660, the nature of belief, its sectarian divisions, and clerical hierarchy competed with politics, literature, manners, and
public personalities as legitimate satiric material. With parson-
baiting and creed-sniping high on the list of blood sports, satire
was sometimes indistinguishable from the invective once described by Robert Burton. "Religion itself," he wrote, "is brought
into ridicule and contempt, and the clerical calling is rendered
vile. And in view of these facts, I venture to repeat the abusive
expressions which some vulgar fellow has applied to the clergy,
that they are a rotten crowd, beggarly, uncouth, filthy, melancholy, miserable, despicable, and contemptible." Or, as in the
more moderate words of Samuel Butler, religious truth could

not elude diminution by hordes who approved "of no satire but that which is written against the Gods."[1]

On the one side, then, stood those who found in satire a justifiable means of fostering or negating sectarian principles; for them religious satire was valid as genre and propaganda. On the other side, however, stood their opponents—orthodox as well as dissenting, clerical as well as secular—who maintained that religious satire abraded an already fragmented Christianity. This group, so heterogeneous in its makeup, was seemingly divided beyond reconciliation. How, without bringing religion into further disorder, could significant differences among sects and even among disbelievers be debated? How could reason and piety prevail in an atmosphere clouded by extremism and ill will? In the minds of many fearful of spiritual waste, satire exacerbated feelings beyond the limits of intellectual and moral decorum; it increased divisiveness and so threatened true Christianity. That was at least the nominal position of Stillingfleet, who frequently jousted against both Catholics and Deists. An able preacher-rhetorician, he knew how to turn scriptural authority into Anglican channels. He could, for example, invoke Proverbs 14:9 to reprove scoffers—and anyone outside the religious Establishment bore that epithet—who "make a mock at sin."

Advocating religious dignity, he expected "persons of civility and honor" to treat theological problems, if not with reverence, then with respect. But propriety was lacking and he protested about satiric "wit grown so schismatical and sacrilegious, that it can please it self with nothing but holy ground." Boldly assured, he let it be known that the time had come for the emollient wisdom he could offer. As the subtitle of his first book, *Irenicum* (1659), hints, England basked in good fortune to have Stillingfleet the healer and his *Weapon-Salve for the Churches Wounds*. In that treatise he wrote "not to increase the controversies of the times, nor to foment the differences that are among us." And there also he objected that "the generality of men let all their

---

1. Burton, *The Anatomy of Melancholy* (Oxford, 1621), pt. I, sec. 2, mem. 3, subsec. 15; Butler, *Characters and Note-Books,* p. 408.

religion run up into briars and thorns, into contentions and parties, as though religion were indeed *sacramentum militiae*, but more against fellow-Christians than the unquestionable hindrances of men's eternal happiness." Despite his avowed yearning for spiritual quiet, Stillingfleet became entangled in satiric thorns and briars of his own. His taunts about heterodox questioning and Catholic premises of infallibility reveal an Anglican warrior bound metaphorically by a *sacramentum militiae*. Although he openly stated his aversion to irony employed in apologetics, he did not hesitate to apply it himself in a context favorable to the national church. With heavy, insistent repetition he hurled himself against *infallible* faith, *infallible* church, *infallible* Pope, *infallible* tradition; against "those mountebanks who pretend to the most *infallible* cures." He capitalized on a widespread antipathy to authoritarian dogma and to superstition, which Anglicans equated with Catholicism. His repetitions, deliberately tedious, work well as irritants. Meant to annoy through mockery, they reduce to hubristic charlatanism any assumption of infallibility. Time and again he scores hits, even while abjuring "the science of controversy," which "like the throwing vinegar upon hot coals . . . gives a quick scent for the present, but vanishes immediately into smoke and air."[2] The antimilitant claims become but another smoke screen, as easily penetrated as that surrounding his use of satire in religious controversy. For this reason one of his Catholic adversaries could charge: "Peruse the Doctor page after page, you will find the man all along in peevish humor, when you see his book brimful of tart biting ironies, drolleries, comical expressions, impertinent demands, and idle stories."[3] Even if Stillingfleet disclaims peevishness and impertinence, his practice in much of his polemic belies an innocence of satiric intention.

    2. *The Works of that Eminent and most learned Prelate, Dr. Edw. Stillingfleet, late Lord Bishop of Worcester, together with his Life and Character*, 6 vols. (1710), especially 1:19-26, 117-18; 2:147-49; 4:484-85; 5:A3ᵛ. Cf. *Hudibras*, for example, I. i. 187-204: Sir Hudibras brags about the "infallibility" of his Presbyterianism. In modern times James Joyce depicts a mildly bibulous satiric scene whose dialogue centers on "the infallibility of the Pope." See "Grace," in *Dubliners* (London: Grant Richards, 1914), p. 208.
    3. Quoted by Anthony Collins, *A Discourse concerning Ridicule and Irony*, p. 8.

This double game was a popular form of rhetorical dexterity. Wily debaters who professed hostility to religious satire shuffled phrases, rearranged ideas, loaded syntax, pretended whimsy, and pursued any other ironical course that might embarrass the opposition. Few satirists could have been less reluctant than Andrew Marvell to identify their purpose. Nevertheless he went through a metaphoric ritual of concealment by denouncing an enemy who "never oils his hone, but that he may whet his razor; and that not to shave, but to cut men's throats."[4] The thesis of satire's antisatire forwarded by Stillingfleet and Marvell is a gamelike fiction that carries into the next century. It appears, for example, in the theological pronouncements of Benjamin Hoadly, one of the most argumentative of the Low Church prelates. As early as 1709, almost a decade before his embroilment in the rancorous Bangorian Controversy, Hoadly was questioning High Church claims for divine authority. Thus, even before his elevation to the first of his four bishoprics, this parish rector was taking on such well-placed adversaries as the bishops of Rochester and Exeter. The quarrel with the latter made him especially visible when Hoadly's friend Steele turned it to satiric advantage for him in four *Tatler* essays.[5]

In numerous sermons and pamphlets, Hoadly's zest for conflict and ridicule fails to square with his formal objections to "raillery and banter [as] the best way of handling even the most sacred matters." He contradicted his own plea for tolerance when he repudiated the eccentric Irish baronet Sir Richard Bulkeley and his endorsement of visionary claims set forth by a group of French pseudoseers. Hoadly's taste for ironic stricture emerges in a commentary on Bulkeley's interpretation of the Second Coming: "We acknowledge a belief of His coming necessary, and a constant holiness of life necessary. This is the preparation He expects. But whether He will come at noon, or at midnight, today or the following, we leave to Him as a thing not necessary to be determined, nor necessary to be believed. And

---

4. *The Rehearsal Transpros'd: or, Animadversions upon a late Book, Entituled, A Preface shewing what Grounds there are of Fears and Jealousies of Popery* (1672), p. 41.

5. *Tatler* 44, 45, 50, 51; Calhoun Winton, *Captain Steele: The Early Career of Richard Steele* (Baltimore: Johns Hopkins Press, 1964), pp. 112–14.

methinks we might hope that *others* should leave the world as undisturbed and free in this matter as our *Lord* hath commanded them to be."[6] In equating the necessary with what is nonsensical, he cleansed an article of faith from the dross of zealotry and he belittled the "New Prophets" until they vanished into the miasmata of their own absurdity.

Like the oracular Ralpho of *Hudibras,* such visionaries had to be hooted at

> For mystic learning, wondrous able
> In magic, talisman, and cabal,
> Whose primitive tradition reaches
> As far as Adam's first green breeches.
>
> [I. i. 523-26]

Hoadly's derisive attack upon claimants of vatic power had sources imbedded in the foundations of religious satire. In the second century Lucian, for instance, had jeered at mortals like the quack Alexander, who pretended to be a prophet. Tongue-in-cheek, he further dramatized the struggle between certain lesser gods—Apollo, Aesculapius, Artemis, to name a few—who fobbed themselves off as oracles and a chagrined Zeus who was forced to compete with them for sacrifices. In later European culture antivatic cynicism became so fixed that assertions of divine prescience were condemned by writers as various as Sebastian Brant, Erasmus, Jonson, Swift, and Burns, among many others. Satirists like these feared the questionable adjuncts of prophecy; vision, fanaticism, enthusiasm suggested to them the morally reprehensible, the corruption of brotherhood and rational piety. As a portent of pride, prophecy reduced the fount of belief to egocentricity; as superstition, it elevated persecution to a virtue.

Bluntly and disdainfully, Hoadly decried Sir Richard's ignorance of sacred matters and simultaneously paraded his own righteousness:

I am sure, if [ridicule] should be generally embraced, the world must come at length to be made up of creatures perpetually grinning, and

---

6. *A Brief Vindication of the Antient Prophets from the Imputations and Misrepresentations of Such as Adhere to our Present Pretenders to Inspiration. In a Letter to Sir Richard Bulkeley, Bart.* (1709), "Preface" and p. 4.

mimicking, and playing mountebank-tricks at one another: and they must always be in the right, who can get the longest and loudest laugh on their side. A serious countenance must be a monstrous sight: and an honest enquirer into truth the greatest jest imaginable. And let any one judge what a *blessed state* of things must succeed![7]

But while denying his dependence upon "raillery and banter" for the settlement of theological disputes, Hoadly resorts to precisely those devices as a way of dispatching Bulkeley. That kind of ironic pretense is of course traditional, and Hoadly should have been content to stop there. Instead, he belabored scoffers and thereby weakened the credibility of his assault on the "New Prophets" and their Irish patrons. Indeed, his assault was sufficiently deflected to lose its center. Specifically, he created a new area of contention by deriding religious satirists; and he proved himself a hypocrite.

Hoadly relished the give-and-take of polemics; and it must be admitted that he had as much to take as to give. Seldom, if ever, has a clergyman been subjected to such intense, abusive attack. This should not be surprising, however: no one entertaining such extreme latitudinarian attitudes as Hoadly did could reasonably expect gentler treatment, least of all from the smarting Tories and members of the High Church party. Neither, for that matter, did he leave room for tolerance among the Dissenters, to whom his insistence upon conformity had been a longtime source of anger. In the still smoldering heat of the Bangorian Controversy, Defoe vigorously assailed Hoadly's Anglicanism. Mockingly personal, Defoe reduces the prelate to the status of a quack doctor who "deserves to be demolished for administering poison instead of physic." The "Mountebank," as he is constantly addressed, is opposed by Defoe in the guise of "Merry-Andrew." And the center of the confrontation, patently enough, is "Bangor-Bridge." The destructive element prevails, for Defoe's mockery is bitter, its vengeful sounds crying down any possible conciliation. The occasional spark of humor is more forced than real, as when Hoadly's friendship with Steele is recollected: "The

7. "Preface," *A Brief Vindication.* For a later example of scoffing (at Bishop Edmund Gibson et al.), see *The Courtier's New Book of Common Prayer, Containing the Army's New Te Deum, the Courtier's New Creed, the British Litany* [1745?].

brightest men in town, Master, even *Men of Steel,* that we thought would never grow rusty, (pardon me ONE Pun, Master,) yet we find them tarnish, lose their lustre, and grow quite out of fashion."[8] Even Defoe, we sense, was here more interested in the unequivocal meanings of invective than in the dubious subtleties of fun and wit.

The satiric energy generated by Hoadly's controversial sermons and essays is intriguingly topical, and the same is true of their ripostes. When we think of durable effect, however, unrestrained satire like Defoe's achieves greater historical than literary appeal. Similarly, Hoadly's antisatiric pretense is nullified by posturing that finally exhausts the reader's patience. But there were also other deeply concerned men for whom religious satire was *de facto* unacceptable, who were—like Isaac Watts— alienated by the substance and spirit of such satire. A nonconformist of impeccable spiritual commitment, he earned the regard of Anglicans and fellow Dissenters alike for his "meekness of opposition and his mildness of censure." These qualities not only helped turn him against satire but made him always more comfortable as the patient "teacher of a congregation" than as the quarrelsome ironist. "When I have felt a slight inclination to satire or burlesque," he wrote, "I thought it proper to suppress it."

Still he knew that not everyone responds identically to religious influence; for some, fear, coercion, or wit was more conducive to understanding and obedience than chaste reasonableness. While therefore admitting that he would seize "any handle of the soul to lead it away betimes from vicious pleasures," he backed away from "the grinning and the growling muses." In theory he kept the door fractionally ajar, prepared to admit satire if he recognized its necessity. But that alternative would rarely have been exercised by one of Watts's temperament. "Could I persuade any man by a kinder method," he acknowledged, "I should never think it proper to scold or laugh at him."[9]

---

8. *Merry-Andrew's Epistle to his Old Master Benjamin, a Mountebank at Bangor-Bridge, on the River Dee, near Wales* (1719).

9. "Preface," *Horae Lyricae,* in *Eighteenth-Century Critical Essays,* ed. Elledge, 1:159–60; *English Poets,* 3:307–8.

The admission is rhetorical because he always managed to find a "method" gentler than satire for exhortation. Thus he stood with that minority of pious Englishmen who not only declared themselves against satire but lived up to their declaration.

Conversely, religious satire attracted others as a dangerous yet effective persuasive. They were uneasy about its use, fearful of the cliché of impiety associated with it. Driven by such uncertainty, they fumbled to have it both ways, like one anonymous essayist who began in compromise and ended in sophistry. With Shaftesbury as a lever, he commented: "Ridicule, or true jesting, is, with regard to sincerity, as much serious as any other method of reasoning; and the more apt to promote both its desired consequences of conviction and laughter, the more the sentiment of the dispenser is sincere, and his deportment grave." But then, conceding that truth remains the only valid test of ridicule, he poses this hairsplitting proposition: "How is it possible that an instrument, whose professed use is to pull down, should be employed in supporting any sect of religion, except there were only two sects of religion in the world, and one of them necessarily true; whereas it is possible there may be five hundred, and all but one false and ridiculous." By some process of verbal legerdemain, he concluded that religious satire had no relevance in his time, George II having established an exceptional level of toleration: "Religion is now become in England, almost what it was first intended to be; not a tool for the politic and the seditious to work withal, but a matter entirely of private concern, subject to no jurisdiction but that of conscience or private opinion."[10] By 1753, then, to follow such a tenuous line of reasoning, religious satire was permissible but no longer necessary or really operable.

Were we to acknowledge this essay as evidence, then we should also be obliged to concede that the energy of the controversy over such satire had already waned. Yet neither in practice nor in theory was this so. The matter that gives sustenance to

10. *An Essay on Ridicule* (1753), pp. 30, 49, 54-55. For an "official" justification of religious satire, see *The Young Gentleman and Lady Instructed in . . . Principles of Politeness, Prudence, and Virtue* (1747), 1:299-300 ["authorized" by King George II]. Deterrence is the key.

religious satire continued in abundance; and—except for the normal attrition to which any fashionable or long-standing mode of expression is prey—signs of radical depletion would be hard to discern. The prejudices against Catholicism, Dissent, and Deism that had nurtured much satiric polemic remained alive. And to these old biases were added new ones generated by the popularity of the evangelical movement both in and outside the Church of England. A traditionalist such as Matthew Bramble reveals the polarity between what he regards as the genuine "light of reason" and Humphry Clinker's specious claims for the "new light of God's grace." In the opinion of his irascible master, Humphry's sermonizing cannot be excused as the action of either "an hypocritical knave, or a wrong-headed enthusiast." To preach Methodism, Humphry must be the victim of a seductively "disturbed imagination" or of a fanatic stubbornness as a result of which preacher and congregation "will be misled by a will-i'the-wisp, from one error into another, till . . . plunged into religious frenzy."[11] Bramble's outrage, bursting forth in irrepressible—yet comic—violence reduces evangelicalism to a serious aberration, if not madness, worthy of the satirist's art.

In fact, the evangelicals resisted such intolerance, and their resistance constituted the steel within the "meekness" exemplified by Isaac Watts and his successors. A contemporary of Matthew Bramble's creator, for instance, the gentle, meditative William Cowper responded overtly to religious satire instead of turning the other cheek. Especially in a group of poems written between 1781 and 1783, despite a few lapses of his own into the mode, he states his disenchantment with satire as a whole because he sees nothing but decline since the grand days of Arbuthnot and Swift (and even the latter "Too often rails to gratify his spleen"). Much like Dryden a hundred years earlier, Cowper complained,

> Satire has long since done his best; and curst
> And loathsome ribaldry has done his worst.

11. Tobias Smollett, *The Expedition of Humphry Clinker,* letter from Jery Melford to Sir Watkin Phillips, 10 June. Bramble is perhaps recalling Swift's "mere light of nature," *Mechanical Operation of the Spirit,* sec. ii.

Speaking out of a moral repugnance that cannot be dissociated from aesthetic sensibility, he harshly concludes that in his day "most sat'rists are . . . a public scourge," sour, "wild assassins . . . Prepar'd to poignard whomsoe'er they meet." He equates satire with scandals and lies, its wit with cruelty. Analogically, he relates the genre to the "guns, halberts, swords, and pistols, great and small" displayed symmetrically "in starry forms" upon the walls of the Tower of London. Despite "the exact designer's skill" these weapons must, like satire itself, be accounted "implements of mischief still."[12]

For Cowper, a once valuable mode had collapsed in spirit as it had in execution, its constructive worth surrendered to ugly vindictiveness. All of his humanistic aversion to the "implements of mischief" may be reasserted against religious satire. Lacking "love of virtue," such a mode became in Cowper's opinion—as in Watts's—too saline to benefit man's faltering religious convictions. To be corrected of his "mulish folly" he must be moved by "softer methods" and "gently tutor'd." Yet at times even Cowper's high-flown principles retreated before his bias. In 1781 the conflict between theory and practice—with the latter triumphant—made its point when he animadverted in the poem *Truth* on Catholicism and the life of monastic withdrawal.

Initially his intention could be mistaken for a descriptive account of simple piety. But a series of nouns and adjectives derogating the fervor that he associated with Rome soon dispels that impression:

> See the sage hermit, by mankind admir'd,
> With all that bigotry adopts inspir'd,
> Wearing out life in his religious whim,
> Till his religious whimsy wears out him.
> His works, his abstinence, his zeal, allow'd,
> You think him humble—God accounts him proud.
>
> [87-92]

As he continues, Cowper becomes progressively remote from a

12. *Charity* (written 1781), ll. 491-516, 533-56; *Table-Talk* (written 1781), ll. 728-29. See *The Poetical Works of William Cowper*, ed. H. S. Milford, 3rd ed. (London: Humphrey Milford, 1926). Cf. "Prologue," *The Kind Keeper* [1678], ll. 1-6, in Dryden's *Poems*, ed. Kinsley, 1:174-75.

"love of virtue." And with unusual severity he satirizes the quest
for sanctification implicit in the Catholic's "penitential stripes"
and "streaming blood" of self-mortification.

If Cowper allowed himself caustic release on this occasion, he
restrained his anger thereafter. By 1783–1784 in *The Task* he
took up his original position and flatly denied that satire could
come to terms with either the needs or questions of faith. He had
only pity for the satirist who

> Strutting and vap'ring in an empty school,
> Spent all his force and made no proselyte.

Whatever faults the religious establishment might be guilty of,
religion itself—and only religion—could remedy them:

> I say the pulpit (in the sober use
> Of its legitimate, peculiar pow'rs)
> Must stand acknowledged, while the world shall stand,
> The most important and effectual guard,
> Support, and ornament of virtue's cause.
>
> [II, 330–34]

His visionary peace fused with religious awe and owed nothing
to the persuasion of any ironist. Like many other men, then,
Cowper would ultimately have agreed that while satire could be
potent in controlling worldly trifles, "the freaks of fashion" (II,
317), even then he had misgivings. And certainly the image of
the "lunatic clergyman,"[13] the religious satirist who fought complacency with shock and extravagant statement, alienated the
poet's spirituality. Cowper, in short, rejected satire as a specious
way of guiding the human heart to a choice between good and
evil, justice and wrongdoing. The very term *religious satire* and
the various ideas it embraced constituted for him a semantic
absurdity.

## II

Satire in theological discussion created cruxes for anyone convinced that the subject itself was too fundamental and solemn to

13. Christopher Isherwood, in *Lions and Shadows* (London: Hogarth Press,
1938), created this image of W. H. Auden as a deliberately outrageous satirist.
For an excellent view of the poet's satiric affinities, see the essays by Monroe K.
Spears, ch. 3, fn. 8.

admit of ironic reversal and jest. On the other hand, adherents of satire's curative power—its persuasive force—took advantage of its controlled wit and the scruples it raised. In *Satire III*, for example, Donne transmitted his intense devotional need through metaphor that illustrates the impulse to question and analyze:

> To adore, or scorn an image, or protest,
> May all be bad; doubt wisely; in strange way
> To stand inquiring right, is not to stray:
> To sleep, or run wrong, is.
>
> [76-79]

Religion, in short, insists upon the full exercise of spirit and mind; and Donne utilizes satire allegorically to tell us how belief will help us attain the finality of human apprehension. For

> On a huge hill,
> Cragged and steep, Truth stands, and he that will
> Reach her, about must, and about must go;
> And what the hill's suddenness resists, win so;
> Yet strive so, that before age, death's twilight,
> Thy soul rest, for none can work in that night.
>
> [79-84]

The soul or core of Donne's satire is his injunction to "doubt wisely," a call for rational examination; it is an important stage in his religious development. Roman Catholicism lay behind him and his highest authority at the moment (about 1594–1595) resided in conscience. He did not direct his "doubts" against formal religion; they indicated neither skepticism nor uncertainty. Rather he made them his means of skirting impediments before his progress toward the "Truths" of the primitive church. Eventually, as he said in the later *Sermons,* he would discover them by leaving "natural reason and human arts at the bottom of the hill, and climb up only by the light and strength of faith." But now, still youthful, he evinced confidence that his intellectual resources, assisted by the "brave scorn" of satire, would enable him to define properly the center of his devotion, his "Mistress, fair Religion."[14]

14. *The Satires, Epigrams and Verse Letters,* ed. W. Milgate (Oxford: Clarendon Press, 1967), pp. 10–14; *The Divine Poems,* ed. Helen Gardner (Oxford: Clarendon Press, 1952), pp. xviii–xix.

If wise doubt can be the satirist's appeal to conscience, so
equally can wise laughter, as Donne asserted in "Paradox 10."
Wise laughter, further, was the method Milton employed during
his confrontation with Bishop Joseph Hall:

> Now that the confutant may also know as he desires, what force of
> teaching there is sometimes in laughter, I shall return him in short, that
> laughter being one way of answering *a fool according to his folly*, teaches
> two sorts of persons, first the fool himself *not to be wise in his own conceit;*
> as Solomon affirms, which is certainly a great document, to make an
> unwise man know himself. Next, it teaches the hearers, in as much as
> scorn is one of those punishments which belong to men carnally wise,
> which is oft in Scripture declared; for when such are punished *the simple
> are thereby made wise*, if Solomon's rule be true. And I would ask, to what
> end Eliah mocked the false prophets [I Kings 18:27]? Was it to show his
> wit, or to fulfill his humor? Doubtless we cannot imagine that great
> servant of God had any other end in all which he there did, but to teach
> and instruct the poor misled people. And we may frequently read, that
> many of the martyrs in the midst of their troubles, were not sparing to
> deride and scoff their superstitious persecutors.[15]

As Milton stated his proposition, satiric laughter *is* wise laughter: it discredits the fool, it induces self-scrutiny, it instructs the
misguided. Milton's assurance impresses. And so also do his allusions to Solomon and Eliah, which give every sign of being in-
controvertible arguments for religious satire. Yet with true
rhetorical cunning Milton withheld evidence that would have
damaged his position. Of necessity, if his argument were to convince, he drew a curtain over biblical passages proscribing satire,
such as "Fools make a mock at sin."[16] He chose instead to remind
his antagonists that even a saint or a prophet may be driven to
ironic utterance when his deepest commitments are in the balance. And we may wish to remind ourselves that a good man, if
he is also a good rhetorician (and Milton was both), may make as
free with Scripture as does the Devil.

Some controversialists, indeed, advanced their arguments as
though they were writing in finely ironic turns of scriptural discourse. They liked often to emulate the bitter yet victoriously

15. Milton, *An Apology . . . Smectymnuus, Works,* 3:317.
16. Proverbs 14:9; see also 1:26–33; 2 Chronicles 36:16; Jeremiah 15:17.

ennobled tone of the Psalmist. "Why do the heathen rage, and the people imagine a vain thing?" he had asked. "The kings of the earth set themselves, and the rulers take counsel together, against the Lord, and against his anointed, saying, Let us break their bands asunder, and cast away their cords from us. He that sitteth in the heavens shall laugh: the Lord shall have them in derision. . ." (2:1-4). The religious satirist frequently seems to be a judge who sitteth in his own sectarian heaven laughing scornfully at wayward mortals. In so doing he ideally expresses a genius that derives from both frustration and the need to hope; from tensions of love and hate; from a compulsion to hurt and heal. The product of such contrarieties, religious satire undertakes their reconciliation through antitheses: when it thunders, it does so to compassionate; when it derides or shames it means to evoke humility; when it laughs, it proposes to educe good intention; when it questions complacency, it insinuates the nearness of eternal authority.

Often, we have already seen, the Christian satirist embellished his *saeva indignatio* with language intended to connote divine inspiration. Joseph Hall, for example, predicated that the verses in the *Virgidemiae*, "Begot long since of truth and holy rage," lay menacingly like a bundle of switches for use against "the broils" of any "unquiet age." Even more passionate in The *Scourge of Villainy* and choking with heavenly fury, John Marston pleaded:

> O that a satire's hand had force to pluck
> Some floodgate up, to purge the world from muck:
> Would God I could turn Alpheus' river in
> To purge this Augean oxstall from foul sin.
> 			[*Proemium in librum tertium,* 17-20]

And, lest the hieratic point be missed, he underscored it:

> Methinks some sacred rage warms all my veins,
> Making my spright mount up to higher strains
> Than well beseems a rough-tongued satire's part.
> 			[Bk. III, Sat. 9, 7-9][17]

17. Hall, *Poems*, p. 47; *The Poems of John Marston*, ed. Arnold Davenport (Liverpool: University of Liverpool, 1961), pp. 149, 158.

Indignation voiced by Hall and Marston can be stirring; but the epithets "holy" and "sacred" are formulaic, literary and rhetorical rather than sacerdotal. Thus verbally armed, many a Christian satirist hoped his righteousness would reverberate with supernal approval. Shaftesbury harbored no such hope. And where others thundered, he was a bland Pied Piper, exhorting with polite prose. Extending the limits of Donne's wise doubts and Milton's wise laughter, he urged that ridicule be made to unmask pride and deception. In response to a common fear that mockery augments irreverence, he argued contrarily that it strengthens religious liberty with its correlatives of piety and virtue. In the constant battle against repression or even spiritual debility, no strategy functions better than controlled, decent-minded derision, "that which borders most on the manner of the earliest Greek comedy." Specifically he alluded to *Hudibras* as a model of satiric disputation "written on the subject of our religious controversies in the last age."[18]

### III

Through diminution, overstatement, and fantasy, Butler had already achieved the "tolerated manner of criticism" that in time underlay Shaftesbury's theory of ridicule. Although a variety of popular subjects—including politics, law, pedantry, the Royal Society—contribute to Butler's involvement with τὸ γελοῖον (the laughable), we are concerned now with the ways in which he played with and upon religious prejudices. An Anglican by profession, he reacted more or less favorably to the principles of natural religion enunciated by such theologians as Hales, Chillingworth, and Tillotson. By temperament a skeptic, he saw little in religious establishments to make him optimistic. If, as *Hudi-*

18. *Characteristics*, 1:169; also 10-12, 61, 74-75. La Bruyère had complained that satirists liked to inflate the importance of trifling subjects: *Oeuvres de La Bruyère*, ed. G. Servois, 3d ed., 3 vols. (Paris: Libraire Hachette, 1922), 2:61. See also R. L. Brett, *The Third Earl of Shaftesbury* (London: Hutchinson's University Library, 1951), pp. 165-85; Thomas B. Gilmore, Jr., *The Eighteenth-Century Controversy over Ridicule as a Test of Truth*, Research Paper no. 25 (Atlanta: Georgia State University, Jan. 1970); on ridicule, ch. 3 above.

*bras* has made clear, he warred with Puritanism, his notebooks as well as the poem reveal an equally strong anti-Catholic bent.[19]

In this long poem, which pays more attention to dialogue than to action,[20] ridicule imparts a distinction to the wit interwoven with many strands of irony, hyperbole, and parody. These have all been combined to produce a semblance of joviality, but Butler's light touch deceives; his satire often disguises the cruelty of debasement and innuendo. The poem is nevertheless rich in laughter that helps to soften incipient rancor. This ambivalence becomes especially apparent as the Knight prepares for action against bear-baiting, but not until—still mounted—he makes a speech from his Presbyterian perspective. In a comic oration reminiscent of upstart aspirations in a tatterdemalion time,

> When tinkers bawl'd aloud, to settle
> Church discipline, for patching kettle.
> No sow-gelder did blow horn
> To geld a cat, but cried *Reform*.
> The oyster-women lock'd their fish up,
> And trudg'd away, to cry *No Bishop*.
>
> [I. ii. 535–40]

Dissent, in this hudibrastic vision, is served shabbily by "a Gospel-preaching-ministry" who are more partial to the old clothes they hawk than to canonical vestments. The grotesque Knight's run-on peroration makes his appeal to religious principle as ludicrous as the jingles of a music-hall routine.

He is Butler's persona for antiheroic diminution through whom everything is leveled. For "poor Hudibras, his poet had no tenderness: he chooses not that any pity should be shown or respect paid him: he gives him up at once to laughter and contempt, without any quality that can dignify or protect him." When Butler allows his mock hero interludes of lofty or seemingly reflective discourse they sound so affected that they

19. Quintilian, VI. iii. 22–23; *Hudibras,* ed. John Wilders (Oxford: Clarendon Press, 1967). See introduction, especially pp. xxi–xliii, and commentary, pp. 322–449. On the laughable, *Coleridge's Miscellaneous Criticism,* p. 441.

20. *English Poets,* 1:211. For an interesting view of satiric energy, see Michael A. Seidel, "Patterns of Anarchy and Oppression in Butler's *Hudibras,*" *ECS* 5 (1971): 294–314.

emphasize and reemphasize the *faux dévot*.[21] These same harangues also magnify other qualities—for instance, a bumbling, amorous vulgarity—that the poet wishes remembered about the Knight as a parody of the courtly suitor:

> Quoth he, to bid me not to love,
> Is to forbid my pulse to move,
> My beard to grow, my ears to prick up,
> Or (when I'm in a fit) to hickup;
> Command me to piss out the moon,
> And 'twill as easily be done.
>
> [II. i. 343–48]

Although the lover swaggers as ineptly as the preacher, Hudibras has—if nothing else—mastered the use of the low metaphor. The language of chivalry and religion alike remain beyond his capacity to articulate.

From the precepts of Renaissance and later rhetoric, Butler derived several principles of *elocutio* to which *Hudibras* owes its comic intensity.[22] Low words are thematically important; they bring the Presbyterian hero down to gutter level. And so likewise is his absurd oratory, its very excess abusive of all meaning:

> For rhetoric, he could not ope
> His mouth, but out there flew a trope.
>
> [I. i. 81–82]

The rhetorician becomes analogous to the courtier and bigot as an object of scorn. With usual obtuseness about his own failures of comparison, thus, Hudibras warns Ralpho against the dangers of comparison:

> Thou canst at best but overstrain
> A paradox, and th' own hot brain.
> For what can Synods have at all
> With bears that's analogical?
> Or what relation has debating

21. *English Poets*, 1:210. See Auerbach's commentary on the *Tartuffe* of Molière, ch. 15, *Mimesis;* Edwards, *Imagination and Power*, pp. 39–44, for a consideration of Hudibras as a symbol of the foundered Renaissance heroic ideal. "Theriophily" as a satiric theme is discussed by Bertrand A. Goldgar, "Satires on Man and 'the Dignity of Human Nature,'" *PMLA* 80 (Dec. 1965): 535–41.
22. Ian Jack, *Augustan Satire: Intention and Idiom in English Poetry 1660–1750* (Oxford: Clarendon Press, 1957), pp. 15–42.

> Of Church affairs with bear-baiting?
> A just comparison still is,
> Of things *ejusdem generis.*
>
> [I. i. 843–50]

Jog-trot rhythms, antic uninhibited rhymes, "unpoetic" diction, and an unabashedly pedantic and redundant closing couplet— all these make Hudibras his own unwitting judge, as prone to incriminate himself through self-revelation as Dogberry was.

Moreover, insect and animal imagery both complements and stretches the possibilities of human denigration beyond Hudibras the individual. Allusions that evoke disgust—"maggots bred in rotten cheese" and gin-drinking rats—graphically symbolize everything that is squalid in experience and contrary to religious expectation. The man steeped in theological error not only corrupts his own kind, according to Butler, but actually infects animals with his vices:

> For, as some late philosophers
> Have well observ'd, beasts that converse
> With man, take after him, as hogs
> Get pigs all th' year, and bitches dogs.
> Just so by our example cattle
> Learn to give one another battle.
> We read in Nero's time, the heathen,
> When they destroy'd the Christian brethren,
> They sow'd them in the skins of bears,
> And then set dogs about their ears:
> From whence, no doubt, th' invention came
> Of this lewd, Antichristian game.
>
> [I. i. 783–94]

The "Antichristian game" is bear-baiting, which provides through the recurrent imagery of dogs and bears the likeness of religious division. Equally symptomatic of faulty religious observances is the willingness to be taken in by superstition. To make his point, the poet created Sidrophel, a trickster who substitutes the pseudofindings of astrology for Christian miracles. Parodic of episodes in Homer and Virgil, the satirist has the protean Sidrophel transform himself first into a bear and then, when the courageous Hudibras is too much for the sorcerer, into a goose who escapes by diving below the pond's surface (III. i. 289–96).

A dealer in magic and transference for the amazement of the gullible, Sidrophel spins out what appears to be a mockery of the immersionists. In any event, the metamorphosis violates both reason and Christian belief. Butler uses it for a tacit attack upon the vulgar acceptance of play-acting ritual and pseudoprophecy. The satire on Puritanism dominates, but the poem encompasses other failures equatable with religion's inadequacy, chief of which is dissimulation or fraud. In the sixty-odd years following publication of *Hudibras*, in Dennis's judgment (1720), nothing could approximate it as "a very just [satire] on hypocrisy."[23] Looked at from a viewpoint that posited the oneness of church and state, truthfulness—political and religious—in characters like Sir Hudibras and his squire exudes mere expedience at best. Ralpho feels no shame in the premise that "oaths are but words, and words but wind, / Too feeble implements to bind" (II. ii. 107–108). "Reformado Saints" (figuratively, leaders without followers), typified by the Knight, contract obligations under vows and yet "know little of their privilege." Honor, says Ralpho with Falstaffian candor, stays "but a word / To swear by only." Even in love the standard of hypocrisy prevails: " 'tis not what we do, but say" (II. i. 341).

The poet himself brands the hero's consummate duplicity: "As if hypocrisy and non-sense / Had got the advowson of his conscience" (I. i. 233–34). Like Spenser's Huddibras in *The Faerie Queene* (II. ii. 17), Sir Hudibras proves "not so good of deedes, as great of name." And in a provocatively analogous sense, he too is "all arm'd in shyning brass." Derivatively, then, the name describes one who seems at first glance worthier than he is in fact: the surface appearance covers an unattractive reality. The possible Spenserian connotations of "hubris" and "brazen" are, perhaps, relevant to an interpretation of the Knight's role in the later poem.[24] But another dyslogistic echo here should be underscored. "Hudibras" readily becomes "hue of

23. See Richmond P. Bond, *English Burlesque Poetry 1700–1750* (Cambridge, Mass.: Harvard University Press, 1932), pp. 5–7; *The Characters and Conduct of Sir John Edgar . . . Letter III. To Sir John Edgar*, in Dennis's *Critical Works*, 2:201.

24. *Hudibras*, p. 322. Additionally a pun may be involved: "Quoth he, my head's not made of brass" (II. i. 531).

brass" (suggestive in tone if not in meaning of *hue de bras* or even *Hugh de Bras*), a mocking nonce-word that, hinting at Anglo-French courtliness, endorses the hero's chivalric calling. By extension, the name implies a brassy coloration that could be mistaken for gold and thus allow the false or hypocritical to triumph. And brass, in the scriptural epithet, is "sounding," the echo of emptiness and deceit.

As a trait of the religious pretender, militancy irritated Butler, who deplored the violence of sectarian zeal. Palpably scornful, he denounced the "true-blue" Presbyterian as one of the "Errant Saints" of the "Church Militant." The poet rose up in feigned horror that faith should be built upon "the holy text of pike and gun," that there were those who would

> Decide all controversies by
> Infallible artillery;
> And prove their doctrine orthodox
> By apostolic blows and knocks;
> . . . . . . . . . . . . . . . . . . . . . . . . . . . .
> More peevish, cross, and splenetic,
> Than dog distract, or monkey sick.
> [I. i. 187–210]

And the "infallible" Independent Ralpho—as much a hybrid as his master—is equally prepared "to fit himself for martial deed." An amateur warrior, he glibly mouths professional terms, "van, main battle, rear." Punning is shamelessly explicit:

> Both kinds of mettle he prepar'd,
> Either to give blows, or to ward,
> Courage within, and steel without,
> To give, or to receive a rout.
> His death-charg'd pistols he did fit well,
> Drawn out from his life-preserving vittle.
> [I. ii. 83–88]

Whatever their religious differences—and they are many—this oddly mated quixotic pair share a belligerence of spirit and rhetoric.

As Johnson describes them: "The hero . . . is a Presbyterian Justice who, in the confidence of legal authority and the rage of zealous ignorance, ranges the country to repress superstition and correct abuses, accompanied by an Independent Clerk, disputatious and obstinate, with whom he often debates, but never conquers him."[25] Each in his own way is an ineffectual clod through whom Butler satirizes the follies of religious zealotry, pretense, and aspirations built upon inadequate substance (I. i. 65–186). Sir Hudibras, for example, with his hairsplitting incompetence was a makeshift logician who could confute himself or, indebted to Aristotle, prove finally that "a man's no horse." An addlepated philosopher, he could twist a tough "rope of sand." His squire Ralpho stands forth a memorable caricature (I. i. 451–616), the most amusing and satirized features of his personality being compressed into religious idiosyncracies. He parades as a mystic guided by inspiration, his "dark lantern of the spirit." His inner light comes to him from on high. It is

> An *ignis fatuus,* that bewitches,
> And leads men into pools and ditches,
> To make them dip themselves, and sound
> For Christendom in dirty pond.

Butler's mockery of the Dissenters' ritual of baptism reduces immersion to absurdity:

> To dive like wild fowl for salvation,
> And fish to catch regeneration.
>
> [I. i. 503–508]

Little less profane than the diving scene in Book II of *The Dunciad,* this one exemplifies in all the brilliance of belittlement the satirist's antagonism to Christian zeal.[26]

Borrowing from the imagery and idiom of chivalric romance, he defined his moral purpose. Satire, he wrote, is "a kind of Knight Errant that goes upon adventures, to relieve the distressed damsel Virtue, and redeem honor out of enchanted castles, and oppressed truth, and reason out of the captivity of giants or magicians."[27] Moved by the spirit of his own poem and theory,

---

25. *English Poets,* 1:210.
26. *Characters and Note-Books,* p. 163. Butler describes an Anabaptist as one who "does not like the use of water in his baptism, as it falls from Heaven in drops, but as it runs out of the bowels of the earth, or stands putrefying in a dirty pond."
27. Jack, p. 16; *Characters and Note-Books,* p. 469; *Hudibras,* p. xlii.

he wrote satire because he felt driven to it by a gloomy distrust of man's religious institutions. In the act of writing he assumed that he created something positive, perhaps even spiritually and humanely restorative. If he thought of himself as a knight errant, he was closer to Don Quixote than to Lancelot, and like the good mad knight—although he never lost touch with experience—transfigured dull reality into the shimmer of make-believe. We must concede Butler's special brand of pessimism, one ameliorated by *humanitas*, enough of which shines through to affirm his regard for man's possible worth.

## IV

The unequivocally orthodox Addison generalized in *Spectator* 445 that he had always been ready to aim "the batteries of ridicule" at whatever was "in some measure criminal." They became the weapons he relied upon to fight "the battles of impiety and profaneness." And in the *Review* (15 February 1709), with a more specific target in sight, Defoe had deemed ridicule a proper agent for correcting "the vicious clergy." He wished "to rouse up and excite those gentlemen, whose right it is, and have power in their hands, that they would restore the discipline of the Church to its uninterrupted exercise, and that they would remove the scandalous, the ignorant, and the insufficient from the altar." Soon thereafter, in *An Essay on Criticism* (550-51), Pope took a similar if more elegant tack:

> Pulpits their sacred satire learned to spare,
> And Vice admir'd to find a flatt'rer there!

However satirists—Anglicans, Dissenters, and Catholics— argued about doctrine, in at least one respect they discovered common ground. They insisted that ridicule, soberly used, encouraged reform by pointing out the silliness of deficient conduct and avoided the dangers of alienation by maintaining an air of impersonality and good nature. Shaftesbury amplified this argument with the assertion that man's abiding virtue reduced evil to illusion. Since vice, the act of evil purpose and a contradiction of man's best interest, can have no ultimate being, it is laughable and innately absurd. Why, then, not laugh?

Morally exuberant opinions like these were more than offset by a popular taste for the bloodletting of threat and innuendo. The religious divisions of the eighteenth century created a responsive audience for nearly savage disputation. Simultaneously, however, they created a dilemma for the propagandists charged with winning sectarian battles. The dichotomy between the supposed charitable ends of religion and verbal extremism was manifest, and yet, somehow, the polemicists had to achieve an acceptable reconciliation unless religion itself were to be reduced to a sordid exercise. That reconciliation, however, was easier recommended than made, for the battlegrounds were more readily definable by raw emotions than by reason or even faith. Within the Anglican Church itself, for example, a fierce struggle for power was taking place between the High-Church-minded prelates in their country parishes and the Whiggish bishops.

As a hired journalist in the Whig camp, John Dunton understood the psychological necessity of reviling an opposition that—he charged—viciously set out to divide and destroy a sanctified institution (of which his clients were obviously the guardians). Dunton turned to satire as the appropriate vehicle for designating blame and implying praise, but his idea of satire is curiously ambivalent. That is, he is the vindictive muckraker, but he is also the platitudinous champion of virtue and truth. The split is startlingly apparent in a satire on "pulpit fools," in which he piously declares of himself: "I love church rites, and cannot think it fit / To have 'em banter'd by a pulpit wit" (p. 33). This seems harmlessly traditional until we turn back to the introductory prose statement. There the borderline is not even imaginable for Dunton is the fanatic accuser, indicting an intolerant, hypocritical, trouble-making clergy.

By "pulpit fool" he means "a Levite, that rails in the pulpit, and plots out of it. . . . He is . . . stupid and censorious . . . (a mere incendiary), a wolf in sheep's clothing, a professed enemy to Church and State, hid under canonical vestments," and so on. This is unalloyed diatribe aimed directly at winning over congregations from their parish priests; so far removed is Dunton's intention from a basis of rational, theological discussion. And yet, in the poem itself (essentially a 66-page roster of identifiable pulpit fools), Dunton softens the pitch. Seldom bland, to be sure, he at least makes occasional stabs at ironic wit as though to compensate for the destructive pole-axe he brandishes. In addition, he borrows almost verbatim (page 1) from the 1679 Mulgrave-Dryden *Essay upon Satire* (11–14) the customary formula of protest and retribution:

> Satire has always shin'd among the rest,
> And is the boldest way, if not the best,
> To tell men freely of their blackest faults:
> Then pulpit fools, come here and purge your thoughts.[28]

If you wish to believe him, in Dunton's satire there will be "no coarse lampoon, uncivil or obscene" (p. 2):

> No—Satire will in brighter colors shine;
> Her form is dreadful, but 'tis all divine:
> In her true shape she always will appear
> Just, and impartial, as she is severe:
> The Church and State to her remarks belong,
> She will but seldom touch a private wrong.

Between the preface and the poem, in short, is a satiric no-man's-land, that peripheral world of furious imprecation which briefly subsides into the idiom of formal satire. We know what mischief the prose writer is up to; yet he is neither more nor less convincing than the versifier, once the niceties of satiric form have been taken into account. It is difficult, after all, to make a choice between out-and-out *médisance* and pat scolding.

A form of journalistic opportunism similar to Dunton's is evident in the writings of Tom Brown ("of facetious memory"). Wittier and coarser than Dunton, Brown, still in the Grub Street tradition, exemplifies the brash satirist *manqué* who capitalized on prejudices, borrowing causes without fretting over principles. As the self-styled "Moralist," he became a stereotype who invariably specified his punitive intention toward the "Hypocrite in

28. *The Pulpit-Fool. A Satyr* (20 May 1707). Dunton's piece was occasioned by a seditious sermon preached at Whitehall (26 Feb. 1706/7) which charged that preferment had been given to those responsible for the execution of Charles I. [Foxon, *Catalogue*, 1:207, lists a 2d part, pub. 15 July.] See ch. 5.

Black," toward falsifiers of theological doctrine, and toward obvious related targets:

> Only to such its rage my satire shows,
> To all the rest my humblest duty bows.[29]

The accents of Swift and Juvenal impart righteous, credible indignation. Those of Tom Brown, on the other hand, exhibit lively but still noisy bombast. Conceptually, he can merely convert argument into cliché: satire "is not less proper for discourses, that recommend virtue, than to those which are designed against vice." He assumed the role of a reformer, but even the familiar words were not to be trusted, for he simply took over as his own—unencumbered by acknowledgment—what he had translated from Dacier.[30]

Tom Brown is facile in the mechanics of satire although wanting in its artistic and spiritual legacy. Restricted by his own journalistic expedience, his effusions are generally empty of believable positive intention. But although we can dismiss Brown's strident idiom, we cannot dismiss the dedication that animated much other religious satire. Nor was this dedication a strictly English phenomenon. Erasmus, significantly, was so repelled by the indiscretions contaminating the possibilities of faith that he derided "all Christian religion [for it] seems to have a kind of alliance with folly, and in no respect to have any accord with wisdom." Even more radically, he attacked the effects of zeal as a perversion, both pernicious and self-destructive.

---

29. *The Moralist: or, a Satyr upon the Sects* (1691), p. 4. Cf. Addison, *Spectator* 567; *English Poets,* 1:381. Brown liked to inject himself into religious controversies that helped assure his notoriety: for example, *The Reasons of Mr. Bays Changing his Religion. Considered in a Dialogue between Crites, Eugenius, and Mr. Bays* (1688); *The Stage-Beaux Toss'd in a Blanket: or, Hypocrisie Ala-Mode* (1704). The epigraph of Burns's *Holy Fair* comes from *The Stage-Beaux.*

30. *The Works of Mr. Thomas Brown, in Prose and Verse, Serious, Moral, and Comical,* 3 vols. (1707, 1708), 1:25–26; André Dacier, *Remarques Critiques sur les Oeuvres d'Horace, avec une Nouvelle Traduction* (Paris, 1681–89). The translation of Dacier's "Préface sur les Satires d'Horace" appears in *Miscellany Poems upon Several Occasions* (1692), and is attributed by the editor Charles Gildon to "a very ingenious friend of mine." The "friend," according to Benjamin Boyce, was probably Brown. See *Tom Brown of Facetious Memory, Grub Street in the Age of Dryden,* Harvard Studies in English 21 (Cambridge, Mass.: Harvard University Press, 1939), p. 38.

Unsurprisingly, Erasmus identified himself with the ascetic, contentious St. Jerome (?340–420), who had "indulged in" satiric writing freely and sharply. And he also imagined that if "you might look down from the moon, as Menippus did of old, upon the numberless agitations among mortal men, you would think you were seeing a swarm of flies or gnats, quarreling among themselves, waging wars, setting snares for each other, robbing, sporting, wantoning, being born, growing old, and dying." Like his predecessors, Erasmus allowed himself the privilege of mordant satire:

This liberty has always been permitted to men of wit, that in their jests they may poke fun at the general manners of men with impunity, so long as their license does not extend to outrage. . . . he that censures the lives of men in such a way that he points at no individual by name—I ask whether he does not seem to teach, and to warn, rather than to bite? . . . he who spares no class of men would seem to be angry at no person, but at the vices of all. Hence if anyone turns up complaining that he has been libelled, he betrays his bad conscience or, at best, his fear.[31]

Following this principle, Erasmus proposed a condition for religious satire that in time became quintessential: to sting men for perversity and irreligion has sacred validity if the animadversion shuns the coarse and the personal, and if the taunting intention is redemptive.

A gallant foe of secularism in religious orders, Erasmus had many followers who agreed that it menaced the simplicity and altruism of Christian belief. For practical effect, however, they were outnumbered by a materialistic clergy. Much later, as a case in point, Samuel Parker (1640–1688) represented one kind of worldly pietism that long offended church critics. A religious turnabout, Parker wrote satires falling so short of literary merit and conviction that they can now be treated as little more than

31. Desiderius Erasmus, *The Praise of Folly* [1509], trans. Hoyt Hopewell Hudson (Princeton: Princeton University Press, 1941), pp. 70, 3–4. See also Sebastian Brant's *Narrenschiff* [1494], *The Ship of Fools*, trans. Edwin W. Leydel (New York: Columbia University Press, 1944); Pope's *Correspondence*, 1:118, 128; 3:81; *An Essay on Criticism*, l. 693; Collins, *A Discourse concerning Ridicule and Irony*, p. 10; Cowper, "To Erasmus." For discussion of Jerome: John Peter, *Complaint and Satire in Early English Literature* (Oxford: Clarendon Press, 1956), pp. 15–30.; David S. Wiesen, *St. Jerome as a Satirist* (Ithaca, N.Y.: Cornell University Press, 1964).

oddities in the warlike history of the opposition to nonconformism. In their day, however, his satires carried the threatening authority of the Episcopal-Cavalier party. He began his conscious religious life as a Puritan but saw the Anglican light so brilliantly during the Restoration that he became the scourge of those whose "testimony of the spirit" he once had witnessed. In 1686, with the personal blessing of James II, he was elected Bishop of Oxford as a reward for long years of Erastianism and Dissenter-baiting. Parker's quarrelsome satire resorts to stock metaphors notable only for abrasive cynicism. It is the work of a man described by Bishop Burnet as "covetous and ambitious," a man who "seemed to have no other sense of religion but as a political interest, and a subject of party and faction."[32] The values that provoked Parker's satires have little to do with the exaltation, the pity, and anger that give lasting vitality to the satire of Erasmus.

Burnet's words may exaggerate; yet they do not fall too wide of the mark. Parker's rhetoric will not be confused with the wit, sophistication, or implicit idealism of satire as a universal art form. He may protest loudly against the "pharisaic hypocrisy" of the Dissenters and their dissembling "visor[s] of holiness." Slogans, however, do not inspire confidence that he speaks in "the spirit of true religion." What he calls "high indignation" is no better than vindictive self-righteousness and inquisitorial bullying, as when he exclaims: "Now to lash these morose and churlish zealots with smart and twingeing satires is so far from being a criminal passion, that 'tis a zeal of meekness and charity, and a prosecution of the grand and diffusive duty of humanity, and proceeds only from an earnest desire to maintain the common love and charity of mankind." In this verbal flood, invective alternates with metaphoric brutality. Parker said of nonconformists, "We must lance their tumor, and take out the core of their proud flesh before we can cure them." Nothing softer will do in rhetoric that relies on such locutions as "rat divines . . . peevish Grub-Street divines . . . push-pin divinity." Parker, well versed in

32. Gilbert Burnet, *The History of His Own Time*, 2 vols. (1724, 1734), 1:696; see also 1:260, 700, 740.

semantic violence, was also an adept apologist on behalf of religious satire. Yet the unrestrained language that laced his "reproofs with sharp invectives" makes his satiric pamphlets self-defeating. They neither amuse nor probe the scruples of the human heart; they arouse neither wrath nor regret over error, neither guilt nor fear. They argue on the side of those who are already convinced and irritate those who will not be; in their venomous simplicity they reduce reason to scurrility. Piety had an odd champion in one who insisted that even "anger, malice and bitterness are holy fervors in the cause of God."[33]

The popularity of the embroilment between Parker and his Puritan adversaries swelled with the entry of Andrew Marvell, who wittily disparaged Parker and maximized the Catholic bent of his High Church attitudes. Marvell explicitly identified his feelings about Parker's intolerance in *The Rehearsal Transpros'd: or Animadversions upon a late Book, Intituled, A Preface shewing what Grounds there are of Fears and Jealousies of Popery* (1672). The main title of the pamphlet—a thin disguise for Parker's ease in sliding from Puritanism to Episcopacy—was well taken. Even such a nominal connection with *The Rehearsal* (1672) helped to signal Marvell's satiric intent. The author of that popular play, further, was known to advocate the right of dissent. Although *The Rehearsal* primarily satirizes drama and dramatists, Villiers's religious tolerance would have been a matter of contemporary inference. And what would have been recognized as Parker's repudiation of this liberal spokesman became just as obviously

33. See Parker, *A Discourse of Ecclesiastical Politie; wherein the Authority of the Civil Magistrate over the Consciences of Subjects in Matters of External Religion is Asserted; the Mischiefs and Inconveniencies of Toleration are represented, and all Pretences Pleaded in Behalf of Liberty of Conscience are fully Answered* (1670), pp. vi, x. Cf. Parker's preface to Bishop Bramhall's *Vindication of himself and the Episcopal Clergy, from the Presbyterian Charge of Popery* (1672); *A Reproof to the Rehearsal Transpros'd* (1673). Violence like Parker's engendered counterviolence and helped to popularize a dogmatic feud. One result of this may be seen in a retort by John Owen to Parker's vituperation: *Insolence and Impudence Triumphant; Envy and Fury Enthron'd: The Mirrour of Malice and Madness, in a late Treatise, Entituled, A Discourse of Ecclesiastical Polity . . . A brief View of his Tame and Softly, Alias, Wild and Savage Humour: . . . Being (in short) a Collection of some of his Intemperate Railings and Prophane Satyrs; wherein he hath abused Religion and the Power of Godliness, Droll'd on Piety, and all things Sacred* (1670?).

Marvell's flaunting opposition to the religious establishment. Insidious word-play and boisterous romping merge in the epithet "Buffoon-General to the Church of England." By adroit linkage of pejoratives ending in *ism—cardinalism, nepotism, putanism—* Marvell brands Parker as a harsh authoritarian who indulges in self-seeking, favoritism, and lewdness. Their battle, as described by Wood, was a public entertainment, even though it was fought between "two such right cocks of the game so keenly engaging with sharp and dangerous weapons." Parker would doubtless have protested that his methods were positively curative; and Marvell, disavowing raillery in religious dispute, would likewise have described as righteousness what we now see as contrived vehemence. Nevertheless, his unrelenting derision of a "scold crying whore first, and having the last word," of a self-appointed "prolocutor . . . a synodical individuum," must have titillated a contemporary audience.[34] The contest was further spiced by the shifted loyalties of both Parker and Marvell. Parker, a monarchist, found himself in the ambiguous position of abetting a repressive ecclesiastical policy against the toleration of Charles's Declaration of Indulgence (March 1672). Obversely, Marvell, a passionate republican, shone forth as the King's stout supporter. Conscience prodded his feud with Parker. But so too did political expedience: as the member from Hull, Marvell seized the advantage of defending an unpredictably short-lived royal mandate and of ridiculing a blatant, intractable court-party man. His satire reveals a religious commitment equally intense and pragmatic.

Even Swift, his Anglicanism softened by hindsight, conceded that Parker's bludgeoning strikes were no match for Marvell's wit. Swift theorized that the general admiration elicited by Marvell nullified the effectiveness of Parker's *Ecclesiastical Polity.* The observation occurs in *A Tale of a Tub* during an otherwise con-

---

34. *The Rehearsal Transpros'd,* pp. 11, 42–45, 184, 261–63; Anthony à Wood, *Athenae Oxonienses* [1691, 1692], 4 vols. (1813–20), 4:231. For the Donneybrook atmosphere created by the Marvell-Parker affair, see for instance the piece sometimes attributed to Dryden: *S'too him Bayes: or some Observations upon the Humor of Writing Rehearsals Transpros'd* (Oxford, 1673). In *The Rehearsal* Bayes (Dryden) was said to have mastered the art of "transprosing," of putting "prose . . . into verse" (I. i.).

temptuous discourse upon "common answerers to books, which are allowed to have any merit." Beneath metaphoric foliage, he compares answerers to "annuals that grow about a young tree, and seem to vie with it for a summer, but fall and die with the leaves in autumn." But because exceptions crop up, "we still read Marvell's answer to Parker with pleasure, though the book it answers be sunk long ago."[35] Swift's dislike of Parker's crude intolerance doubtless contributed to his assertion; but so too did his critical judgment that Marvell's was a superior talent. Despite theological differences, Swift appreciated his intellectual and creative agility.

He practiced his own ironic talents with an exceptional vigor and wit against those who threatened or slighted his religious values. During 1710 and 1711, thus, he attacked in the *Examiner* "the Tribe of Free-Thinkers," that is, all "Atheists, Deists, Socinians." He could apply words as though they were knouts, but not all of the opponents he singled out for punishment trembled or capitulated. Among his would-be victims, Anthony Collins merely laughed at him as "one of the greatest drolls that ever appeared upon the stage of the world." On 25 January 1712/13 Swift published an extended essay, *Mr. Collins's Discourse of Free-Thinking*, his answer to Collins's "brief compleat Body of Atheology." Although Swift called his own essay a "little whim," he took it seriously enough to attribute to Collins a dangerous corruption of biblical and theological history.[36] In an odd reversal of intention, Swift enhanced Collins's reputation by taking notice of a work that linked the relatively unknown young man with figures as familiar as Tindal and Toland.

For almost twenty years thereafter Collins feuded with Swift and other priests, surviving with self-possession and humor to become a leading anti-Establishment satirist. No matter how Swift might have chafed and scolded, Collins was neither fool

35. "Apology," *A Tale of a Tub*, and "Marginalia," both in Swift's *Prose Works*, 1:4-5, 5:273. Cf. John Eachard, *The Grounds and Occasions of the Contempt of the Clergy* (1670).

36. See Collins's *Discourse concerning Ridicule and Irony*, pp. xiv, 39; Swift's *Prose Works*, 4:27 ff., commenting on Collins's *A Discourse of Free-Thinking, Occasion'd by the Rise and Growth of a Sect call'd Free-Thinkers* (1713).

nor knave. While he made the orthodox smart under his anti-clericalism and impudent analysis of Anglican dogma, they had to admit his unswerving defense of rational piety. Although he had no confidence in vision, he affirmed the primacy of conscience in all questions of belief and crises of the spirit. He strode into controversies with sometimes elephantine force. He was opinionated and even blustery at the outset of his career; but with growing maturity he used wit and supple rhetoric to smooth the rough surfaces.

Building upon Shaftesbury's *Essay on the Freedom of Wit and Humor,* Collins summarized his own concept of religious satire in *A Discourse concerning Ridicule and Irony in Writing* (1729). In this final work he intended to repudiate Nathaniel Marshall's argument that responsible men have no right to attack civil or canonical laws with "ludicrous insult." Nonsense, Collins retorted at length, in his own name, in the name of Scripture, and in the names of all those Anglican divines whom he delighted to embarrass by enlisting them as coadjutors. Ridicule, he insisted, ferreted out truth and punished error evident in hypocrisy, superstition, self-righteousness, and persecution. Collins had long since completed his apprenticeship to Shaftesbury; and he had proved his ability to write in his own manner a hybrid of intelligent causerie, irreverent wit, and jesting parable. Behind the mask of a hyperreligious conservative, he had cleverly invented a rhetoric of "*Insult, Buffoonery, Banter . . . Irony, Mockery and Bitter Raillery*" to preach his deistic message. In 1729 he was no less certain than he had been in 1713 that "the opinions and practices of men in all matters, and especially in matters of religion, are generally so absurd and ridiculous that it is impossible for them not to be the subject of ridicule." For only through mockery that arouses appropriate laughter can one "remove out of [men's] minds all bigotry contracted by ignorance and an evil education, all peevishness, hatred, and ill-nature towards one another, on account of different sentiments in religion; and to form in them the natural principles of moderation, humanity, affection and friendship" (p. 12).

Frequently the most visible record of a religious satirist's ethical or ideological position consists in what he fulminates against: *anti*papacy, *anti*-Socinianism, *anti*-Arminianism, *anti*-Puritanism, *anti*deism, *anti*clericalism, *anti*-high church, *anti*-low church, *anti*-evangelicalism. Renunciation alone, however, is insufficient. It would be at best mischievous were it not offset by a determination to substitute good for bad, intelligence for stupidity, order for anarchy, true belief for irrationality and fanaticism. To determine how well the satirist has fulfilled his *pro* aims, the critic may have to penetrate a mask worn as self-protection against "those who are disposed to do [the satirist] a mischief."[37] Contrarily the critic may have to deal not with a defensive fiction but with an aggressive one, a shamanlike cover behind which the satirist may utter his incantations. In any event, as a cover it helps to liberate customary inhibitions and encourage free expression. Thus Johnson agreed with a remark in Castiglione's *Courtier* (II. 11), that "'a mask confers a right of acting and speaking with less restraint, even when the wearer happens to be known.' He that is discovered without his own consent, may claim some indulgence, and cannot be rigorously called to justify those sallies or frolics which his disguise must prove him desirous to conceal" (*Rambler* 208).

Just as concealment, however it varies in kind and amount, is intrinsic to satiric structure, so normal curiosity makes us restless to uncover the face behind the mask. Part of the experience of reading satire requires that we establish possible attitudinal relationships between the author and the work he has created. A commonly voiced question is: where is the demarcation between fiction and authorial self, between invention and fact or truth? Customarily satirists keep their own counsel, insisting that answers must be speculative, perhaps totally dependent upon contextual interpretation. At times, however, satirists do provide hints that help to unfold certain of the mysteries about their theories of satire.

Burns, to take one instance, wrote religious satires whose truths, though evident even when masked, become more reso-

37. Quoted from Shaftesbury by Collins, p. 24.

nant, and their credibility and connotative richness deeper, by knowledge of his private convictions. In the first Commonplace Book, for March 1784, he soberly commented:

I have often observed ... that every man even the worst, have something good about them. ... Let any of the strictest character for regularity of conduct among us, examine impartially how many of his virtues are owing to constitution and education; how many vices he has never been guilty of, not from any care or vigilance, but from want of opportunity ... how much he is indebted to the World's good opinion, because the World does not know all; I say any man who can thus think, will scan the failings, nay the faults and crimes of mankind around him, with a brother's eye.[38]

The philosophical recognition of man for what he is and the consequent theme of benevolence, stated as self-conscious abstractions, are not evocative. But translated into the idiom of the *Address to the Unco Guid, or the Rigidly Righteous,* they acquire a power in which satire controls thought fused with feeling: overt scorn alternates with a sentimentalized but richly metaphoric plea for tolerance. Deriving his epigraph from Ecclesiastes 7:16 ("Be not righteous overmuch"), Burns created a mood and tone not sanctified, certainly, yet indebted to religious search and good will. The poem as a whole, like the unadorned prose of the Commonplace Book, is self-contained. Each can stand by itself and each is enunciated by the same man looking at the world's failings "with a brother's eye." But what the satire embellishes with imagination, the prose simply asserts.

Satire for Burns became a creative extension of his daily war against religiosity. "Of all nonsense," he told Alexander Cunningham, "religious nonsense is the most nonsensical ... will you, or can you tell me ... why a religioso turn of mind has always a tendency to narrow and illiberalize the heart?" Like many of his satiric predecessors, Burns also felt prompted to justify himself. Not only did he outline the principles of his Christian belief, but he denied that he would "despise or ridicule

38. *Robert Burns's Commonplace Book 1783-1785*, ed. David Daiches (London: Centaur Press, 1965), p. 7. See Alexander Scott, "The Satires: Underground Poetry," *Critical Essays on Robert Burns*, ed. Donald A. Low (London and Boston: Routledge & Kegan Paul, 1975), pp. 90-105.

so sacredly important a matter as real Religion." The statement supports the impression of a satirist who always repudiated whatever he thought spurious in order that he might defend the "real." Yet Burns, sensing that he had to vindicate himself, declared—as had Erasmus—in the words of Paul that he was not mad. Burns's meaning, had he chosen to restate the entire quotation, suggested that through his satire he spoke "forth the words of truth and soberness" (Acts 26:25). Inferentially, that allusion to Paul places Burns, if only lightly, in debt to the hieratic tradition identifying satire with divine inspiration. But even more important than a debt of which Burns himself may have been unaware is the conscious *humanitas* of his poetry and expository remarks. Perhaps, he confessed in words that recall us to a disillusioned Pope, "I am too tired with and shocked at a life, too much the prey of giddy inconsistencies and thoughtless follies; by degrees I grow sober, prudent, and statedly pious."[39]

Satirically Burns conveys the tensions of a strained morality: an empiric grossness impinges on his idealism; a contorted piety like Holy Willie's, visible everywhere about him, contends with his hopes for man's salvation. But Burns proclaimed what many in his world barely whispered, that brotherhood must be both a social and religious good. He was far from being alone in his view of responsibility "to his fellow creatures." In this he had the sanction, among others, of his countryman Adam Smith, who insisted that

a moral being is an accountable being. . . . [It is] a being that must give an account of its actions to some other, and that consequently must regulate them according to the good-liking of this other. Man is accountable to God and his fellow creatures. But though he is, no doubt, principally accountable to God, in the order of time, he must necessarily conceive himself as accountable to his fellow creatures, before he can form any idea of the Deity, or of the rules by which that Divine Being will judge of his conduct.[40]

Burns and Smith alike noted the vanities that distract the fool from supernal obligation; and both justified the contempt

39. *The Letters of Robert Burns*, ed. J. De Lancey Ferguson, 2 vols. (Oxford: Clarendon Press, 1931), 2:120; 1:18–19, 153.
40. *The Theory of Moral Sentiments* (London and Edinburgh, 1759), p. 257.

thereby provoked in dutiful men. Whether the satirist laughed at and pitied moral obstinacy or the philosopher somberly evaluated it, they shared a need to get at the human conscience. Only in this way could they prove to man, as an "accountable being," that he must pay his debts to society in order to find lasting grace.

To this same thesis of religious accountability Edward Gibbon brought historical perspective and his own skeptical intelligence. The result—synthesized in the famous fifteenth chapter of *The Decline and Fall of the Roman Empire*—became the monumental metaphor of his observation that "man is the greatest fool of the whole creation." Gibbon in his story of the beginnings of Christianity dramatizes the cosmic irony he discovered while exploring "the inevitable mixture of error and corruption which [religion] contracted in a long residence upon earth, among a weak and degenerate race of beings." Despite the "melancholy" conclusions of his research, he abandoned historical objectivity to satirize a prolonged spiritual collapse. In so doing he compiled a vast record of human blunder and fraud, and he exhibited a complexity of feeling that ranged from indignation and loathing to scorn and laughter. Gibbon eulogized Pascal as the tutor from whom he "learned to manage the weapon of grave and temperate irony, even on subjects of ecclesiastical solemnity." But also in the background of his satiric manner and attitudes is an affinity with the sterner writings of Juvenal, which he had read with intense sympathy as early as 1763. The Roman's values— manifested in his "love of liberty, and loftiness of mind"—were therefore precious to the historian.[41]

Gibbon's wit is intricate, its mocking disparagement often camouflaged as candid reporting:

It is a very ancient reproach, suggested by the ignorance or the malice of infidelity, that the Christians allured into their party the most atrocious criminals, who, as soon as they were touched by a sense of remorse,

41. *The History of the Decline and Fall of the Roman Empire*, 3 vols. (New York: Modern Library, 1932), 1:383; and cf. the angry concluding sentence of ch. 6, "A Voyage to Brobdingnag." For the importance of Juvenal to Gibbon, see Harold L. Bond, *The Literary Art of Edward Gibbon* (Oxford: Clarendon Press, 1960), p. 16.

were easily persuaded to wash away, in the water of baptism, the guilt of their past conduct, for which the temples of the gods refused to grant them any expiation. But this reproach, when it is cleared from misrepresentation, contributes as much to the honor as it did to the increase of the church. The friends of Christianity may acknowledge without a blush that many of the most eminent saints had been before their baptism the most abandoned sinners.[42]

The reader who has followed Gibbon's reductive comparison is forced into a series of beliefs damaging to confidence in Christian superiority: that infidelity is not necessarily to be associated with intellectual blindness or spite, but organized church membership sometimes is; that repentance is all too readily born of expedience; that "saint" and "sinner" are mere labels without substantive distinctions; that Christianity is a fallible institution because it is a human one and so a "mixture of error and corruption." The meanings of this satiric passage devastate the carefully guarded Christian ego—but without authorial pontification.

Here as elsewhere in Gibbon, the deceptive reasonableness and innocence, the banter and ironic smile, the seemingly guileless display of crushing authority or frankness, all become methods that expose a chronicle of human weakness and perversity. We have indeed little to choose between the decline of the Romans and the rise of the Christians. The lesson in either case remains the persistent, haunting jest of man's uneasy pride in himself, his sovereignty, and his institutions. It is a lesson taught best in the skewed world of satire where "the lame walked, the blind saw, the sick were healed, the dead were raised, daemons were expelled, and the laws of Nature were frequently suspended for the benefit of the church."[43]

Like Juvenal and Swift, although they were less temperate

---

42. *The Autobiography of Edward Gibbon*, ed. Dero A. Saunders, rev. ed. (New York: Meridian, 1961), p. 103; *Decline and Fall*, 1:411.

43. *Decline and Fall*, 1:443. For an analysis of Gibbon's irony, see Bond, *The Literary Art of Edward Gibbon*, pp. 110–35. And for some contemporary retorts: Henry Edward Davis, *An Examination of the Fifteenth and Sixteenth Chapters of Mr. Gibbon's History* (1778); Davis, *A Reply to Mr. Gibbon's Vindication* (1779); William Disney, *A Sermon Preached before the University of Cambridge on Sunday, June 28, 1789, with Some Strictures* (1789).

tutors than Pascal, Gibbon permitted his intellectual aesthetic to mature in an aura of wit and disenchantment. He also shared with them a humanity that brooded over man's imperfections as the enemies of all the ideals he might have put into beneficial play. For all they had in common, they did not possess the same focus of discontent. "The race of beings" who vexed the historian he saw framed in the hard permanence of the past, whereas Swift was outraged more immediately by neighbors in time. The Christian ethic upon which Swift built his dark meliorism repudiates Gibbon's skepticism. Swift, to be sure, had doubts about the individual's readiness to grasp from "celestial wisdom" the happiness, let alone the grace, that might lie in reserve for him. But Gibbon, wandering through the corridors of history, rejected even the concept of a "celestial wisdom" as foreign to his vision of man's dismal temporality.

At his most contemptuous Gibbon waved away his fellow creatures in insect imagery comparable to Erasmus's or Pope's. Plagued by perception gained from hindsight, he did not assume that after centuries of self-persecution and intolerance Christian society could be liberated from the profligate cost of inhumanity. Yet he was goaded by conscience to desperate hope. The present seemed better than the past and the future could not be foretold. The satire of *The Decline and Fall* is tragic: its implicit pathos and compassion are as much Gibbon's measure of man as are his dry mockery and disdain.

v

All religious satire, when well placed, causes discomfort, for it attacks mores consecrated by time, culture, and awe. A lancet for complacency, it cuts into mysteries that adhere to religious systems and probes for answers to the presumably inviolable. Illustrative of this truism, Blake parodied his former mentor Swedenborg as an "Angel sitting at the tomb." His writings Blake disparaged in the imagery of "linen clothes folded up" uselessly, shrouds without meaning after death. The mystic philosopher "shews the folly of churches, & exposes hypocrites," but despite the concession, Blake could no longer accept as anything but error the limitations of one who "conversed with Angels" yet "not with Devils who all hate religion." At other times more rompish and colloquial in his iconoclasm, Blake ridiculed the excesses of organized worship. The voices of "Mrs. Sinagain" and "Mrs. Sigtagatist" sound the praises of such as "Mr. Huffcap" who "cry & stamp & kick & sweat, and all for the good of their souls." Whether the souls are those of the clergy or the congregation Blake—in a display of satiric ambiguity that would have been congenial to Burns and Gibbon—left the answer dangling. The hypocrite and the pulpit-thumping parson remain as inseparable as Swift's strident Enthusiasts.[44]

Religious satire has always thrived because spiritual and ecclesiastical uniformity contradicts diverse human nature and man's tendency to reject or discredit whatever challenges his scheme of values and heritage. The vigor of opposition and inquiry alters in proportion to the intensity with which the satirist feels committed to his belief or, for that matter, disbelief. His vehicle, hence, is a rhetoric of protest that can range from laughter to rage, from comedy to tragedy. Within this spectrum, further, his intention may vary from the simple and clamorous to the multiple and deliberately obscure. Satire as harsh-sounding as that of Hall and Marston represents one function of the mode; it amplifies personal biases often with a semblance of bad temper. Occasional bursts of wit and metaphor do little to modify abusiveness when the dominant tone is so vengeful that the audience may transfer its sympathy from satirist to ostensible culprit. And yet at the same level of personal involvement, the satirist may engage his enemy vindictively but with a risible cleverness that entertains even while it contends. Marvell, for instance, may not convert us to his Puritan argument that sectarian multiplicity premises the triumph of individual conscience and liberty; nevertheless we enjoy the suppleness with which he dances about the heavy-breathing Parker.

Religious satire develops out of paradoxes, beginning with the

44. "The Marriage of Heaven and Hell" [ca. 1790-1793], plates 3, 21-22; "An Island in the Moon" [ca. 1784-1788] (ch. 4), *The Poetry and Prose of William Blake*, rev. ed. by David V. Erdman; commentary by Harold Bloom (Garden City, N.Y.: Doubleday, 1970), pp. 34, 41-42, 443-44. See also S. Foster Damon, *A Blake Dictionary* (Providence, R.I.: Brown University Press, 1965).

militant formulations designed to forward the teachings of the Prince of Peace. The theme of brotherhood is celebrated, but frequently in a setting of derision or hostility and denigration. The terms of such satire encourage intolerance; if an equality of sects or of moral systems were admissible, most religious controversies would be harmlessly defused. The norm, rather, comes closer to that mockingly postulated by Pope:

> (Thus wit, like faith, by each man is apply'd
> To one small sect, and all are damn'd beside.)

Humility, moreover, is fundamental to the Christian ethos; yet its satirical practitioners, whether Anglican, Catholic, or Deist, can be snide, even arrogant.

Authorial presumption—hard-voiced in a tonal idiom of deliberate crudity—marks Swift's refutation of enthusiasm, the fragmentary *Mechanical Operation of the Spirit.* Barely concealed in the persona of a carping letter-writer, Swift hounds the nonconformists, as Ehrenpreis comments, not "for having bodies, passions, faeces," but rather "for confusing these with religion, for describing themselves as inspired when they are windy, or as charitable when they are lustful." Enthusiastic preachers, the narrator says, argue in vain as to whether their gifts came from "possession, or inspiration." It is, he goes on, "a sketch of human vanity for every individual to imagine the whole universe is interested in his meanest concern. If he hath got cleanly over a kennel, some angel, unseen, descended on purpose to help him by the hand ... this mystery of venting spiritual gifts is nothing but a trade."[45] Every word that the commentator utters, as far as Swift is concerned, may be taken for his own literal certainties. The hyperbole and extravagant figuration merely add salt to these truths and preserve them in their satiric form. The letter-writer, then, is permitted to leave no doubt of his conscious purpose, which is to snuff out irretrievably (albeit vulgarly) confidence in the effulgence of the inner light.

45. Pope, *An Essay on Criticism,* ll. 396–97; *A Discourse concerning the Mechanical Operation of the Spirit,* in Swift's *Prose Works,* 1:180–81; Irvin Ehrenpreis, *Swift: The Man, His Works, and the Age,* 2 vols. (Cambridge, Mass.: Harvard University Press, 1962–1967), 1:245; Ricardo Quintana, *Swift: An Introduction* (London, New York, Toronto: Oxford University Press, 1955), p. 58.

Much of the satire that centers in religious debate owes its power to a paradoxical union of skepticism and authority. One incentive for satiric expression, indeed, springs from a desire to promote scruples as a counteraction to unreasoning acceptance of creed or ritual. At times, as in Donne's third satire, the questioning is intrinsic, leading to a renewal and enforcement of faith. In other instances satirists may phrase questions that prompt disbelief, that deny any and all religious systems. This is the crisis into which the study of history drove Gibbon. Anticipating Bluphocks, the menippean vagabond of *Pippa Passes,* Gibbon had "abjured all religions."[46] And eventually, through the oblique intercession of a masked character, Joyce passed radically beyond abjuration to an active assault upon Catholic dogma. He opened *Ulysses* with a disturbing integration of comic shock. "Stately, plump Buck Mulligan" looks like a vain, well-fed medieval prelate and lives up to his appearance as he intones the Mass and mocks the ritual. His irreverent parody sounds initially and uncomfortably like the whim of a world-weary college student.

The comedy—if such it be—vanishes almost immediately, however, with the arrival of a bereaved Stephen Dedalus, the "fearful Jesuit," as he is greeted. The shock mounts, for Mulligan confirms himself as a smugly satanic hypocrite who faults his friend for failure in the very Christian observance which he has been deriding: "You could have knelt down, damn it Kinch, when your dying mother asked you.... I'm hyperborean as much as you. But to think of your mother begging you with her last breath to kneel down and pray for her. And you refused. There is something sinister in you."[47] The pun "hyperborean" clinches Mulligan's hypocrisy at several degrees of tension and meaning. It possesses first of all a bookish flavor that emphasizes the elegant sophisticate who struggles to maintain the pose. As

46. Robert Browning, *Pippa Passes and Shorter Poems,* ed. Joseph E. Baker (New York: Odyssey Press, 1947), p. 34.

47. James Joyce, *Ulysses* (New York: Modern Library, 1934), pp. 3–7. According to Weldon Thornton, Mulligan's use of "hyperborean" to imply that he and Dedalus are superior beings derives from *The Antichrist* of Nietzsche (sec. 1). *Allusions in "Ulysses": An Annotated List* (Chapel Hill: University of North Carolina Press, 1968), p. 13.

an uncommon word, further, it makes us grope through its ambiguities, for "hyperborean" has associations shifting from the specific to the mythic. At one level, then, the word literalizes the fact that the two young men dwell in a northern region. It is simply an academic way of saying that they are countrymen with the same national or social traditions. More subtly, however, Mulligan wants Dedalus to assert their moral affinity. Since the fabulous Hyperboreans were a happy race situated beyond the north in a land of sunshine, Mulligan implies that he and Dedalus stand apart from ordinary men and that, by extension, both are imbued with the good of their virtuous environment. The irony is that Mulligan, the self-identified hypocrite, attributes to himself qualities that belong to Dedalus. The makeup of the hypocrite contains no virtue, whereas Dedalus, who respects the age-old force of the religion he has forsworn, eschews deceit. Mulligan, standing apart only through his capacity for affectation, is happy, as Dedalus—the eternal seeker—is not. From the very outset, therefore, Joyce grants his fiction freedom, permits it to plummet and rise, to move from parody to sham, from tragedy to blasphemy, all and always in a need to express, however indirectly, his quest for an inner truth beyond the ambience of religious discipline.

The trail from Lucian to Joyce continues a long one but it is blazed plainly with its diversity of tone and theme and purpose. Religious satire, we have seen, is often unwelcome, beginning with the biblical warning that only "fools make a mock at sin." Obversely, however, such satire has its defenders who perhaps even more frequently urge it as a way of appealing to sinners and dissidents. Theologians such as Stillingfleet and Swift, for example, hammer away at those who have not come around to an Anglican piety. Members of the Dissenting laity, such as Marvell and Defoe, engage in comparable methods of persuasion to affirm their own attitudes of faith and conscience. They are all proponents of an absolute outlook: each serves as a disputant either rigidly for or rigidly against certain principles of ceremony and belief. But others promote a judicious temperance. Like Donne, they acknowledge the inconsistencies of human conduct and temptation that may inhibit spiritual commitment. They rely upon a call to reason as well as moral passion. To doubt, they would say, can be efficacious, but it must be wise doubt.

And also in a religious context there remain those scoffers— Gibbon, Joyce, and the like—who do not make a mock at sin, yet who do reject institutionalized piety. Reminiscent of writers like Erasmus and Burns but delighting in their iconoclasm, they stress the incidence of hypocrisy and religious egocentricity without turning their backs on the concept of brotherhood. Nevertheless, by means of ironic language and imagery each of these satirists intends to arouse moral antipathies; each exhibits a longing to repudiate corruption and to exalt the good, whatever its definition, as a way of life. As synthesized by Coleridge: "When serious satire commences, or satire that is felt as serious, however comically drest, the free laughter ceases; it becomes sardonic."[48] Following the Coleridgean premise, we may correlate serious with religious satire, which aims to see man for what he really is. To be seen thus, man must be stripped of all outer disguises, like Lemuel Gulliver standing naked before the master of the Houyhnhnms. Or, it may not be too much to say, like man standing before his God.

48. *Miscellaneous Criticism*, p. 118.

# CHAPTER 5

# "SACRIFICING TO THE GRACES":
## Political Satire

Following the outbreak of monarchical crisis in 1642, English-men responded to the urgencies of change with ideological as well as physical intensity. Satirists no less than the military were drawn into highly volatile circumstances that made for rancor and idealism, distrust and generous nationalism. What could not be done with guns or debate was attempted with innuendo and ridicule. The fortunes of empire, the fall and rise of rulers were intriguing topics. But so later was court gossip, which reached down into the streets where tongues wagged about the private conduct of kings and ministers and their mistresses. No topic of daily conversation was more compulsive or more productive of friction than the interrelated broils of religion and politics. The man in the shop and on the Exchange wanted to know what was going on; the authorities were determined to tell him nothing that was likely to increase bitterness and set off new waves of violence and discontent. Dissent and protest were not agreeable facts of English life, and once Charles II ascended the throne his licensers did whatever they could to dampen controversy. But what repressions inhibited they also made desirable; curbs on free expression opened at least one vein of underground communication.

Between 1660 and 1714 topical satire provided a covert yet fruitful supplement to news reports. From this period alone more than 3,000 verse satires have survived in print, despite the harsh Licensing Act of 1662. Further, many satires—a large number of them still extant—circulated in manuscript. This must have worried the suspicious, ubiquitous L'Estrange, who proposed in 1667 that even unprinted matter be regulated by censorship. All the evidence points to the importance of a near-fugitive mode that could be informative as well as entertaining. The evidence also predicates the grand sweep of the satiric net: no person was too great, no event too portentous for immunity from ridicule. The quantitative impact of occasional satire is often underestimated because of the value accorded by literary history to a handful of works. *Absalom and Achitophel,* to take one instance, has overshadowed almost all other Restoration satire. The temptation has been to focus on the literary celebrity, be he Dryden or—a little later—Pope and Swift. Obviously the superior range of a few satirists will always justify the critical attention they have earned. We must recognize, however, that although they are the center they are not *the* tradition. Rather, they are the major constellations from whom the lesser satellites—to say nothing of the sputtering, fading planetoids—often manage a passing fame. There is a large body of political satire whose value derives less from individual talent than from the voracious, ironic exploitation of public controversies.[1]

Thus, although many well-known authors contributed to an outpouring of satirical literature, many more will always remain unidentified and certainly unsung. They belong to the mercenary army of Grub Street hacks and factional propagandists, badly paid and in constant fear of arrest. But theirs being an age of political awareness, keen public interest encouraged them to hazard reprisals and repressions. Consequently, while disagreement often became synonymous with disloyalty, the

---

1. See introduction, *POAS,* I, and Fredrick S. Siebert, *Freedom of the Press in England 1476–1776: The Rise and Decline of Government Control* (Urbana: University of Illinois Press, 1952), pp. 237–302. French taste for political and religious satires is well documented by Robert Darnton, "Trade in the Taboo: The Life of a Clandestine Book Dealer in Prerevolutionary France," pp. 13 ff., 47–48, in *The Widening Circle: Essays on the Circulation of Literature in Eighteenth-Century Europe,* ed. Paul J. Korshin (Philadelphia: University of Pennsylvania Press, 1976).

"seditious" satires circulating briskly in the coffee houses were equally in demand in Whitehall and Westminster. Almost any ineptly handled or questionable affair of state set satiric pens in motion. And it did not matter whether the pen belonged to an anonymous or a recognized author. When the British fleet, commanded by the Duke of York, defeated the Dutch at Lowestoft in June 1665, Edmund Waller—fulsomely and prematurely—celebrated the event in a poem, *Instructions to a Painter*. Unfortunately, York had let the Dutch slip away and rebuild their strength, as a result of which the remainder of 1665 and 1666 was an inglorious time for British naval fortunes. For Marvell the opportunity to attack the King's politicians, if not the King himself, was fortuitously provided by Waller's *Instructions*, which he parodied in a *Second Advice to a Painter* (1666):

> Nay, Painter, if thou dar'st design that fight
> Which Waller only courage had to write,
> If thy bold hand can, without shaking, draw
> What e'en the actors trembl'd when they saw.
>
> [1–4]

During the next few years, with this and some three other allied poems, Marvell led a company of writers who adopted his satiric design and continued the complaints about mismanagement of state and military affairs in England. The complaints are interesting in themselves because of their historical and political implications. But they also have a literary significance for which Waller, in a perverse way, should be given credit. Even prior to his mediocre if earnestly conceived lines, there had been occasional eulogistic poems wherein the authors consulted with painters—that is, gave them "advice"—on the designs or motifs of their projects. Following Waller's, a stream of advisory poems—satiric and panegyric—achieved the status of a minor genre in which partisan commentaries, variously identified in some such way as "Advice" or "Instructions" or "Directions to the Painter," flourished modestly for the next two hundred years. Among those who gave satiric advice, aside from Marvell, were Denham, Villiers, Oldham, Swift, Peter Pindar, even Dickens. Between 1665 and 1800 topical "Advice-to-a-Painter" poems numbered about eighty, all of them thus in a lineal descent from Waller's oddly perpetuated *succès d'estime*.[2]

Public affairs, then, became a major outlet for satirists, their subjects ranging from high to low, from miscalculations such as the Duke of York's to trivial political squabbles. Factional contests forced surly differences between the court and country parties. At the same time, acrimonious personal divisions invaded privacies having little to do with political debate. Stressing particularity, the quarrels denuded whatever seemed pretentious or false. Attack on individuals in public life and in institutions was free-wheeling; awe of greatness vanished as political satirists wrote tirelessly. And whereas once there had been discussions over such matters as the divine right of kings, these were succeeded by candid admission that monarchs were as susceptible to error as any of their subjects. Ferocity in political satire indeed widened.[3]

Any political authority could expect satiric scourging. As public contempt for the unseated Puritans began to fade, it was followed by fearful yet scornful reaction to the possibility of a Catholic succession. Ideological hysteria created fresh victims, a truth grimly abundant in terrorism associated with the Popish Plot fomented by Titus Oates. In 1679, when religiopolitical frenzy was most feverish, John Oldham prepared his contribution to mass paranoia, a long verse sequence *Satires upon the Jesuits* (published in 1681 and 1682). The energy of his fulmination is exceptional, and so too in the prologue is the semblance

2. *POAS*, 1:20–167; Mary Tom Osborne, *Advice-to-a-Painter Poems, 1633–1856: An Annotated Finding List* (Austin: University of Texas Press, 1949). As an example of Marvell's continuing parodic popularity, see A. Marvell, Junior, *Satirical and Panegyrical Instructions to Mr. William Hogarth, Painter, on Admiral Vernon's Taking Porto Bello with Six Ships of War Only* (1740).

3. C. V. Wedgwood, *Poetry and Politics Under the Stuarts* (Cambridge: Cambridge University Press, 1960), p. 138; cf. Ruth Nevo, *The Dial of Virtue: A Study of Poems on Affairs of State in the Seventeenth Century* (Princeton: Princeton University Press, 1963). John Dunton converts the slogan *humanum est errare* into praise whereby virtues outweigh flaws: *A Satyr Upon King William; being the Secret History of His Life and Reign* (1703); *A Cat may Look on a Queen: or, a Satyr on Her Present Majesty* (1705).

he creates of himself as the bitterly indignant satirist who stands alone, no longer able to bear ineffectual English resistance to the Roman threat:

> In vain our preaching tribe attack the foes,
> In vain their weak artillery oppose:
> Mistaken honest men, who gravely blame,
> And hope that gentle doctrine should reclaim.

Nothing judicious can be found in these *Satires* wherein, a nineteenth-century editor observed, Oldham "assailed the whole system of the Jesuits with a fearlessness of invective scarcely paralleled in the language."[4] We would substitute "vindictiveness" or "malice" for "fearlessness."

One of the most savage of the *Satires,* the third, on "Loyola's Will," begins:

> Long had the famed impostor found success,
> Long seen his damned fraternity's increase,
> In wealth, and power, mischief, guile improved,
> By popes, and pope-rid kings upheld, and loved;
> Laden with tears, and sins, and numerous scars,
> Got some i' the field, but most in other wars,
> Now finding life decay, and fate draw near,
> Grown ripe for hell, and Roman calendar,
> He thinks it worth his holy thoughts, and care,
> Some hidden rules, and secrets to impart,
> The proofs of long experience and deep art,
> Which to his successors may useful be
> In conduct of their future villainy.

What comes afterward is a shrill play upon public feeling, rabble-rousing diatribe disconnected from tolerance or humanity. Theatrically exaggerating, Oldham envisages Loyola on his deathbed, a mad, terrifying figure "by fiend possessed." Gathered around him like demonic legacy-hunters are the "firm associates of [his] great design" to whom the testator bequeaths an inheritance that represents him as the shocking vilifier of his own order.

The roster of sins is too long and repetitious for detailed ac-

---

4. Robert Bell, ed., *Poems of John Oldham* [1854, 1871], reproduced, introduction by Bonamy Dobrée (London and Carbondale: Centaur Press and Southern Illinois University Press, 1960), pp. 80–81, and 80n. *POAS,* 2:17–81, substitutes "years" for "tears" in l. 5 of the poem below.

count here. Oldham projects Loyola as a blind idolater of papal authority and, by the same token, as implacably hostile to any non-Catholic sect. In the familiar mode of unintended self-revelation, Loyola's legacy turns into a blasphemous confession of hypocrisy, tyrannical cruelty, and immorality. The Jesuit priests emerge as sybarites made wealthy by indulgences; they are as guilty of lewdness and simony as they are of betraying the mobs with religious myths and false miracles. Loyola has more to say, but—in an echo of the Faust legend—his time runs out and *Satire III* ends abruptly when "scrambling spirits seize his parting soul."[5] A self-righteous Oldham, in short, wrote with the assurance of one addressing a sympathetic audience more predisposed to an inflammatory message than to the niceties of tropes.

And as once the Puritans had been the chief butts of satiric humor, now, under a barrage of doggerel wit and crude jibes, the followers of Cromwell were being made to stand aside for the "converts apostolic" of James II. Appeals to ignorance and intolerance continued to set standards for satiric attack and counterattack, sometimes even helping to chart the course of history. One of the most influential of such popular satires was *Lilli burlero,* a ballad of sorts written in 1687 by Thomas Wharton against papists and King James's representative in Ireland, Richard Talbot, Earl of Tyrconnel. The initial appeal presumably lay in the pseudo-Gaelic words, which, as Swift morosely observed, were "not Irish . . . but better than Scotch." The force of the ridicule was enhanced after Henry Purcell set the ballad to brisk music, and it began to be heard all over England in the autumn of 1688. Then the foolish lines—like a mock incantation—were used against the Irish troops brought into England as part of James's desperate effort to save his crown.[6] The arrogantly simplistic verses acquire a supposedly comic emphasis from the brogue. For instance:

> Ho, brother Teague, dost hear de decree,
> Lilli burlero, bullen a-la;

5. *Poems of John Oldham,* pp. 104, 123.
6. *POAS,* 4:309–19; Swift, *Prose Works,* 5:289.

> Dat we shall have a new debittie,
> Lilli burlero bullen a-la,
> Lero lero, lero lero, lilli burlero, bullen a-la;
> Lero lero, lero lero, lilli burlero, bullen a-la.

Talbot has the distinction of being attacked by low-comedy invective that annoys more than it hurts:

> Ho, by my shoul, it is a Talbot,
> And he will cut de Englishman's troat.

> Though, by my shoul, de English do prat,
> De law's on dare side, and Chreist knows what.

> But if dispense do come from de Pope,
> Weel hang Magno Cart and demselves on a rope.

As propaganda, such lines are too raw to be taken seriously. Nevertheless, perhaps owing to Purcell's catchy air, the ballad became so infectious that its imitations were soon rampant. (The air was in fact still serviceable in 1798 when English troops ordered to Ireland to quell the Rebellion revived it.)

In *Tristram Shandy* that seasoned antipapist warrior, My Uncle Toby, frequently derived comfort from whistling "Lillabullero." Indeed the mere misapprehension that Tristram's baptism might be related to a Catholic ritual prompted in the old soldier the need to drive out demons. And when Walter Shandy, curious to hear more of the discourse that had set off these unfortunate associations, became impatient with the melodious interruption, "My uncle Toby gave a nod—resumed his pipe, and content[ed] himself with whistling *Lillabullero* inwardly" (IV, xxix). Well past the midpoint of the eighteenth century Sterne, and doubtless many of his readers, still recollected this tuneful talisman, a roistering charm against a Catholic enemy who periodically disrupted Anglican complacence. My Uncle Toby's musical serenity is but another of the charming idiosyncrasies that give density to *Tristram Shandy*. Considered in the historical afterglow of Restoration and Revolution politics, Sterne's seemingly random use of "Lillabullero" vibrates with nuance.

The satiric role, when directed at religion and politics, has always been ambivalent. Whether jester or avenger, the satirist doubles as entertainer and critic, as clown and pundit. Like a gladiator in a Roman arena, when the satirist performs well his judges spare him and bestow honors. To perform well artistically means to write well both aesthetically and intellectually, to entertain and yet to strike appropriate targets. Aesthetic failure courts censure and oblivion. Intellectual failure—the selection of inappropriate targets or mismanagement of satiric attack—can be equally disastrous. The satirist, knowing he risked retaliation should his satire be too openly offensive, employed art and artifice to satisfy practical as well as literary need. To minimize sanctions, as we have already seen, he often transparently disguised his victims' identities and his own. And sometimes he donned masks as a mere pretense to point up the absurdity of masking, even while he damned individuals or institutions. He might take additional cover behind allegory and beast fable. And he might shield himself in metaphor or other linguistic armor. Often as cunning as his own *eiron,* the satirist either erased the visible authorial self or created himself anew through a sheltering persona.

Occasionally, however, he would be carried away by enthusiasm for the assault, abandon subterfuge, and fall victim to his own audacity. This may be what happened to Dryden on 18 December 1679, when thugs waylaid him in Rose Alley to administer one of the most notorious beatings in literary history. After all these years the circumstances remain clouded, but reconstruction goes something like this: Dryden was suspected of responsibility (at least in collaboration with the Earl of Mulgrave) for a libelous poem, *An Essay upon Satire,* which had been circulating in manuscript. As two irritated victims, according to speculation, Rochester and the Duchess of Portsmouth had particular reason to take offense and instigate the severe drubbing. But Dryden—assuming that he did indeed have a hand in the poem—was vulnerable also for having risked the enmity of other great people: the first Earl of Shaftesbury, the Earl of Pembroke, and even the King himself, "saunt'ring Charles, between his beastly brace" of mistresses. Shaftesbury, "our little Machiavel," becomes an interesting anticipation of Achitophel;

and Rochester is despicable "for his mere want of wit / (Though thought to have a tail and cloven feet)."[7] Dryden's widely publicized thrashing, and its assumed reason, must have sobered many another writer with rash thoughts of "satire bold." The hazards of political satire, at least nominally, continued on into the eighteenth century; but, as the third Earl of Shaftesbury noted, there were ways to promulgate dissident opinions and yet skirt risks: "If men are forbid to speak their minds seriously on certain subjects they will do it ironically. If they are forbid to speak at all upon such subjects, or if they find it really dangerous to do so, they will then redouble their disguise, involve themselves in mysteriousness, and talk so as hardly to be understood, or at least not plainly interpreted, by those who are disposed to do them a mischief." Shaftesbury concedes that a "persecuting spirit" may result in extremes of raillery and buffoonery, and that consequently genuine wit and humor may be corrupted.[8] The *Craftsman* (No. 31, 24 March 1727) later corroborated this opinion, granting "that it would be more honorable, as well as more useful, to write without disguise, provided it were equally safe. But would not any man be esteemed a lunatic, who should in plain terms attack such a monster as Wolsey or Buckingham, in the plenitude of their power; especially, if he has any parallel instances at hand, or can throw the same thoughts under shades and allegories?" Caleb D'Anvers (that is, Nicholas Amhurst) is an astute satirist. He states an unarguable truth, reaches into the safe past for "parallel instances," and blandly lets his readers infer that the analogous "monster" is in fact Robert Walpole.

D'Anvers's technique, simple but effective, seeds an idea to set

---

7. *POAS*, 1: 396-413. Confusing the aftermath of *An Essay upon Satire* (1679) with that of *Absalom and Achitophel* (1681), Defoe told in the *Review* (17 May 1712) how Dryden "had described the Duke of Buckingham with a great deal of wit, but in one line [550] had given him ill names, as fiddler and buffoon." Dryden's reward, according to the prudent Defoe, was a caning for his ill manners and thirty guineas for his wit. "Now [Defoe] would recommend to all those gentlemen who take upon them to write satires on great men, that they would take care to merit the guineas without the cane." See also *POAS*, 1:396-97.

8. "A Letter concerning Enthusiasm," sec. iii; "Essay on the Freedom of Wit and Humour," p. 1, sec. iv: *Characteristics*, 1:15, 50.

off a possible growth of associations that the reader may readily understand. Another common associational device relies upon the substitution of blanks, dashes, or asterisks for words, phrases, or lines. A generation earlier the fine art of the asterisk appears frequently in *A Tale of a Tub*. Equating madness and public life, Swift's persona solemnly recommends attempts to "produce admirable instruments for the several offices in a State, ******† civil and military." Swift applies asterisks as a rude boy would a thumb to his nose. The correlation is obvious, and yet the absurd blank (marked for annotation with the crosslike dagger) hints at something so sanctified as to be ineffable.[9]

Swift's lacunae paradoxically help reveal his satiric game. Not only do the blank spaces cause the objects satirized to be laughable, but they also burlesque concealment seriously intended by other writers. He was deriding the ineffectuality of penetrable disguises. Yet that did not discourage the use of the technique, as Addison demonstrated in *Spectator* 568 (16 July 1714), where he brilliantly combined the absurdity of omitted letters with caricature to create "an angry politician." Playing the congenial narrator, Mr. Spectator, Addison produces a coffee-house setting, "not far from the Royal Exchange," where he meets three gentlemen passing the time of day. Remaining incognito in their midst, Mr. Spectator turns the conversation to No. 567 (14 July), which happens to be at hand, and which deals with the subject of disguise in political writing. When he comments in feigned innocence on the essay's wittiness, the Tory politician wrathfully takes the bait.

"This fellow"—the author of No. 567—the satirized politician snaps, "can't for his life keep out of politics. Do you see how he abuses four great men here?" Mr. Spectator looked "very attentively on the paper and asked [his unwitting adversary] if he meant those who were represented by asterisks." Increasingly choleric, the Tory responded: "Asterisks . . . do you call them? They are all of them stars. He might as well have put garters to

---

9. "A Digression concerning Madness," *Prose Works*, 1:111. Hawkesworth in his editorial zeal compounds the joke when he decodes the obvious asterisks as "ecclesiastical." See also ch. 3.

'em. Then, pray, do but mind the two or three next lines! Ch-rch and P-dd-ng in the same sentence! Our clergy are very much beholden to him." At this moment one of the three gentlemen, Whiggish and mild, attempts to mollify the infuriated companion and yet justify the stratagem of the periodical. Mr. Spectator, he explains, "is very cautious of giving offence, and has therefore put two dashes into his pudding." Far from being satisfied, the Tory retorts vehemently, "A fig for his dash. . . . In his next sentence he gives a plain innuendo, that our posterity will be in a sweet p-ckle. . . . Why does he not write it at length if he means honestly?"

Mr. Spectator, his identity still concealed, inflames the Tory even more by pretending "the parenthesis in the belly of" one sentence more dangerous than what is spelled out. "But who," he insinuatingly asks, "is my Lady Q-p-t-s? . . ." Having raised the question, the narrator slyly "owned that . . . the *Spectator* had gone too far in writing so many letters of my Lady Q-p-t-s's name; but . . . he has made a little amends for it in his next sentence, where he leaves a blank space without so much as a consonant to direct us; I mean," went on Mr. Spectator, "after those words, 'The Fleet, that used to be the terror of the ocean, should be wind-bound for the sake of a—;' after which ensues a chasm, that in my opinion looks modest enough." Thereupon the Tory renewed his complaint against such Spectatorial tricks. "Sir," he said, "you may easily know his meaning by his gaping." Perhaps unaware of his own pun, the politician supposed the essayist "designs his chasm, as you call it, for an hole to creep out at, but I believe it will hardly serve his turn. Who can endure to see the great officers of State, the B—ys and T—ts, treated after so scurrilous a manner." Well, said the cloaked narrator, "I can't for my life . . . imagine who they are the *Spectator* means?"

All of the matter in these paragraphs comments on the putative scandal printed in No. 567 two days earlier. Both essays sought to provoke inferences about certain state events and individuals. The result is Addison's two-part satire, the first in the mask of Mr. Spectator and the second in the adversarial Tory voice (chiefly) of the "angry politician." The latter is indeed so angered by No. 567 that he misses its satire and, hence, its purpose. So doing, he unconsciously offers himself up as a butt for mockery, as the unthinking, sputtery public figure. The politician's ire, though equatable with Tory stupidity, becomes a sardonic reflection upon any obtuse political reaction. At the same time his banality, as an attribute of the rank-and-file placemen, counterpoints the scandalous activities that occur in the higher reaches of authority.

We suggest that the "four great men" represents satiric license for one or two, that "Ch-rch and P-dd-ng" is a not so cryptic allusion to the High Church party, and that "my Lady *Q-p-t-s*" is Lady Masham: at the time Nos. 567 and 568 appeared the "great officer of state" was Robert Harley, first Earl of Oxford. Even a dull politician could surmise his presence, for the brilliant lord treasurer and first minister had been elected a Knight of the Garter 25 October 1712, and had been installed 4 August 1713. So the ancient symbol of elevation was still in the mind of Mr. Spectator's adversary. But Oxford was also in trouble with a High Church Queen, already displeased because of the casual style in which he discharged personal and public obligations. At this point in Addison's narrative another personage assumes dramatic proportions. This time it is Lady Masham, Oxford's cousin, successor in the royal household to the Duchess of Marlborough and ultimately a supporter of Bolingbroke's successful effort to seize Oxford's staff of office.

The Whigs—and therefore the *Spectator*—distrusted the Tory Lady Masham as a powerful, conspiratorial threat to their ambitions. Enigmatically masked as "Lady *Q-p-t-s*," she evokes all kinds of associations, ranging from the quizzical to the questionable. A playful Latinist could have had in mind the manifold possibilities of *quem putas*.[10] This becomes literally "Lady Whom do You Suppose," as though she is so well known that mention of her name would be superfluous. The language game may then be taken at least one step further to correlate *Q-p-t-s* with

10. See Swift, "An Enquiry into the Behaviour of the Queen's Last Ministry," for the favorable Tory view of Lady Masham. *Prose Works*, 8:153. *Quem putas* was first suggested in 1905 by Wendell and Greenough. See also the speculation, "Her Majesty's Quarter Part," in relation to the Assiento Contract, Donald F. Bond, ed., *The Spectator*, 4:538n.

*qui putes,* from *putere* ("to stink"). The vulgarism perhaps exists as no more than a vague hint; yet it brings the riddle into focus without dangerously explicit allusions. The final impression damns satirically, for Lady Masham—according to Whig opinion—was the Queen's corrupt or rotten (hence *qui putes*) counselor. In any event, dashes and asterisks encourage sly completions; they sustain innuendoes compounded by such *double entendres* as "the parenthesis in the belly . . . wind-bound . . . a— . . . chasm . . . an hole to creep out at."[11]

Oxford tendered his resignation to the Queen 8 June, though he was not relieved of his duties until 27 July, a few days before her death. From 14 to 16 July, thus, there was doubtless resentment among his followers—including our irritable politician—that he had been "treated after so scurrilous a manner." Conveniently his champion forgot that the earlier *Spectator* had described an important man as "an ill man . . . a B—y or a T—t." Oxford, the consummate intriguer, was in other words also "bully" and "tyrant." These epithets, we see in No. 568, went unchallenged, although it should also be noted that they would have been applicable to any tough first minister. And by this time Bolingbroke, as the ascendant Tory politician, could just as easily have been heir presumptive to the Whig denigrations of "bully" and "tyrant." Tilting with asterisks and dashes, Addison has the last word. Or at least Mr. Spectator has, reflecting "upon the difficulty of writing any thing in this censorious age, which a weak head may not construe into private satire and personal reflection." Addison made it reasonably easy for almost any head to construe this satire at will, as long as it worked against the Tories.

Satire can benefit from concealment, even when subterfuge frustrates those who are satirized and those who wish to exact sanctions against satirists. One can almost sympathize with the annoyed writer who, some fifty years later, searched for Junius's identity as though his own salvation depended upon the discovery. Junius, he wrote, "is determined to keep his advantage by

---

11. See Pope, *Correspondence,* 3:265–66; "Epilogue to the Satires, Dial. II": "F. Yet none but you by name the guilty lash; / Ev'n Guthry saves half Newgate by a dash" (ll. 10–11).

the help of his mask; it is an excellent protection, it has saved
many a man from an untimely end. But whenever he will be
honest enough to lay it aside, avow himself, and produce the
face which has so long lurked behind it, the world will be able to
judge of his motives for writing such infamous invectives. . . .
Junius delights to mangle carcases with a hatchet. . . . One would
imagine he had been taught to throw it by the savages in
America." As irritating as a tick under the skin, the unseen
Junius scoffed: "Masks, hatchets, racks, and vipers dance
through your letters in all the mazes of metaphorical confusion."[12] While the frenzied enemy searched, Junius compla-
cently chided him with suffering from the aberrations "of a disturbed imagination; the melancholy madness of poetry without
the inspiration." No doubt Junius was tightening the screw on
his adversary, teasing him where he was most vulnerable, and
hoping to make him howl with frustration and rage. In this he
appears nearly to have succeeded. But he also added his to the
many political voices that had long been crying out for satirical
wit.

## II

In Addison's provocative phrase, even the satirist dealing with
sober state matters should "sometimes sacrifice to the graces."
The idea is an attractive one that Edmund Burke—another professed enemy of dullness—liked so well he borrowed the terminology.[13] Sacrificing to the graces connotes the best features
of satiric rhetoric: intellectual substance supported by cogent
imagination. Elegance prevails over bald language only if the

12. Response to the pamphleteer by William Draper (17 Feb. 1769) in *The
Letters of Junius*, ed. C. W. Everett (London: Faber & Gwyer, 1927), pp. 36–37.
For Junius's retort, see pp. 43–44 (3 Mar.). It is reminiscent of Pope's metrical
glissade in which "ductile dulness new meanders takes; / There motley images
her fancy strike, / Figures ill pair'd, and similes unlike. / She sees a mob of
metaphors advance, / Pleas'd with the madness of the mazy dance" (*The Dunciad*,
I, 64–68).
13. See Addison, *Freeholder* 45; *Reflections on the Revolution in France*, in *The
Works of the Right Honorable Edmund Burke*, rev. ed., 12 vols. (Boston: Little,
Brown, 1866–1867), 3:559. The phrase "sacrificing to the graces" has a history of
usage that includes Plato, the seventeenth-century divines, and Lord Chester-
field. See Tave, *The Amiable Humorist*, p. 11.

elegance complements critical intention. Language, in short, must support the arguments being espoused.

Among the traditional resources of persuasion is figurative analogy used to call forth classical, literary, or biblical associations. A particularly apt metaphor in political satire is that of the Eumenides, those serpent-wreathed Furies who punish breaches of state law. The satiric point is vigorously if not profoundly enunciated by Robert Wild in "Iter Boreale" (1660), where he has enlisted the support of a Fury ("Alecto with her flaming whip") against Cromwell and John Bradshaw, presiding officer of the commission that had tried Charles I. Wild's phrasing doubtless borders on the malicious. Still, without embarking upon a poetical evaluation of "Iter Boreale," we can nonetheless take account of Wild as a satirist who brightens a fairly barren style with charged metaphor and so lends colloquial, imaginative spice to his argument. Eager to catch this lively spirit, some anonymous wit a few decades later reduced the menacing "hell-born dame" to caricature, turning a conventional metaphor into that of a head "periwigg'd with snakes."

Swift also manipulated Alecto as a near-comic stock device. The name itself was useful to indicate the three Furies (the others are Megaera and Tisiphone). Alecto exemplies the relentless pursuit described in "An Epistle to a Lady" (1733):

> Poultney deep, accomplish'd St. Johns,
> Scourge the villains with a vengeance.
> Let me, tho' the smell be noisome,
> Strip their bums; let Caleb hoyse 'em;
> Then, apply Alecto's whip,
> Till they wriggle, howl, and skip.
>
> [175–80]

Scatology apart, this is the simple, effective writing that Swift was pleased to think an Irish footman could understand. And so for the most part he could. But Swift was also writing for a more discriminating audience. The contrived vulgarity may be what catches the immediate attention; at the same time, almost naturally, it draws us into the metaphor so that comic simplicity merges with punitive shock: the scourge alive with venomous creatures is a poetically apt weapon to inflict upon venomous men, to set them dancing and writhing in pain. But it is also a degrading source of punishment, the hoysed rascals being subjected to treatment generally reserved for wayward schoolboys.[14] An even more vividly affective satirist than Wild, Swift builds the metaphor into the situation. Figurations like those of Alecto's whip intrigue imagination and mind. Satirically they function as powerful, compressed signals, associational tricks to further moral and censorious intention. When extended, they may also have allegorical interest, as in Isaac Bickerstaff's rendering of "Ithuriel's spear." Milton created the narrative incident for *Paradise Lost* (IV. 786, 812), in which the spear (perhaps a variation of Achilles' spear, which could both kill and cure) becomes a means to expose corruption and evil. Subsequently, Steele manipulated the instrument carried by Ithuriel—whom Milton described as "a strong and subtle Spirit"—so that it achieves satiric transformational powers:

It would be tedious to describe the long series of metamorphoses that I entertained myself with in my night's adventure, of Whigs disguised in Tories, and Tories in Whigs; men in red coats that denounced terror in their countenances, trembling at the touch of my spear; others in black, with peace in their mouths, but swords in their hands. I could tell stories of noblemen changed into usurers, and magistrates into beadles; of free-thinkers into penitents, and reformers into whoremasters. I must not, however, omit the mention of a grave citizen that passed by me with a huge clasped Bible under his arm, and a band of most immoderate breadth; but upon a touch [of the spear] on the shoulder, he let drop his book, and fell a-picking my pocket.

[*Tatler* 237][15]

Ithuriel's spear represents an ingenious borrowing for the politically minded satirist: it carries multiplex sanction, from quasi Scripture (for Ithuriel in Hebrew literally means imbued "with

14. *POAS*, 1:4 (ll. 9–10); Swift, *Poems*, 2:635; Herbert Davis, "Alecto's Whip," in *Jonathan Swift: Essays on his Satire*, pp. 249–50. To "hoyse" is "to hoist," as a bare-bottomed pupil is hoisted onto an usher's back in readiness for a flogging. Cf. *POAS*, 3:464–65 (ll. 1–16); Hall, *Virgidemiae*, in *Poems*, bk. V, Sat. 3; and anon., *A Satyr against Common-Wealths* (1684).

15. Cf. *Tatler* 258; John Brown, *An Essay on Satire*, ll. 126–28, describes Ithuriel's spear as revealing "the cloven hoof" of diabolism and "lengthened ear" of asinine folly. D'Anvers, *Craftsman* 83, acknowledges Bickerstaff as his metaphoric source, using the spear to expose the lies a great man tells his lackeys.

the superiority of God") and myth to Milton; owing to its magical properties, it recalls the primitive origins of satiric incantation; it becomes central to a dream fantasy in which the satirist is omnipotent, transforming reality into fiction and fiction back into reality. Paradoxically, then, Bickerstaff uses the spear both to mask and reveal; it creates an opaque cover for his moralizing function and still it *un*masks hypocrisy and other forms of human perversity. Bickerstaff, spear in hand, becomes the agent of truth and decency.

Another use of figuration is the beast metaphor, through which human shortcomings are placed in an animal context or are viewed by animals with a clarity denied to erring man. In *The Hind and the Panther* Dryden analogically reduces republican sectarianism and disbelief to inferior forms of life whose conduct seems directed by irrational impulse: devouring instinct (the "insatiate wolf" of Presbyterianism), slyness (the "false Reynard" of Socinianism), predatory cruelty (the "bloody bear" of the Independents and the "bristled Baptist boar"), ineffectual timidity (the "quaking hare" of the Quakers), and smirking mimicry (the "buffoon ape" of atheism).

The man-animal equation provided an apt allegorical frame for Addison, who in *Guardian* 71 (2 June 1713) spun out an elaborate fiction to disguise political spying as a subhuman activity. Assuming the quiet assurance of one familiar with the government's secret service, he told the "rural reader, that we polite men of the town give the name of a lion to any one that is a great man's spy." To enlarge upon a distaste for espionage, cultivated while he was undersecretary of state, he introduces the jackal as the odious scavenger who hunts with the lion. The jackal—so the myth goes—earns his keep by flushing quarry for the lion's kill, part of which is doled out to the parasitic partner.[16] Mockingly grave, Addison examines the etymological basis of the leonine designation. This he traces, in the reign of Elizabeth, to Walsingham's barber, a presumably apocryphal man named Lion, "who

16. Cf. Dryden's metaphor in "Annus Mirabilis" of jackals who "on their lions for prey attend" (st. lxxxii). For another statement on this subject, see E. A. and L. D. Bloom, *Joseph Addison's Sociable Animal* (Providence, R.I.: Brown University Press, 1971), pp. 108–9.

had an admirable knack of fishing out the secrets of his customers, as they were under his hands." So skillful was he in his trade of extracting intelligence, that his name became synonymous with the master spy's. Spying, Addison made no bones about remarking, had become a commonplace occupation. The lions, unambiguously branded "beasts of prey," boldly roam the streets of London, consorting in one coffeehouse after another, "and seeking whom they may devour." Ironically, "a lion in our British arms is one of the supporters of the crown." But it is the crown of a government dependent on "factions and intrigues, none of which could "subsist without this necessary animal."

If the satire wants exceptional subtlety, it nonetheless cleverly mingles mockery with reprehension. The historical mask functions superficially, for Walsingham, as Elizabeth's great man, is not significantly more unscrupulous in ferreting out intelligence than are Queen Anne's great men, Oxford and Bolingbroke. The discovered secrets of rivals and parties, traditionally the nerves and sinews of political survival, depend upon the master spy. And even as the Addisonian jackal benefits from subordination to the lion, so the lion profits from satisfying the wants of *his* master: "As the lion generally thirsts after blood, and is of a fierce and cruel nature, there are no secrets which he hunts after with more delight, than those that cut off heads, hang, draw, and quarter, or end in the ruin of the person who becomes his prey. If he gets the wind of any word or action that may do a man good, it is not for his purpose; he quits the chase, and falls into a more agreeable scent." The two animals—lion and jackal—thus unite in an unholy alliance, but for Addison the lion, the epitome of treachery, is distinctly abhorrent. He is, in Job's lament (30:29), "a brother of jackals," with all that these animals connote morally. The chief target of Addison's opprobrium, the lion must be "hated both by God and man, and regarded with the utmost contempt even by such as made use of him." Emblematic of the error of pride, the humiliating comparison of man with animals shows individuals that they are no wiser than nonrational creatures and no more deserving of respect.

As we have noted earlier, Butler had reached the bitter conclusion that man perverts everything he touches, even the animals he controls:

> For, as some late philosophers
> Have well observ'd, beasts that converse
> With man, take after him, as hogs
> Get pigs all th'year, and bitches dogs.

Equally bitter, Swift was to declare that "beasts may degen'rate into men." Nature itself, in short, may be infected by man's deluded belief in his own superiority. By pushing beast similitudes as far as possible, Butler and Swift insisted that human institutions, religious or political, are endangered by bestial irrationality. With offensive resignation, thus, Swift descended "as low as he well could, by specifying four animals: the wolf, the ass, the swine, and the ape; all equally mischievous except the last, who outdoes them in the article of cunning: So great is the pride of man."[17] No rule-of-thumb has been devised to determine whether any of these metaphoric approaches will work as their authors intended—or, indeed, to define precisely what their authors intended. Certainly, when the satiric vision becomes this bleak, the misanthropic implications are unsettling, and the appeal to reason may then be less convincing than the instinct to retreat from such an appearance of grinding contempt.

As is true of all satire, however, the dramatically exaggerated metaphors should not be insisted upon as the satirist's literal understanding of the world. Rather, some common objective ground exists upon which we may be able to come to terms with animal satire even as provocative as that which we have just seen. All three—Butler, Swift, Addison—share at least these attitudes: that communal man has failed; that his social and political institutions no longer reflect the best of which the human spirit

---

17. *Hudibras*, I. i. 784–85; Swift, "Beast's Confession," *Poems*, 2:601. For a milder equation of men and animals, see "The Twa Dogs," *The Poems and Songs of Robert Burns*, ed. James Kinsley, 3 vols. (Oxford: Clarendon Press, 1968), 1:137–45. Also cf. Bernard Mandeville, *The Fable of the Bees: or, Private Vices, Publick Benefits* (1714), and Pope's consistent fondness for metaphors using insect and animal images.

and will are capable. But for the alienated satirist this recognition often accompanies a reassertion of that capability. And often, paradoxically, it also confirms a longing for some vaguely defined Golden Age—some Cockaigne, Utopia, Never-Never Land—where man may fulfill his ideal nature.[18] Other satirists who do not look backward may also envision a golden future even without drafting its blueprint. For such the implication remains strong that change is desirable in political mores whose degeneration they like to blame on the misuse by, or the inadequacy of, a "Great Man." Authority satirized is the almost invariable synonym for oppression and corruption.[19]

So interwoven with innuendo, the epithet "Great Man" was generally understood to subvert the classical assumptions of *fortis animus et magnus,* a popular theme of eighteenth-century moral writing. As reversed by the satirists, the Stoic ideal of "Greatness" was their cuckoolike creation, nesting where it had no business—among words of praise. Best exemplified in a serious context by Cicero, true greatness magnifies the satirically conceived deterioration of that virtue into sham and treachery:

> The soul that is altogether courageous and great is marked above all by two characteristics: one of these is indifference to outward circumstances; for such a person cherishes the conviction that nothing but moral goodness and propriety deserves to be either admired or wished for or striven after, and that he ought not to be subject to any man or any passion or any accident of fortune. The second characteristic is that, when the soul is disciplined in the way above mentioned, one should do deeds not only great and in the highest degree useful, but extremely arduous and laborious and fraught with danger both to life and to many things that make life worth living.

In these terms, especially relating to the first characteristic of excellence, the modern Great Man of the satirists had nullified every trait of moral courage, including unselfish ambition, in-

18. For a reconciliation of satire and utopia, see Robert C. Elliott, *The Shape of Utopia: Studies in a Literary Genre* (Chicago and London: University of Chicago Press, 1970), esp. chs. 1 and 3. Isaac Kramnick provides a political context for utopian nostalgia in *Bolingbroke and his Circle: The Politics of Nostalgia in the Age of Walpole* (Cambridge, Mass.: Harvard University Press, 1968), pp. 205-35.

19. For example, *The Fatigues of a Great Man, or the Plague of Serving One's Country* (1720?); *The Art of Railing at Great Men: being a Discourse upon Political Railers Ancient and Modern* (1723); *Craftsman,* 7 Feb. 1727.

tegrity, and justice. The polarity between genuine and false greatness is further accentuated by those contemporary moralists who evinced their admiration for the pure ideal. Steele, for example, owes much to Cicero for a celebration of "Greatness Among the Moderns" (1705–1707).[20] And though Fielding was to immortalize the satiric possibilities of "Greatness," he found the primary concept anything but laughable, as in his distinctions between the real and the bogus, which inform his poem "Of True Greatness, An Epistle to George Dodington, Esq." (1741):

> Where shall we say then that true greatness dwells?
> In palaces of kings, or hermits' cells?
> Doth she confirm the minister's mock-state,
> Or bloody on the victor's garland wait?
> Warbles, harmonious, she the poet's song,
> Or, graver, laws pronounces to the throng?
> To no profession, party, place confin'd,
> True greatness lives but in the noble mind;
> Him constant through each various scene attends,
> Fierce to his foes, and faithful to his friends.

[245–54]

That same concern, but much elaborated, sets the theme for most of the *Miscellanies* (1743) in which the verses to Dodington are reproduced. The preface of that collection (some of it virtually a thematic explication of *Jonathan Wild,* which occupies volume three), holds that "an idea of goodness" must be a part of true greatness. But without any of the elements of goodness (benevolence, honor, honesty, charity), greatness is like "the false sublime in poetry." It then consists of bombast, which "is, by the ignorant and ill-judging vulgar, often mistaken for solid wit and eloquence.... Thus pride, ostentation, insolence,

---

20. Cicero, *De Officiis,* trans. Walter Miller (London and New York: Heinemann and Macmillan, 1913), I. xx. 66–69; *Tracts and Pamphlets by Richard Steele,* ed. Rae Blanchard (Baltimore: Johns Hopkins Press, 1944), pp. 618–25. See also by Steele, *The Christian Hero* (1701), pp. 1–62, for his Christian interpretation of greatness. For further commentaries on greatness, see: William Robert Irwin, *The Making of* Jonathan Wild: *A Study in the Literary Method of Henry Fielding* (New York: Columbia University Press, 1941); Henry Knight Miller, *Essays on Fielding's Miscellanies,* pp. 42–54, 144, 185; *Miscellanies by Henry Fielding, Esq; Volume One,* ed. Henry Knight Miller (Middletown, Conn.: Wesleyan University Press, 1972), pp. xix–xxvii, 19–29.

cruelty, and every kind of villainy are often construed into true greatness of mind."[21] And Fielding professes to expose "bombast greatness."

Although custom dictated that any important politician be dubbed Great Man, the prototype was long assumed to be Robert Walpole. It is doubtful that he paid much attention to the unflattering implications of tags, for absolute success effectively anesthetized any feelings he might have had for external appearance. By 1732 he had become "so used to his own greatness that he no longer bothered to adjust himself to circumstances." Ostentatious and corpulent, Walpole was the consummate model for caricature: "His sensibilities hardened. His language, always coarse, became brutal; his attitude to friends and foes franker, more unguarded. Flattery, no matter how gross, sweetened a vanity grown monstrous with a decade's sycophancy. The bright, gay, ever-laughing Robin Walpole of the Kit Cat had vanished in the vast, square-jowled hulk of a man who talked and acted as if power were his to eternity."[22]

Ridicule of Greatness during Walpole's two decades as England's reigning politician has tended—on usually speculative grounds—to be interpreted as an attack upon the first minister himself. Fielding's mock-hero Tom Thumb, a case in point, is frequently seen as a reductively scaled Walpole,[23] his pettiness magnified by grandiloquent comparison:

21. *Miscellanies*, pp. 11-12, 28.

22. J. H. Plumb, *Sir Robert Walpole: The King's Minister* (Boston: Houghton Mifflin, 1961), pp. 249-50. "The *Great* Man," as blandly emended by Pope ("Epilogue to the Satires, Dial. I," l. 26): "A phrase, by common use, appropriated to the first minister." For an excellent account of "Pope's private satirist's war with Walpole," see Maynard Mack, *The Garden and the City*, p. 172. Another, speculative chapter in Pope's private war concerns the prosecution in 1723 of his brother-in-law Charles Rackett for violation of the forestry laws. See E. P. Thompson, *Whigs and Hunters: The Origin of the Black Act* (New York: Pantheon Books, Random House, 1975), App. 2.

23. Among the critics who see traces of Walpole in Tom Thumb: Irwin, p. 36; Martin C. Battestin, "Fielding's Changing Politics and *Joseph Andrews*," *PQ* 39 (1960): 53; Miller, ed., *Miscellanies*, p. 56n. The identification is rejected by Goldgar, *Walpole and the Wits*, pp. 104-5. The mock-heroic play first appeared in 1730 as *Tom Thumb. A Tragedy*. The revision of 1731 was titled *The Tragedy of Tragedies; or the Life and Death of Tom Thumb the Great*. For an identification of Fielding as author of *Pasquin* and *Tom Thumb*, see *The Church Yard: A Satirical Poem* (1739).

Not Alexander, in his highest pride,
Could boast of merits greater than Tom Thumb,
Not Caesar, Scipio, all the flow'rs of Rome,
Deserv'd their triumphs better than Tom Thumb.

[I. iii]

Proof for the presence of Walpole is not demonstrable. But
enough reason exists to assert that one aim of *Tom Thumb* is
political deflation. Fielding relentlessly mocks Thomas Thumb
riding "some cock-sparrow in a farmer's yard," or huzzahs "the
welcome hero, giant-killing lad." His antics argue for the ludicrous rather than the harmful, for the mighty midget creates nothing effectual according to the norms of human aspiration. Fielding here treats the Greatness of any politician as an affectation to
which we should react with amused superiority. Normal human
beings may not be inclined to laughter at the hero's stature *per se,*
since that is an accident of nature. Rather, if they laugh at all, it
will probably be at the pettiness symbolized by his size: Lillipu-
tian pretense conspires to deceive. The aberration that provokes
the unsympathetic response is a moral one. The self-evident
quality of the joke accentuates it, for Tom Thumb's diminutive-
ness mirrors an incongruity between real and pretended capability.

When Fielding moves from overt fabrication to the
pseudobiography of *Jonathan Wild,* he significantly extends the
limits of his concern with false greatness. Now a brutally "real"
thief-taker succeeds the childlike, harmless Tom Thumb.[24] The
result, thematically, becomes a search for some kind of realistic
yet ethically viable median between gross evil like Wild's and
undiscriminating goodness like Heartfree's. As in *Tom Thumb,*
the ironically distorted agent of Greatness is the Great Man himself, a recognizably human figure whose ruling passion is political authoritarianism. To that extent, verisimilitude shapes

24. For a good factual account, see Gerald Howson, *Thief-Taker General: The
Rise and Fall of Jonathan Wild* (New York: St. Martin's Press, 1970). See also
Defoe's pamphlet biography, *The Life of Jonathan Wild, from his Birth to his Death*
(1725). Among the candidates tentatively suggested as models for Wild (aside
from Walpole) have been William Pulteney, Charles Townshend, John Carteret.
See Irwin, pp. 40–41.

*Jonathan Wild.* Again, we face a well-tried assumption that Wild is an allegorical equivalent for Walpole, an assumption, however, which should be qualified in the light of Fielding's shifted political allegiances. For reasons plausibly described by Battestin, "circumstances which . . . when taken together, strongly suggest that in the latter half of 1741 Fielding, disillusioned by the hypocrisy and ingratitude of the Patriots and desperately needing money to care for a sick wife and dying child, may well have accepted Walpole's patronage" (p. 40).

The novel, though published in 1743, was probably written prior to his defection—while he remained an articulate voice of the Opposition—and Jonathan Wild bears a suspicious resemblance to the first minister. Fielding, however, attempted to make the satire applicable generally to unscrupulous politicians at any time. In the preface to the *Miscellanies* (p. 9), he disavowed specificity, protesting that he had not "intended to represent the features of any other person [than the hero]. Roguery, and not a rogue, is my subject; and . . . I have been so far from endeavoring to particularize any individual, that I have with my utmost art avoided it." Yet he would not deny such an opportunity to the reader, "especially if he knows much of the great world, since he must then be acquainted, I believe, with more than one on whom he can fix the resemblance." The distance from a plainly identifiable Great Man appears even more strikingly in the edition of 1754, which incorporates "considerable corrections and additions" to help soften topical analogies. The reigning figure was by then fixed as a token of sham greatness. Fielding, it must seem, had elevated his concerns to far-reaching moral issues correlative with abuses of governmental power.[25]

As fictionally consistent in his outrageous reversal of moral standards as, say, Swift or Defoe, Fielding throws down the traditional satiric challenge to corruption: he plays a risky game in assuming he has the capacity to persuade his readers that what he calls black is in fact white. He can succeed only if he assumes further that they too distinguish black from white, that they

25. For a convenient text of the 1743 edition and the 1754 alterations, consult the World Classics ed. (London: Oxford University Press, 1932; rpt. 1951, 1961).

need to have their minds stretched for them, and that most are disposed toward white. The Great Man's conduct seems unexceptional until its infamy comes home as a result of the satirist's irony, metaphoric exaggeration, or other rhetorical means. Fielding catches us up in his "biography" by making its inversions lively and teasingly credible.

But however entertaining the fiction or realistic the allegorical details, Fielding also has other business to occupy him. He never loses sight of an omniscient role that makes him a palpable moralist and didact as well as creative shaper. To cite an example (III, xiv), in both the original and revised editions of *Jonathan Wild* he lays out prevailing political disagreements in a spirit transparently and censoriously his own. The context sets up a dialogue between Blueskin, who has refused to surrender booty, and Wild, who insists upon deference to his authority. The dialogue thereupon becomes a confrontation on the origins and manipulations of power.

With cool reasonableness, Wild distinguishes between a band of thieves and "a legal society, where the chief magistrate is always chosen for the public good, which, as we see in all the legal societies of the world, he constantly consults, daily contributing, by his superior skill, to their prosperity, and not sacrificing their good to his own wealth, or pleasure, or humor. But in an illegal society or gang, as this of ours, it is otherwise, for who would be at the head of a gang, unless for his own interest? And without a head, you know, you cannot subsist." Subsequently, Blueskin objects to Wild's presumptuously designating him a captain. "The ribbon, or the bauble, that you gave me, implies that I have either signalized myself, by some great action, for the benefit and glory of my country; or at least that I am descended from those who have done so. I know myself to be a scoundrel, and so have been those few ancestors I can remember, or have ever heard of. Therefore I am resolved to knock the first man down, who calls me Sir, or Right Honorable."

The two thieves see eye to eye in differentiating their callings from those generally associated with "legal societies," but their apparent honesty of statement is made suspect by an ironic authorial presence. The words Fielding has Wild utter possess a surface accuracy, yet the disabused reader understands that legality as here represented is only relative. He must believe in fact that the gang leader and the "chief magistrate" have a great deal in common, since the latter—as connoted here—*does* sacrifice the public good to his own benefit even as Wild would do. And like any self-seeking politician, Wild assigns power in ways distasteful to equally ambitious henchmen. Blueskin too knows the principle of self-interest and would gladly become a leader to advance his privileges. Yet at the same time—and no matter how feloniously—his greater candor emerges, for he eschews Wild's hypocritical pretense. He has no illusions about trading pounds for the empty titles that a Great Man wishes to fob off on him as a reward for allegiance or obedience. Blueskin with his own pride of station wishes cash, not honor.

Coleridge, although he admired *Jonathan Wild*, had reservations about "the transposition of Fielding's scorching wit . . . to the mouth of his hero." He wondered whether the novelist's trick is "objectionable on the grounds of *incredulus odi*, or is to be admired as answering the author's purpose by unrealizing the story, in order to give a deeper reality to the truths intended." This, Coleridge said, "I must leave doubtful, yet myself inclining to the latter judgment."[26] The conclusion is surprisingly hesitant for one whose inclination coincides with Fielding's self-evident heuristic purpose. As head of an illegal society, Wild uses seized authority not only for personal gain but also to express contempt of legally constituted society. The unsuccessfully rebellious Blueskin has just as keen insight as Wild into the illegitimacy of the latter's distribution of honors—that is, spoils. Ironically, Fielding allegorizes in this duel of understanding and words the extent to which politicians overreach their legal prerogatives. Truly, then, he has "unrealized the story," bringing it into normative perspective by allowing his villains to expose the illegality of Greatness.

Fielding not only demonstrates in *Jonathan Wild*, as he does in his other fiction, that he is a master teller of picaresque tales, he

26. *Miscellaneous Criticism*, p. 306.

also confirms the conscience that contributes so substantially to the creation of these tales. An important byproduct of his moral vision—a social sympathy—is the talent we have already discerned for transcending particularity in order to show that the faults of Greatness become the legacy of many public figures. Toward this end, in an expertly compressed chapter (II, vi), he develops a thesis—not unlike Swift's on coats or on high and low heels—that adornment does not make the man and his ideas; nor does it safeguard his individuality. The members of Wild's gang "wore different principles, i.e. hats," and as a result "frequent dissensions grew among them. There were particularly two parties, *viz.* those who wore hats fiercely cocked, and those who preferred the nab or trencher hat, with the brim flapping over their eyes; between which, jars and animosities almost perpetually arose." Like any ruling politician, Wild resolved the issue high-handedly. "Is a Prig less a Prig in one hat than another?" he demanded.[27] "It is the mark of a gentleman to move his hat on every occasion." With the declaration that the best hat is that "which will contain the largest booty," Wild grandly ended divisions for the moment and brought the gang together under his dictatorial leadership.

Coleridge conceded that "the mind weary of, shrinks from, the more than painful interest, the μισητόν of utter depravity." Chapters such as "On Hats" serve as philosophic and moral relief, "like the chorus in the Greek tragedy." We may not agree with him that the chapter, "brief as it is, exceeds any thing even in Swift's Lilliput, or Tale of the Tub." But when he exclaims, "How forcibly it applies to the Whigs, Tories, and Radicals of [his] own times," surely he makes a telling point.[28] That Fielding

27. Prig is to be read as *either* thief or Great Man.
28. Cf. *The Works of Lord Byron, Letters and Journals,* ed. Rowland E. Prothero, 6 vols. (London: John Murray, 1898–1901), 5: 465: "I have lately [1821] been reading Fielding over again. They talk of Radicalism, Jacobinism, etc., in England (I am told), but they should turn over the pages of 'Jonathan Wild the Great.' The inequality of conditions, and the littleness of the great, were never set forth in stronger terms; and his contempt for Conquerors and the like is such, that, had he lived *now,* he would have been denounced in 'the Courier' as the grand Mouth-piece and Factionary of the Revolutionists. And yet I never recollect to have heard this turn of Fielding's mind noticed, though it is obvious in every page."

created a vivid story and even a local set of satiric references is a high mark in his favor. He deserves an even higher mark, however, for expanding details of character and circumstances with durable meanings. He levels time and place. He may create laughable digressions on the anatomy of hats; the episode itself may suggest the ludicrous; but the fundamental good sense and seriousness are inescapable.

Fielding's fictional reliance on clothing imagery serves further to develop his certainty that arbitrary power, inseparable from money, dictates right and wrong without relevance to truth or justice. At a primary level the discussion of hats provides comic and reflective respite; and it helps to assert the superficiality of party labels and distinctions. But also, as Coleridge intimates, Fielding wished to emphasize greater profundities at stake here and throughout the "biography." The argument viewed thus is meant to be progressive, beginning with the finite and temporal and culminating in allegorical truths that transcend political bickering. That, at least, is the insistence in the revision of 1754. There, an "Advertisement from the Publisher to the Reader" (presumably written by Fielding) reiterates the earlier denial of personal, malicious intention, rationalizes Newgate as the proper *topos* for moral indoctrination, and calls special attention to the speech of "the Grave Man in pages 195, 196" (that is, IV, iii).

The Grave Man, identified further as a "Debtor," represents a victimized public. Belonging to neither party and yet foolishly prepared to serve either, he is the dupe of both, plundered by them at will. The speech alluded to occurs in Newgate immediately after Wild's party has defeated that of Roger Johnson. As a right of victory, Wild strips the opposing leader "of all his finery" and instead of selling it to share the profits with the debtors, who had helped him, he preempts everything for his own use. Incensed beyond further restraint, the Grave Man bitterly complains to his fellows: "What a wolf is in a sheepfold, a Great Man is in society. Now, when one wolf is in possession of a sheepfold, how little would it avail the simple flock to expel him, and place another in his stead? Of the same benefit to us is the overthrowing one Prig in favor of another. And for what other

advantage was your struggle? Did you not all know, that Wild
and his followers were Prigs, as well as Johnson and his?"

Belatedly then, the Grave Man discovers what Wild had long
known: a Prig is ever a Prig. In making this discovery, however,
the debtor makes still another that (futilely) promises to be his
moral awakening. "Every Prig," he observes, "is a slave. His own
priggish desires, which enslave him themselves, betray him to
the tyranny of others. To preserve, therefore, the liberty [that is,
plunder] of Newgate, is to change the manners of Newgate. Let
us, therefore, who are confined here for debt only, separate
ourselves entirely from the Prigs . . . from Priggism. . . ." The call
for liberation by the Grave Man, who appears to be Fielding's
persona, is only illusory. Nobly rhetorical, he urges these amor-
phous have-nots: "When we separate from the Prigs, let us enter
into a closer alliance with one another. Let us consider ourselves
all as members of one community, to the public good of which
we are to sacrifice our private views. . . . Now, Gentlemen, when
we are no longer Prigs, we shall no longer have these fears or
these desires." Brave words, but alas—as the author cynically
makes us aware—only words and never destined to be more.
Wild "continued to levy contributions among the prisoners, to
apply the garnish to his own use." Even so, his new ornaments
did not fit him very well, and everyone hated or envied him.
Such is the lot of the insensitive, autocratic victor, Fielding implies, and he leaves us to ponder for ourselves the heavy price of
alienation paid for power.

Political—like religious—satire thrives on contention, expressing an eternal struggle between the instincts for self-realization
and communal needs, with individualism the more apparent
victim. But political satire functions not so much as a quixotic
contest—a joust between a lone idealistic warrior and countless
faceless philistines; rather it engages groups in battle. Strong
leaders inevitably invite personal notoriety and assault; but at
the same time they stand identifiable as leaders of factions. In
a practical sense political satire operates for mass objectives.
Mainly it addresses itself to competitive desires of those in power
to consolidate their strength, and of those with an appetite to
wrest power from those who already have it. Satire is prop-

aganda whose business it is to display those conflicting aspirations prominently and to implant its bias so as to create an appropriately partisan audience.

Party politics becomes animated, at time brutalized, by opposition even when little exists to oppose. Walpole's government was not irreproachable, but while it fostered much that was blameworthy, many of its actions and policies deserved praise. Hyperbolic by nature, satire always singles out whatever appears to be faulty. Political power becomes a satiric equation for political misuse, of which Walpole was the visible symbol. When Johnson declared himself in *London* about crime and disorder, he did so with cause, even if we concede that violations of the law were not exceptional during the current ministry. Yet Boswell, more kindly disposed toward the lord treasurer than Johnson, argued: "There was, in truth, no 'oppression'; the 'nation' was *not* 'cheated.' Sir Robert Walpole was a wise and benevolent minister, who thought that the happiness and prosperity of a commercial country like ours, would be best promoted by peace, which he accordingly maintained, with credit, during a very long period." Eventually Johnson modified his criticism, even speaking favorably of him. Walpole, who did prevail for two decades, had treats to offer his constituents as well as tricks, positive social and economic gains as well as hokum and felony.[29]

For many politicians one party affiliation will in the long run serve as well as another. If this be cynicism, then it has been kept shiny with experience and much use. When political principles are changed as readily as hats, principles soon cease to count for anything and politics readily becomes the source of satire. No really objective standards exist whereby the critic can satisfy himself that the satirist has written to rectify public wrongs rather than disburden himself of personal irritations or enhance his own reputation at the expense of a Great Man's. Probably an element of each lurks in the best satire: a compulsive instinct to trample on large, therefore vulnerable, feet; twinges of indigna-

---

29. Boswell's *Life*, 1:131; *Political Writings*, ed. Donald J. Greene (New Haven and London: Yale University Press, 1977), 10:5, in *The Yale Edition of the Works of Samuel Johnson*, 10 vols. (1958–1977); Plumb, pp. 325–33.

tion that make the private ethic a part of the public one and enlist the *humanitas* of public outrage.

A symbolically and physically massive figure like Walpole invites imaginative attack, and he gave to *The Beggar's Opera* a full store of public sin. For Gay's purposes no one character could support the load of mockery he wished to heap upon the first minister, and so he distributed the satiric booty as Walpole himself might have disbursed favors for services rendered: among the many. More explicitly, Gay developed several characters—each a criminal—whose shoddy traits of vocation and personality were quickly attributed to Walpole. Within little more than two weeks after the first performance (29 January 1728), the author of a brief "Key" in the *Craftsman*—probably D'Anvers—virtually confirmed an early popular opinion that Lockit ("Keeper or Prime Minister of Newgate") represented the lord treasurer. D'Anvers himself preferred to see Macheath as Walpole and Peachum as Jonathan Wild. A few months later D'Anvers struck again with the opinion that "the ministers of our most august monarch . . . [had been] ridiculed under the prime characters of a thief-catcher, a jailer, and a highwayman."[30]

Conjecture since then, urging a composite intention, has caused Lockit to make way for Robin of Bagshot, who sits with Peachum and Macheath for the portrait of a venal and sensual man. From these three or four faces, we deduce a complex but grossly exaggerated scoundrel: thief, betrayer, suborner, womanizer. The political element, it should be noted, is only part of a satiric mélange, dominated by a motif of moral imperfection. Political circumstance is as obviously important as the isolation of a verifiable villain. But Gay ultimately transcribed topical details into a comic symbolic literature for social and ethical and cultural reflection. The emergent characters resem-

---

30. *A Compleat Key to the Beggar's Opera. In a Letter to Caleb D'Anvers, Esq;* by "Peter Padwell of Padington" and signed "Phil. Harmonicus." First appeared in the *Craftsman,* 17 Feb. 1728; appended to *Woman's Revenge: Or, a Match in Newgate. A Comedy,* by Christopher Bullock (1728); Caleb D'Anvers, *The Twickenham Hotch-Potch, for the Use of the Rev. Dr. Swift, Alexander Pope, Esq; and Company. Being a Sequel to the Beggar's Opera, &c.* (May 1728). See William Eben Schultz, *Gay's Beggar's Opera: Its Content, History & Influence* (New Haven: Yale University Press, 1923), p. 198. Schultz suggests Lockit is a possible allusion to Townshend, Walpole's brother-in-law.

ble Walpole closely enough—or any other high official of the reader's choice—to produce an amused shock of recognition.[31] Modify the costumes and language, and *The Beggar's Opera* can stand for shady gropings after power in almost any era of Western history.

Not everything written against Walpole entertained as did *The Beggar's Opera*, but the politician created a magnetic field around himself that drew and energized some vigorous polemic satires.[32] The bold Opposition journalist Caleb D'Anvers practically abandoned camouflage in constructing "The History of the Norfolk Steward" for the *Craftsman* (No. 41) of 2 September 1727. The technique—simple, disputatious, repetitious—sets current events and individuals into an easily penetrable narrative. Thus the situation grows out of the obvious, the recent lamented death of "Sir George English, our landlord," the succession of his son, "one of the finest gentlemen in Europe," and young George's esteemed lady.

But now, as in a modern soap opera, the villain—no one less than Mr. Lyn . . . steward of the manor"—defeats all hopes of his being removed from office. Of Mr. Lyn, the *Craftsman* reports with astonishing candor that he had broken open a certain strongbox "and gutted it; and when he was found out, said he had applied it to secret service; a cant expression always used by him, when he had committed felony." These and other innuendoes bring the *Craftsman* to the brink of libel. They indicate, further, that satire inclines toward subtle levels of disguise and ingenuity only when the satirist must be responsible for his own safety. Contrarily, satiric attack tends to be bold and frontal when the writer finds support from powerful friends, as the author of the *Craftsman* found from Bolingbroke and Pulteney. Gay pirouettes in the *Opera* through scenes of gracefully

31. Swift made an ironical game of this opacity: *Intelligencer* 3, *Prose Works*, 12:34. See also Fielding's imitation, *The Genuine Grub-Street Opera. As it was Intended to be Acted at the New Theatre in the Hay-Market* (1731), ed. Edgar V. Roberts (Lincoln: University of Nebraska Press, 1968). For further commentary, see Bronson, *Facets of the Enlightenment*, pp. 60–90; Goldgar, *Walpole and the Wits*, p. 66; Jean B. Kern, *Dramatic Satire in the Age of Walpole, 1720–1750* (Ames: University of Iowa Press, 1976), pp. 42–45.

32. Goldgar, "*Gulliver's Travels* and the Opposition to Walpole," in *The Augustan Milieu*, ed. Miller et al., pp. 155–73.

ritualized deception; D'Anvers stands sturdily, taunting his opponent.

Still another to join the satiric hue and cry against the "obnoxious prime minister" was Samuel Johnson. The urban experiences and associations that preceded the composition of *London* had likely given him a taste for political propaganda; but in 1738 he was still a relative novice not yet prepared to wage more than a limited factional campaign. Then, in the spring of the following year, apparently more committed to an Opposition role, he undertook a *Craftsman*-like fiction that put him somewhere between subterfuge and statement. The "uninterrupted irony" of *Marmor Norfolciense*, which annoyed the prominsterial Hawkins, is conventional and heavy-handed, but Johnson despite his anonymous authorship required at least this much shelter to avoid detection. His Walpole is largely an implied presence, for the main issue of the satire is the Hanoverian monarchy and the upper reaches of English government in general. A double-talking persona, Probus Britannicus, describes how a farmer in Norfolk (a county certain to conjure up thoughts of Walpole) unearthed a marble slab on which appears a revolutionary poem in Latin, the climax of which is a couplet, "Plurima tunc leges / Mutabit, plurima reges." But Probus Britannicus questions the reliability of the translation:

> Then o'er the world shall Discord stretch her wings,
> Kings change their laws, and kingdoms change their kings.

Dogmatically attached to outmoded concepts of government, he repudiates the prophecy that evil times will fall upon the country now that the stone has been uncovered.[33]

He speaks in such assured casuistical slogans that England's

---

33. Boswell (*Life*, 1:141-43) reported that Pope enjoyed the humor of the essay. Not so Hawkins, however, who complained that Johnson was concentrating on "all the topics of popular discontent." The biographer made the unsubstantiated claim that a warrant was issued for Johnson's arrest, as a consequence of which he and his wife fled from the city to "an obscure lodging in a house in Lambeth-marsh, and lay there concealed till the scent after him was grown cold." Sir John Hawkins, *The Life of Samuel Johnson, LL.D.*, 2d ed. (1787), pp. 71-72. Two weeks after *Marmor Norfolciense*, he published another vigorously satiric Opposition tract, *A Compleat Vindication of the Licensers of the Stage*. See Donald J. Greene, *The Politics of Samuel Johnson* (New Haven: Yale University Press, 1960), pp. 96-99.

internal stability and international prestige appear beyond question. Barely disguised, however, sounds the voice of a politician most unlike the good and honest Englishman whose name he bears. The expedient hypocrite, he twists rhetoric so as to enunciate not a statement of fact but one of wish-fulfillment. He concocts a verbal mirage, a word picture of national tranquillity and strength congenial to an acquiescent audience. Some fifty years after the Revolution of 1688, Probus Britannicus intimates that the political hopes engendered by that tumult have been effected, and that only a disloyal prophet would support the disquieting words of "To Posterity." For Johnson—the invisible satirist—the Hanoverian monarchy has not lived up to the inherited "glorious" promises of 1688. Any reasonable, open-eyed man, he wants us to believe, will reverse everything said by Probus Britannicus and thus recognize his delusive and dangerous optimism.[34]

### III

As practitioners of a craft that often hurts, many political satirists have tried to ameliorate their image and justify themselves as impartial proponents of humane necessity. Addison in this vein rejected "abusive, scurrilous styles" of satiric writing (*Spectator* 125). And he protested, further, the difficulty of taming the "angry writer, who"—unable to appear forthrightly in print because of probable government sanctions—"naturally vents his spleen in libels and lampoons" (*Spectator* 451). Like Addison, Steele objected strongly to the "kind of ribaldry [that] passes for wit and humor among the underlings of the party," and to "foul-mouthed ... calumnies" as substitutes for satiric finesse and purpose (*Medley* 23).

We believe objections like these because Addison and Steele rarely wrote satires that contradicted the benignity of their satiric theory. On the other hand, theory does not necessarily square with practice. Such a shrewd debater and controlled

34. In manner and tone *Marmor Norfolciense* has an affinity with *A Modest Proposal* and the projectors of the "Grand Academy of Lagado" (Voyage III, *Gulliver's Travels*). D. N. Smith and E. L. McAdam, Jr., *Johnson's Poems* (Oxford: Clarendon Press, 1941), suggest the scheme of the essay may be an elaboration of Swift's brief poem "The Windsor Prophecy." For text and further commentary, see the *Political Writings*, ed. Greene, 10:19–51.

satirist as Edmund Burke, for example, reproached young, arrogant Philip Francis for his "arguments ad hominem . . . ad verecundiam . . . ad invidiam creandum . . . ad captum." Nevertheless, he himself did not hesitate "to set in a full view the danger from [Richard Price's and Lord Shelburne's] wicked principles and . . . black hearts. . . . If any one be the better for the example made of them, and for this exposition, well and good. I mean to do my best to expose them to the hatred, ridicule, and contempt of the whole world; as I shall always expose such calumniators, hypocrites, sowers of sedition, and approvers of murder and all its triumphs."[35] This is splendid Juvenalian passion, but hardly different in tone or quality from those very faults ascribed to Francis.

A prodigy of rhetorical flexibility, Burke could move easily within an altogether different ambience of satiric attack. Thus he articulated the dark, taut manner just quoted and, with equal facility, the deflationary one of mock-heroic nuance. The latter results when he says of a Whig parliamentary opponent: "The noble lord who spoke last, after extending his right leg a full yard before his left, rolling his flaming eyes, and moving his ponderous frame, at length opened his mouth. I was all attention." Despite Lord North's satanic posture, his speech was only "an overblown bladder [which] has burst, and nobody has been hurt by the crack." Burke regarded the essence of satiric rightness the relation of manner to subject, whether he rebutted a speaker who was "all incoherence and confusion," or explained why "he had not attempted to meddle with the housekeepers of the royal palaces."[36]

If Burke often chose to animadvert with pleasantry, his victims and audience would have had little doubt about the vital force and location of his blows. Traditionally, we have already seen, ridicule need not conflict with seriousness. Swift, for whom the woes of the world could be but inadequately mourned in

35. *The Correspondence of Edmund Burke*, ed. Alfred Cobban and Robert A. Smith (1967), 6:170–71 and 92*n*. Thomas W. Copeland is general editor of the *Correspondence*, 10 vols. (Cambridge and Chicago: University of Cambridge Press, 1958–1978).

36. *The Speeches of the Right Honourable Edmund Burke, in the House of Commons, and in Westminster-Hall*, 4 vols. (1816), 1:14–15; 2:143–44.

tears, wrote in "An Epistle to a Lady" that "Wicked ministers of state / I can easier scorn than hate" (145–46). Hence he resorted to Democritean distance to express his frustration: "In a jest I spend my rage" (172). With an eye toward "courts and ministers," in *Intelligencer* 3, he maintained that humor "is certainly the best ingredient towards that kind of satire, which is most useful, and gives the least offence; which, instead of lashing, laughs men out of their follies, and vices; and is the character that gives Horace the preference to Juvenal." And while he admitted that "some things are too serious, solemn, or sacred to be turned into ridicule, yet the abuses of them are certainly not; since it is allowed, that corruptions in religion, politics, and law, may be proper topics for this kind of satire." He mutes the familiar tone of *saeva indignatio* and adopts in its place a seemingly more tractable one. Although far from complacence, it marks an attitude more dispassionate than usual for him. On this occasion, he finds religious, social, and political institutions both sound and worth defending against defilement. Satire that attempts this goal, he hints, extends the possibilities of constructive human relationships.

The hint itself is often to be suspected as a mere formulaic diversion having little or nothing to do with affirmation. The introductory lines of the Mulgrave-Dryden *Essay upon Satire* (1679),[37] for example, invoke the satirist's art as a corrective, making righteous use of exhortation and ridicule:

> Satire has always shin'd amongst the rest,
> And is the boldest way, if not the best,
> To tell men freely of their foulest faults,
> To laugh at their vain deeds and vainer thoughts.
> In satire too the wise took diff'rent ways,
> Though each deserving its peculiar praise:
> Some did all follies with just sharpness blame,
> While others laugh'd and scorn'd them into shame;
> But of these two the last succeeded best,
> As men aim rightest when they shoot in jest.
>
> [11–20]

While extolling "the boldest way" and deriding court vanities, the authors pay lip-service to the popular doctrine of satiric

37. For Dunton's borrowing, see ch. 4.

efficacy. Initially, in keeping with this illusory show, they avoid excesses of recrimination. The illusion does not last, however, as the *Essay* becomes increasingly personal in its attacks upon those close to the royal household; any semblance of temperance vanishes in spite. Dryden nevertheless cherished restraint as a condition of satire; and in *Absalom and Achitophel,* an infinitely more thoughtful poem, he came closer to reconciling theory and practice. In an address to the readers of the latter poem, he promised to palliate pain and anger with the tickle of good verse and to avoid putting "too sharp an edge" on his satire. The cutting edge is there, we know, but it is carefully sheathed. With an engaging air of moderation linked to self-esteem, he asserted that "no man can be heartily angry with him who pleases him against his will." Dryden either cannot or will not free himself entirely from the clichés of satiric intention. Like almost everyone else, he means to offset political vices by correction. In so saying he uses a traditional metaphor: he will undertake radical surgery only as a last resort: he will if possible "prevent the chirurgeon's work of an *ense rescindendum* [Ovidian excision by sword], which [he wishes] not to [his] very enemies."

By contrast, Churchill forthrightly dismisses such ceremony as nonsense that might have been useful "in less harden'd times." Great then was the force of satire, "and mighty were her rimes":

> But in an age, when actions are allow'd
> Which strike all honor dead, and crimes avow'd,
> . . . . . . . . . . . . . . . . . . . . . . . . . . . . . . . . . . . . . . . . . . .
> Satire throws by her arrows on the ground,
> And, if she cannot cure, she will not wound.

[155–78]

*The Candidate* (1764), Churchill's attack on the fourth Earl of Sandwich, has the immediate topical purpose of balking Sandwich's efforts to become High Steward of Cambridge University; but it also has a more private motive of vengeance against one of Wilkes's enemies.[38] Churchill's achievement is notable, for in a long, essentially spiteful poem he has managed to

---

38. Churchill's *Poetical Works,* ed. Grant, pp. 349–72. Cf. Thomas Gray's satire of Sandwich as "Jemmy Twitcher" in "The Candidate." For the speculative history of this brief (34-line) poem, see Roger Lonsdale, ed., *The Poems of Thomas Gray, William Collins, Oliver Goldsmith* (London: Longmans, 1969), pp. 243-47.

sustain a high level of irony. Some lapses naturally occur—like the invocation to "Sacred Loyalty"—yet a generalized, almost philosophical tone complements a satiric pattern of inversion. The cumulative effect, leisurely unfolded through charge after charge, shows the craft of a poet who confidently unites the formal possibilities of satire with his own creative imagination. The structure of *The Candidate* is schematic, but the poetry and wit are fresh.

The first dozen or so stanzas, cunningly incremental, express the apparent disillusion of a poet wearied by strife and striving. A succession of stanzas thus begins, "*Enough*": enough of actors, authors, critics, Scotland, state, patriots, Wilkes, self, satire. Enough of fruitless anger and recrimination. The time has come for praise. And so commences a briefer, new section enjoining celebration. Here Churchill falls back—ironically, to be sure—on the Renaissance tradition of blame and praise. "*Come, Panegyric,*" he exclaims in a sequence culminating with mock-epic fervor, "Hail, Sandwich . . . Sandwich, All Hail." Represented by Churchill as a master of hypocrisy, Sandwich waited until Bute was brought down. Whereupon,

> . . . like a Mars (fear order'd to retreat)
> We saw thee nimbly vault into his seat,
> Into the seat of pow'r, at one bold leap,
> A perfect connoisseur in statesmanship;
> When, like another Machiavel, we saw
> Thy fingers twisting, and untwisting law.
>
> [283-88]

Insidiously Churchill builds his case against an adversary imagined as wanton, untrustworthy, profligate, intimate with questionable friends:

> To whip a top, to knuckle down at taw,
> To swing upon a gate, to ride a straw,
> To play at push-pin with dull brother Peers,
> To belch out catches in a porter's ears.
>
> [325-28]

Nothing distinguishes carefree childhood from dissipated adulthood: the thoughtless child and irresponsible wastrel become one.

Near the conclusion of the poem Churchill inveighs against

Sandwich's foolishness in language that gives the inverted impression of a man who is independently wise. Sandwich serves as "Wisdom's happy son, but not her slave." This impression of integrity, however, is quickly and audaciously subsumed in the portrait of a creature of change, gay when it is useful to be gay, grave when gravity suits the public mood. And he acts always the fool, "free from the dull impertinence of thought." Is this what it means to be the High Steward of a university? And yet, if he attains investiture, few will protest. Churchill sees university officialdom as corrupt as Sandwich, prepared to greet him in a mockery of pious ritual:

> Divinity, enrob'd in college fur,
> In her right hand a *New Court Calendar*,
> Bound like a Book of Pray'r, thy coming waits
> With all her pack, to hymn thee in the gates.
>
> [763–66]

The pleasure of the poem continues long after the occasion has faded. Political or topical satire as a record of events is one form of history, but virtually by definition it distorts history, having the same persuasive intention as propaganda. At its aesthetic best, nevertheless, satire like Churchill's transcends both the factuality of history and the distortion of propaganda.

Churchill's success depends upon a controlled imagination that gives life to his verses; they exude verve, wit, and poetic assurance. When satire is this good we must listen to Blake's complaint with disappointment: "I am really sorry to see my countrymen trouble themselves about politics. If men were wise, the most arbitrary princes could not hurt them. If they are not wise, the freest government is compelled to be a tyranny. Princes appear to me to be fools. Houses of Commons and Houses of Lords appear to me to be fools; they seem to me to be something else besides human life."[39] Here, precisely, is the matter of political satire, the fools and tyrants who loom large in the chronicles of that subject. Yet about 1810, when he apparently set down

---

39. *The Note-Book of William Blake*, ed. Geoffrey Keynes (London: Nonesuch Press, 1935), p. 106. For a discussion of Blake's satiric poetry, see David V. Erdman, *Blake: Prophet against Empire*, rev. ed. (Princeton: Princeton University Press, 1969), pp. 92–127.

these informal remarks, Blake did not relate them to the poet whose compassion had made the *Songs of Innocence and of Experience* among the most memorable satires in English literature. As part of a counterpointed universe of lamb and tiger, he had imaged a political audience whose design accommodated the gradual but inevitable constriction of innocence in its social enclosure. Mutually dependent, the two sets of *Songs* interact satirically as a commentary on the inner and social lives of common people. But on an altogether different plane, daily politics meant to Blake a hybrid of the foolishness and atavism exercised by men in high places. As such, it was irreconcilable with his own concept of satire applied to a serious, even visionary, approach to understanding man's mortal state.

IV

In an age when Church and State intertwine, theological and political satires are often coextensive. Both, we have observed, are polemic, either dissenting from fixed public doctrines under threat of repression or defending them with the assurance of consensus. Looked at historically, they share the utilitarian quality of a popular forum and peripheral news medium. Occasional in nature, they have a widespread functional appeal: they become vehicles of information, slanted to be sure, but still reflectors of contemporary issues in a way that helps make up for the inadequacy of a restricted press. Topicality thus proves to be a common denominator; and so too, within limits, does a tendency to subordinate reason to emotion.

These among other qualities of purpose and technique link satires of statecraft and of religion. Not all traits can or need be specified. But just as numerous likenesses connect them, enough equally numerous differences exist to give them distinctive entities. And each has its own efficiency, if the generalization may be allowed, which justifies a separation into two kinds of satire. The very focus of religious satire, for example, is such as to encourage the impression—if not always the fact—of an elevated preoccupation. We know that harshness or vulgarity can sometimes dominate even the sanctified subject. On the whole, however, ideology motivates religious satire to a far greater extent than it does political satire. Allusions to Scripture, the deity, or ritual are designed to keep us alert to high purpose. Discussions of ministerial bungling, on the other hand, are generally informed by a sense for the exterior, practical, and earth-bound. The commentator on public affairs may dress up his treatise with political theory or historical analogy, but the ultimate effect for which he strives is one of realistic application. He translates ideals into tangible form, giving them physical propinquity.

Affairs of state, insofar as they relate to economic conditions, civil and religious liberties, social mobility, and the like, have a pervasive impact that satirists exploit in extensively circulated pamphlets, poems, and manuscripts. Theirs is a literature of controversy, propaganda sometimes of a very crude order, which seeks actively partisan commitments from any quarter of society. The rabble stirred to derision by *Lilli burlero* are just as welcome recruits to political causes as the more sophisticated audiences capable of taking in the nuances of *Absalom and Achitophel* or the *Epilogue to the Satires*. The bulk of political satire, indeed, tends to be fugitive, more notable for its pragmatic and contentious temporality than for its niche in history. Thomas Flatman's conversational *Heraclitus Ridens,* as an instance, was a popular serial journal in 1681–1682, enjoying the author's royalist perspective of current events.[40] Like yesterday's newspaper, however, when the public occasion ended the papers were easily forgotten, their localized wit as obscure as their contents.

Better political satirists than Flatman—Dryden, Swift, Pope, Johnson, Churchill, among others—also made better use of schematic devices by which their satires would outlast the moment: myth and beast metaphors, masking, fictional dialogues, symbolic representations—all these and others, when creatively managed, provided a bridge between argumentation and imaginative literature. Yet it cannot be denied that the substance of political satire is topical fact, its source of tension, disagreement (adversarially termed "sedition," just as religious opposition

40. *Heraclitus Ridens: or, A Discourse between Jest and Earnest, Where many a True Word is Spoken in Opposition to All Libellers against the Government* (1681–82).

turns into "impiety" or "atheism"). With detachment as foreign to polemic satire as temperance, the personal element sometimes casts a spell of ambiguity over the intention. The particularity of the *Craftsman*'s attack on Walpole transforms the claims of moderation into ironical nonsense. The notorious Mulgrave-Dryden *Essay upon Satire* charts an uneasy course between the efficacy of boldly shining satire and libelous hits at the court entourage. Defoe's patriotic fervor in *The True-Born Englishman* vacillates between the view of the healing surgeon and the angry xenophobe whose animosity attaches to John Tutchin as "True-Born English Shamwhig" (630), the epitome of national ingratitude.[41]

Name-calling reminds us of militant authorial presence in the design of most political satire. There are also parallel instances in which the author, while presenting himself as an exceedingly angry man, does not speak overtly for self-interest. Rather, he is the loyal organization spokesman who vigorously affirms the policies of his party while undermining those of the other. During the Restoration and eighteenth century, factionalism competed with the abusive quarrels of individuals to provide subjects for party politics. That is by no means to say political rivalry at the party level was not rancorous.[42] Curiously apropos, the names *Whig* and *Tory* connote belligerent division over the right to rule. *Whig*, if etymological speculation is to be trusted, may derive from a word ("Whiggamore") once applied to a Scottish insurgent; and *Tory* was originally a marauding Irishman or Scot hostile to the English. The names, with their taints of Gaelic and

---

41. *POAS*, 6:286. The final "authorized" editions (9th and 10th, 1701) of this much reprinted and pirated poem drop the attack on Tutchin. See John Robert Moore, *A Checklist of the Writings of Daniel Defoe*, 2d ed. (Hamden, Conn.: Archon Books, 1971), no. 28. Cf. another example of Defoe's patriotism: *The Mock-Mourners. A Satyr, by Way of Elegy on King William* (1702), in *POAS*, 6:372–97. [Foxon, *Catalogue*, 1:171–75.]

42. For example, Charles Davenant, *The True Picture of a Modern Whig, Set forth in a Dialogue between Mr. Whiglove & Mr. Double, Two Under-Spur-Leathers to the Late Ministry* (1701); *The True Tom Double: or, An Account of Dr. Davenant's Late Conduct and Writings, Particularly with Relation to the XIth Section of his Essays on Peace at Home, and War Abroad* (1704?); William Shippen, *Faction Display'd. A Poem* (1704); *Some Critical and Politick Remarks on a Late Virulent Lampoon, call'd Faction Display'd* (1704).

Scottish unruliness, could not be more apt for purposes of satiric irony.

There is little in factional satire to persuade the reader that ideological consistency or continuity was the mark of either party, or even that significant differences of conviction separated them. Bolingbroke went so far as to erase all distinction, assuming that honorable men of either Whig or Tory persuasion subscribed to Revolution principles and in general supported like causes: clean government, reduced militarism, and a strong economic position. Pope synthesized the premise within an epigrammatic similitude: "Tories call'd him Whig, and Whigs a Tory." For Defoe, "Whig and Tory, though names of too general use among us, even then [in King William's reign], yet signified little more than what they ought to signify now, (viz.) the friends and the enemies of the Revolution."[43] Like Fielding's prigs, many politicians have been able to alter their positions as they would their hats. The policies of an Opposition member one day may have to be shifted on another when he finds himself in the ruling party. Survival as seen by the satirist becomes a malleable process dependent upon an ability to mold oneself to current political contours.

Comparable to eighteenth-century satire at large, that devoted to state affairs often attempts to conceal its immediate functional aims. Prudence, we have seen, may prompt the satirist to blur the identifying marks of a specific politician in favor of the safer, symbolically transferable euphemism of the Great Man. Disguise not only has the cautionary virtue of affording shelter from possible sanctions. It may also serve as a justification, even when rationalized, for the much-stated claim that satire is a general rather than a particular mode of reproach; and that, further, it is a social or ethical corrective to be advanced against roguery rather than against the rogue, against the faceless many rather than against selected individuals. The reality of political satire

---

43. *Twickenham Pope*, 4:xxxii, 297; Defoe, *The Present State of the Parties in Great Britain* (1712); cf. *Tatler* 232. Ronald Paulson attempts to lay down ideological or philosophical distinctions between Whig and Tory in *The Fictions of Satire*, pp. 120–28, 210–20. But see Keith Grahame Feiling, *The Second Tory Party, 1714–1832* (London: Macmillan, 1938), p. 2.

sometimes eludes reconciliation with the ideal principle, but the recurring emphasis upon generality calls attention to the desirability of a vision that can look beyond the rough-and-tumble of daily politics to lasting standards of social morality. It is also a reminder that the outer skin of much political satire is not so pointlessly abrasive as sometimes appears. The satirist who goes about his task skillfully gives the reader a double reward: the pleasure of an aesthetic experience coupled with the reasonable hope that a stable political order may be attainable.

# CHAPTER 6

# "STUDIED CIVILITY":
## Satire of Manners

Satiric attitudes toward social behavior are conditioned by prevailing convention even as they are in matters of religion and politics. Transgressions, real or imagined, are certain to be deplored as a breakdown of rational community intercourse. Since satire is by precept an art of disagreement, it can be depended upon to take exception to any evidence of disintegrating public mores. Yet it also reserves a right to praise the orthodoxies that insure continuing human values. As we argued in the preceding chapter, the satirist often appears to yearn for a Golden Age because he cannot reconcile himself to contemporary follies and improprieties. Thus he rejects the destabilization of institutions and manners as a threat to social order. And yet he seldom insists that old customs are best simply because they are traditional. Satire, it has been observed, assumes "a special function of analysis, of breaking up the lumber of stereotypes, fossilized beliefs, superstitious terrors, crank theories, pedantic dogmatisms, oppressive fashions, and all other things that impede the free movement . . . of society." The satirist allies himself with those who share his "views as to how normal people can be expected to behave."[1] Ordinarily it follows from this that when the satirist faults public behavior he would like to see some kind

1. Frye, *An Anatomy of Criticism*, p. 233; W. H. Auden, "Notes on the Comic," *The Dyer's Hand*, pp. 384–85. Cf. Henri Bergson on the community of laughter: *Laughter: An Essay on the Meaning of the Comic*, pp. 3–4.

of remedial change take place, even if he himself does not initiate that change.

He sets his reactions to cultural patterns, as to the trends of politics and religion, in a "literary" frame. Nevertheless, he responds empirically to the realities of everyday life. There is, in fact, a valuable historical parallel between satiric attitudes toward public conduct and organized extralegal attempts to reform manners. After the comparatively relaxed atmosphere of the Restoration, both Church and State began to question what had been happening to social standards and did not like the answers. Complaints—often for only hollow, formal show—were plentiful. But others seriously intended could be heard also. About 1690, for example, a handful "of good and zealous citizens," wealthy, respected members of the Church of England, first organized a Society for the Reformation of Manners. As hyperrighteous as they were substantial, they insisted that the laws against sinners be enforced with ruthless impartiality.

Toward this end the society proposed "to control looseness, and to prevent the youth of the city from being spoilt by harlots and loose women, and from spending their time in taverns or alehouses, and distempering themselves by excess of drink, and breaking the sabbath." The members of the Society undertook to deal personally with infractions. Knowing that they could not count on official enforcement, they intended to patrol the streets and with self-assumed authority to make arrests wherever and whenever they deemed necessary. They declared, further, that they would supplement their own efforts by "employing constables and others, to watch ill houses, and take straggling loose persons, and bring them before the magistrates, and inform against them, for the better putting the good laws of the land in execution against all such evil-doers."[2]

The clenched fist of piety appeared once again in England, and high-placed support was enlisted on behalf of aggressive virtue. King William and, later, Queen Anne sanctioned

---

2. John Stow, *A Survey of the Cities of London and Westminster . . . Written first in the Year MDXCVIII . . .*, ed. John Strype, 2 vols. (1720), 2:30–31.

Societies for the Reformation of Manners, and a sometimes bullying clergy gave the movement its orthodox blessings.[3] The
distance between churchly exhortation and secular threat was
very narrow indeed. By 1733 the current Society boasted: "The
total number of persons prosecuted in or near London only, for
debauchery and profaneness, for near 40 years last past, are
calculated at about 98,970. They have also been assisting in
bringing to punishment several sodomitical houses, as well di-
vers persons for sodomy, and sodomitical practices, who have
been prosecuted by the direction, and at the charge of the government." Just a few years later, the prosecutions were estimated
to be 101,683.[4] Such assaults upon public sins speak well for
organized eavesdropping. A vigilante obsession with "lewd and
scandalous practices" is hardly credible today. Among
eighteenth-century Englishmen, however, the severity with
which offenses from sodomy to drunkenness and swearing were
punished must have seemed formidable enough. Decadent behavior that had flourished during the Restoration became the
object of fanatic outrage.

The correlation of the historical and the literary fascinates: in
large part the province of these godly witch-hunters coincides

3. See [Josiah Woodward], *An Account of the Progress of the Reformation of Manners, in England, Scotland, and Ireland,* 12th ed. (1704). Includes Queen Anne's
"Proclamation for the Encouragement of Piety and Virtue, and for the Prevent-
ing and Punishing of Vice, Prophaneness, and Immorality," 25 Feb. 1702/3. She
had issued an earlier proclamation, on her accession to the throne, but noted
that it had "not been executed according to our just expectations and com-
mands."

4. *The Nine and Thirtieth Account of the Progress made in the Cities of London and
Westminster, and Places Adjacent, by the Societies for Promoting a Reformation of Man-
ners* [1733], pp. 36–40 ff. Arthur Bedford, *A Sermon Preached to the Societies for
Reformation of Manners, at St. Mary-le-Bow, on Thursday, January 10th, 1733* (1734).
*The Forty-Fourth Account of the Progress made in the Cities of London and Westminster,
and Places Adjacent, by the Societies for Promoting Reformation of Manners; by further-
ing the Execution of the Laws against Profaneness and Immorality, and by other Christian
Methods* (1739). Appended to *A Sermon Preached to the Societies for Reformation of
Manners, at Salters-Hall, on Monday, October 1st, 1739* [by Timothy Jollie]. Cf.
Swift, *Prose Works,* 2:45; Bernard Mandeville, *A Modest Defense of Publick Stews*
(1724); *POAS,* 6:129–31; W. E. H. Lecky, *A History of England in the Eighteenth
Century,* 3d ed., 8 vols. (London: Longmans, Green, 1883–87), 2:546–47.

with that of the worldly satirist. Reform of manners is the avowedly specific goal of the former even as it is often the professed one of the satirist. But whereas the offenses to be eradicated may be shared targets for zealots and satirists, the weapons of the first consist of plodding, literal interpretation and enforcement. The professional reformers not only invoked the law but also tried to discourage infractions by obvious propaganda: "Many thousands of good books [were] . . . dispersed by these *Societies* throughout the kingdom, and put into the hands of lewd and profane persons, to awaken them to a sense of their sins."[5] If such tactics fell short, the reformers had recourse to the law courts, pillories, and jails. Distrusting the efficacy of reason, they drew upon mandate, prohibition, and fear. At another level of persuasion, the satirists strove to arouse imaginative as well as intellectual reaction to error and foolishness. Not all satirists, we know, succeeded. Generally speaking, however, they tried to engage conscience and mind in a way that would be more persuasive than obligatory, more receptive to wit than to declamation and threat. Through the indirection of irony and metaphor, satirists created fictions that might bring readers closer to self-recognition than they would have been willing to admit in outright confrontation with their accusers. The reformers insisted upon penitential submission. The illusion of relative distance in satire, however, lessened the harsh urgency of obligation.

Reformers and satirists alike hoped to reach large numbers, although the latter could not realistically assume so widespread an appeal for their messages as could the former. These, convinced that they served divine grace in a special role, were optimistic. Satirists, on the other hand—despite formal poetic pronouncements of divine assistance—seemed less sanguine that either force or reason (however wittily enfranchised) could effect lasting rehabilitation. Yet they continued to write profusely. Although they asserted again and again the highly empiric nature of their calling, they also stressed that it coincided with the best interests of social man. Like a missionary who finally must

5. Bedford, *Sermon* of 10 Jan. 1733. Text from Leviticus 5:1.

admit that society has about as much use for him as for any other officious meddler, Defoe laments:

> ... he that first reforms a vicious town,
> Prevents their ruin, but completes his own;
> For if he was an angel from on high,
> He cannot 'scape the general infamy.[6]

Defoe probably knew that his campaign against the erosion of manners was quixotic. But he belongs to a company of satirists who could not help being nags of conscience. They might have their moments of quiescence or even of expedience, but sooner or later, when impatience with social failings can no longer be checked, their protesting voices are heard again.

Manners in the eighteenth century can be associated with a spectrum of human relationships. In one important sense, as defined in Johnson's *Dictionary,* manners are "a general way of life; morals; habits." So perceived, they comprehend a multitude of duties. They connote man's need to fulfill himself as a responsible moral being. Manners taken this way represent tacit cumulative consent. Rationally motivated individuals have often argued that tolerant coexistence contributes to private contentment and to the inner satisfaction of a life well lived. But this concept of naturally harmonious manners also subsumes one that is extrinsic, less speculative, the one that Johnson saw as "ceremonious behavior; studied civility." This is how individuals adhere to formal patterns of polite exchange. However viewed, manners are determined by an impulse for order, and when disorder threatens the social harmony, the satirist intervenes with castigation and ridicule. Two words in particular have become synonymous with attacks on social perversity: one is *dullness,* the catchall enemy of "a general way of life"; the other is *affectation,* the self-conscious artificiality of the fop and the fool.[7]

---

6. "More Reformation, a Satyr upon Himself," ll. 11–14 [16 July 1703], *POAS*, 6:552. Cf. "Manners: a Satire" [1738], *Satires Written by Mr. [Paul] Whitehead* (1739), p. 12: "Pointless all satire in these iron times, / Too faint the colors, and too feeble rhymes."

7. George Etherege's Medley in *The Man of Mode* (1676) has this piece of information for Emilia: "Then there is *The Art of Affectation,* written by a late

*Dullness,* the more infectious fault, also invites more acidulous
condemnation than does *affectation.* But both, we shall see, may
be linked satirically and used as tools for genuine perception.

A tradition of negative associations has grown up around
*dullness* and *affectation.* Unlike abstract philosophical
metaphors—such, for instance, as the Baconian Idols of the
Tribe—the two words adjust to the experiential substance of
manners. Erasmus understood those vitiating qualities of mind
and spirit when he provided the conceit *folly* (translated from his
Latinized Greek *Moriae Encomium*) to express dissatisfaction with
a degenerate world. More economical for certain satirists than
the two separate terms *dullness* and *affectation, folly* embraces
varied sins of character and intention. The semantic mutations
of *folly* satisfied speculative moralists. At the same time their
connotations remained within grasp of practical, uncomplicated
minds. *Folly* is a homely and rigorous word. With foolishness the
least obnoxious of its many meanings, it assimilated errors in an
ascending scale of gravity, from wickedness at large to specifically lewd, wanton, even sacrilegious behavior. For Erasmus and
his borrowers, the word perfectly supports the irrational abuse
of manners and sacred necessity. Toward this definition, in the
guise of a personified *Folly,* he praised himself as "that true
disposer of good things whom the Latins call *Stultitia* and the
Greeks Μωρία."

Thus *Folly* through self-praise damns the gamut of human
aberration, from the temporal to the spiritual, taking credit for
all. The encroachment of moral laxity upon manners is typified
by vanity, sloth, egotism, sensuousness. To these, as to *Folly,*
Erasmus gives uncomfortably human traits. For *Folly*'s wet
nurses he chooses *Drunkenness* and *Ignorance.* Among "other at-
tendants and followers" are *Philautia* (self-love), *Kolakia* (flat-

---

beauty of quality, teaching you how to draw up your breasts, stretch up your
neck, to thrust out your breech, to play with your head, to toss up your nose, to
bite your lips, to turn up your eyes, to speak in a silly soft tone of voice, and use
all the foolish French words that will infallibly make your person and conversation charming; with a short apology at the latter end, in the behalf of young
ladies who notoriously wash and paint, though they have naturally good com-
plexions" (II.i). Cf. *The Laughing Philosopher: or, an Exact Description of the Present
Times, by Democritus Junior* (1729).

tery), *Lethe* (forgetfulness), *Misoponia* (laziness), *Hedone* (pleasure), *Anoia* (madness), *Tryphe* (wantonness), *Comus* (intemperance), *Negretos Hypnos* (sound sleep).[8] Allegorically didactic, Erasmus leaves little to the imagination. His ironies work for deliberate transparency; the moralizing satirist takes care to avoid being misunderstood at any point. As a metaphor *folly* makes fewer demands of the reader than do *dullness* and *affectation*. This is so because Erasmus is less concerned with literary sophistication than with moral clarity, and he sets forth his arguments accordingly.

As a conceit *folly* particularly resembles the implications of *dullness*, although, as we have said, it also includes those of *affectation*. And like them, *folly* implicitly mocks any notion that "he that thinks reasonably must think morally."[9] The byproduct of any era, folly endangers cultures as well as individuals. From the perspective of an eighteenth-century satirist, *dullness* synthesizes the torpid executioners of manners. Personified in *The Dunciad*, it becomes the stupefying daughter "of Chaos and Night" who exists "to blot out order, and extinguish light" (IV. 14–15). The poet ameliorates didacticism by laughing at the blatantly trivial or ludicrous. For more significant effect, however, he enjoins the reader to condemn social atrophy, the paralyzing enemy of manners. Like Dryden's Shadwell—the *mopus*-type of Restoration society—the progeny of Pope's *Dulness* are destructively stupid; of them also it can be said that none ever "deviate into sense." Lacking native wit, they also lack the capacity to identify integration as a reigning principle of the cosmic scheme. Many a satirist would be impelled to cry out with Virginia Woolf's character: "Scraps, orts, and fragments! Surely we should unite!"[10] They should, of course, but cannot except in principle, for the

8. *The Praise of Folly*, pp. 10, 13. The Erasmian *moria* is a phonetic transcription into Latin from the Greek μωρία (generally: folly, error, vanity, vapidity). British readers had ample access to the Dutch humanist's writings. See E. J. Devereux, *A Checklist of English Translations of Erasmus to 1700* (Oxford: Oxford Bibliographical Society, 1968).

9. This is Johnson's phrase, borrowed from the "Preface" to Shakespeare [1765], in *Yale Edition of the Works*, ed. Arthur Sherbo (1968), 7:71. Burke slightly rephrased the aphorism—"where there is no sound reason, there can be no real virtue"—in "A Letter to a Member of the National Assembly" [1791], *Works*, 4:24.

10. *Between the Acts* (London: Hogarth Press, 1969), p. 225.

essence of dullness is fragmentation, with enthusiasm for the parts obliterating respect for the whole. "Book IV" of *The Dunciad,* Reuben Brower remarks, "is the poem of a man acutely sensitive to disorder in a work of art, a life, a society."[11] Throughout the poem, every positive quality attributed to dullness must be reversed as a mockery of truth and esteem: "In clouded majesty," hence, "here Dulness shone" (I. 45-54). The oxymora of "clouded majesty" and shining "Dulness" invite derogation. Pope pursues the absurdity by providing his dimwitted victims with "four guardian virtues" whose intrinsic worth he so qualifies that reduction to a mock-heroic scale is inevitable. Reminiscent of *Folly's* more obvious "household servants," they have the same pejorative utility. *Fortitude* helps these Grubeans to be afraid of nothing—nothing except "hisses, blows or want, or loss of ears." *Temperance* waits upon the author who has learned to expect few rewards other than hunger and thirst. *Prudence* is a euphemism for any expedience to keep the hack out of debtor's prison. And *Poetic Justice* becomes a sorry unreality when the luckless scribbler asks that his belly be filled with "solid pudding" and instead receives "empty praise." Virtue and dullness, then, are antinomies, and to clinch the argument Pope concludes with the oppression of *Science, Wit, Logic, Rhetoric,* and the triumph of the "false guardians" of Morality: "*Chicane* in furs, and *Casuistry* in lawn." The Law and the Church are as vulnerable to Sophistry and Billingsgate as any other creatures under the dominion of Queen Dulness (IV. 20-30).

The Empire of Dulness has never been toppled—that would be too much to expect when contending against "Divinity without a Noûς" (IV. 244)—but her enemies have exposed it relentlessly. Numerous writers between Bacon and Swift, for example, have assaulted the corruption of creative talent, learning, and social institutions.[12] But no one has earned a better

---

11. *Alexander Pope: The Poetry of Allusion* (London, Oxford, New York: Oxford Paperback, 1968), p. 342. For the slang term *mopus,* see Congreve, *The Way of the World* (1700), III. i. 8.

12. Cf. Aubrey L. Williams, *Pope's* Dunciad: *A Study of Its Meaning* (Baton Rouge: Louisiana State University Press, 1955), p. 109. Williams reminds us that duncehood, whose chief trait is dullness, may embrace the perversion of scholastic philosophy expounded by the sixteenth-century Duns Scotus.

right than Pope to be confirmed as the historian of dullness in all its hateful, soporific variety. From about 1728 to 1743 the subject came close to being his ruling literary passion. Successive versions of *The Dunciad* are the cornerstone, but the gospel of dullness according to Pope also found its way into *The Memoirs of Martinus Scriblerus* (1741). And if an epigraph should be wanted, *Peri Bathous* (1728, ch. 10) has it: "... the main end and principal effect of the Bathous is to produce *Tranquillity of Mind,* (and sure it is a better design to promote *sleep* than madness)." Pope navigates among images of intellectual and spiritual weariness; from the great cosmic yawn to the stifling of "sense, and shame, and right, and wrong" (*The Dunciad,* IV. 605–25). He charts the steady decline from genesis into the anarchic chaos of the "uncreating word" to symbolize the impoverishment of manliness. Correspondingly the light of understanding and humanity dims until, finally, "universal darkness buries all."

Johnson questioned whether Pope had introduced any moral purpose into the poem, just as he denied that dullness necessarily offended against morality. In taking exception to Pope's far-ranging metaphor, however, Johnson made a critical bridge to the subject of *affectation:* "Dullness or deformity are not culpable in themselves, but may be very justly reproached when they pretend to the honor of wit or the influence of beauty." Unlike Pope, Johnson could reconcile himself to dullness because he did not regard it as a threat to those manners constituting "a general way of life." Literally, as he indicated in the *Dictionary,* dullness is the mark of stupidity, but nothing significantly worse. The pretense implicit in affectation disturbed him more, however, because it blemished personality to no purpose. It was, he thought, "disguise of the real character, by fictitious appearances." In *Rambler* 20, where he makes this observation, he becomes caustic about any dissimulation as an attempted cheat upon the world. At the same time he modifies his opinion of a disguise that seems merely a contemptible "part of the chosen trappings of folly." Johnson touches upon two points. First, as a voluntary error, affectation is escapable and probably remediable. Second, though worthy of disdain, it merely represents one of those excesses of "ceremonious behavior" that is similar to

Swift's *les petites morales,* the "smaller morals" of social niceties.[13]
A curious correspondence connects Johnson's arguments and
Fielding's celebrated preface to *Joseph Andrews.* Johnson, to be
sure, in the *Rambler* deliberately separates affectation from
hypocrisy. On any gauge of falsity the hypocrite reveals the
villain in himself while the "man of affectation" plays the harmless posturing fool: "Contempt is the proper punishment of affectation, and detestation the just consequence of hypocrisy."
Fielding is equally critical of the hypocrite as one who attempts
"to avoid censure, by concealing . . . vices under an appearance
of their opposite virtues." But he does not measure out distinction between affectation and hypocrisy as does Johnson. For
him, rather, hypocrisy is the modifier, the defining or shaping
trait that he associates with affectation in its most egregious exercise, even as in less culpable circumstances he discovers a connection between vanity and affectation. "Hypocritical affectation" connotes for Fielding abuse of rational morality in its
"violent repugnancy of nature" and is therefore commensurate
with some varieties of dullness. One hears an echo of Horner's
cynical comment that affectation is nature's "greatest monster."[14]
    On the other hand, that "affectation which arises from vanity"
accommodates a tolerance unacceptable to the hypocrisy described by La Rochefoucauld as "a sort of homage which vice
pays to virtue."[15] Vanity is blameworthy, but it relates only to the
"inferior," hence polite, manners of "studied civility." Generally

13. *English Poets,* 3:241; [Harrison's Continuation] *The Tatler* 20 [1710], in
Swift's *Prose Works,* 2:184–87. Cf. Swift, "On Good-Manners and Good-
Breeding," *Prose Works,* 4:214, and "A Project for the Advancement of Religion
and the Reformation of Manners," *Prose Works,* 2:45.
14. According to his own testimony in the *Life* (2:174), Johnson never read
*Joseph Andrews* (1742). That does not, however, preclude the possibility of his
having read the preface. For early remarks by Fielding on affectation, see the
*Champion,* 15 April 1740. See also William Wycherley, *The Country Wife* (1675),
I.i; Congreve, "Concerning Humour in Comedy," *Critical Essays of the Seventeenth
Century,* ed. Spingarn, 3:249.
15. La Rochefoucauld, "Moral Reflections," No. CCXIX. An apparent borrowing from "Protagoras" (323c). See A. E. Taylor, *Plato: The Man and his Work*
(London: Methuen, 1955), p. 243. As expanded by one of John Le Carré's
characters, hypocrisy is "the nearest we ever get to virtue. It's a statement of what
we ought to be. Like religion, like art, like the law, like marriage." *A Small Town
in Germany* (London: Heinemann, 1968), p. 286.

a silly harmlessness pervades our pretending to be something better than we really are, if that pretense borrows from what is innately worthwhile. In short, vanity does "not imply an absolute negation of those qualities which are affected." The telling differentiation proposed by Fielding is between *ostentation* and *deceit*. As an instance, "the affectation of liberality in a vain man differs visibly from the same affectation in the avaricious; for though the vain man is not what he would appear, or hath not the virtue he affects, to the degree he would be thought to have it; yet it sits less awkwardly on him than on the avaricious man, who is the very reverse of what he would *seem* to be." Even misfortune, in Fielding's sense of the paradoxical, can be ridiculed as a form of vanity. To illustrate his point, he creates the analogy of a poor householder who displays elegant but empty dishes, or ornaments the cold grate with flowers when coals are wanting. Thus attempting to impress his neighbors, he substitutes appearance for truth, a denaturalizing act that reduces the manners of social exchange to egotistic pretense. When form takes precedence over an instinctive desire for order and necessity as here, the individual most harmed is the pretender: having deceived society *and* himself, he no longer merits the esteem of his fellows and he has forfeited the right of personal dignity.

As cultures become sophisticated, and as individuals compete increasingly for public recognition, the prospects for success through genuine talent or skill diminish. Concomitantly the temptation to win favor through dissembling grows intense and affectation serves as a major satiric interest. Erasmus, who refused to falsify reality, also repudiated the falsification of manners by resorting to a familiar yet apt theater analogy: "Now what else is the whole life of mortals but a sort of comedy, in which the various actors, disguised by various costumes and masks, walk on and play each one his part, until the manager waves them off the stage? ... Thus all things are presented by shadows; yet this play is put on in no other way." Given this transient uncertainty, he senses the danger of passing off disguise and playacting for the genuine things; and intimations of his warning against the life of illusion are heard frequently thereafter.[16]

When the dictates of fools are suffered, nature is reduced to antic dress. The rise of fools coincides with "the dethronement of Logos," as a result of which all "moral cognition and . . . effort" grow enfeebled.[17] A phenomenon of man's maze-enclosed pursuits, duncely movement knows neither time nor place; and it answers to a variety of names. For the Greeks, it was μωρία; for the Romans, *ostentatio* and *stultitia*; for Erasmus and his contemporaries, *dissembling folly;* for the English, *dullness* and *affectation.* But no matter what the name, we confront in each the same evidence of inner depletion. As a fictional exercise, dullness and affectation prove how entertaining they can be. But beneath their ironic masks in myth, parody, or broad comedy, they cry out for and enforce thought. The reader experiences a certain righteousness—perhaps unvoiced relief also—in the knowledge that offenders other than himself demonstrate the ills of dullness and affectation. The fops and fools of satire, however exaggerated, offer convenient sacrifices upon whom to heap a vicarious burden of guilt or inadequacy. As Timon of Athens reflects about the Poet: "Wilt thou whip thine own faults in other men?" (V. i).

The satirist, recognizing that men err more readily than they reform, contends with a troublesome problem. From one perspective, he thinks that satire can deter when human foibles appear so shameful that we turn away from them in disgust. But antithetically he also assumes that men are self-deluded, apathy and slothful imitation determining the patterns of their lives. It is to such dualism that Sir Carr Scroope responds in a fusion of Horatian metaphor and explicit statement:

> For as a passing bell frights from his meat
> The greedy sick man that too much would eat,
> So when a vice ridiculous is made,
> Our neighbor's shame keeps us from growing bad.

16. *The Praise of Folly,* p. 37.
17. Price, *To the Palace of Wisdom,* pp. 226-27.

> But wholesome remedies few palates please:
> Men rather love what flatters their disease.[18]

Here an ambivalent poet looks off wistfully in two directions. Turning one way, he knows that manners, vain and aimless, should be rectified. Turning the other, he must take account of man's unreliability. Pathetically vulnerable and suggestible, the human creature gives himself over to the fads of the day, and he would rather press himself into the crowd than stand apart as an individual.

Still the satirist must write, he has always insisted, whether because his indignation has no other outlet or because the missionary spirit cannot be suppressed. Ideally, he would argue, his vision of moral and rational energy negated stimulates rebellion against dullness and affectation; and it allows the reader to protest any implication that he too could be infected. As the dunces are stripped of pity, he—subconsciously at least—engages in a countermovement toward increased self-esteem. Thus the satiric play of dullness and affectation boosts his ego while it rips away the tattered worth of its victims. Like waste recycled, dullness and affectation have their uses. Satirically represented, they are self-alienating because they war against imagination and knowledge and design. Yet, even as they invite antipathy, they generate an opposing wish to revive values that they threaten to stifle. Despite themselves, the Smithfield Muses reach up to join a more eminent company.

## II

The egocentric impulse is ordinarily too common for serious condemnation, and yet it may be carried to culpable extremes. Then it becomes an irritant, the unwanted intrusion of another's excesses into our own awareness or a cruel reminder of social

---

18. "In Defense of Satire" [1677], ll. 10–15, *POAS*, 1:365. For a discredited attribution, see "A Satyr upon the Follies of the Man of the Age," *The Miscellaneous Works of his Grace George, late Duke of Buckingham* (1705, 1707), 1:47–48. Cf. Horace, Sat. I. iv. 125–29: "Avidos vicinum funus ut aegros / exanimat mortisque metu sibi parcere cogit, / sic teneros animos aliena opprobria saepe / absterrent vitiis."

injustice.[19] Nowhere, perhaps, is the intrusiveness more flagrant than in the outward symbols of unproductive sumptuousness in which only the privileged few may indulge. The rich man's devotion to luxury, manifested in ostentatious display, becomes an especially apt subject for satire, especially when lacking taste and imagination of his own, he must "purchase what he ne'er can taste." As he develops the theme of prodigality in the *Epistle to Burlington* (1731), Pope attacks those claims to art and learning that, contrary to any aesthetic or intellectual disposition, derive from acquisitiveness and a desire to impress others with bought culture:

> Not for himself he sees, or hears, or eats;
> Artists must choose his pictures, music, meats.
>
> [5-6]

The climax of Pope's attitude toward "the false taste of magnificence" is Timon's country villa, a grotesque collocation of what must surely be the worst in architectural design: "His pond an ocean, his parterre a down" (106). Substituting vastness and ornamentation for proportion and harmony, Timon has authorized vulgar abundance.[20] Instead of the Palladian correctness that Burlington had conceived for his townhouse in Piccadilly, Timon (95-126) could brag of innovative challenges. But instead of "pleasing intricacies" that should have broken the regularity of his garden, he introduced the boring symmetry of lines stretched out to infinity: "Grove nods at grove, each alley has a brother." In still another display of expensive bad taste—"Trees cut to statues, statues thick as trees"—he offended "the suffering

---

19. John Sekora, *Luxury: The Concept in Western Thought, Eden to Smollett* (Baltimore and London: Johns Hopkins Press, 1977); see also Louis A. Landa, "London Observed: The Progress of a Simile," *PQ* 54 (Winter 1975): 275–88. Cf. Plato, *The Republic*, bk. 3: "Luxury and avarice" turn men into "wolves and tyrants."
20. *Twickenham Pope*, $3^2$:123–51; cf. Welsted, *Of Dulness and Scandal;* [James Bramston,] *The Man of Taste. Occasion'd by an Epistle of Mr. Pope's on that Subject. By the Author of the Art of Politicks* (1733); *The Woman of Taste. Occasioned by a Late Poem, Entitled, The Man of Taste* (1733). For the controversial identification of Timon, see $3^2$:142n., 164–68; Mack, *The Garden and the City*, pp. 122n., 272–78.

eye," demeaning nature with his topiary zeal and distorting art with his silly juxtapositions:

> There gladiators fight, or die, in flow'rs;
> Un-water'd see the drooping sea-horse mourn,
> And swallows roost in Nilus' dusty urn.
>
> [124–26]

The character of luxury to which Pope here attends is exhibitionism out of keeping with natural or graceful decorum. Although an indiscriminate Timon remains unawakened, the villa is his most conspicuous offering to bad taste; yet it houses and complements many others. His library, for instance, goes beyond pedantry: its valuable books have been chosen by someone else; their owner will never talk about their substance because he cannot read them. The older the book, the better, and binding counts for more than contents. This vainglory extends to the lavish chapel where "silver bell . . . summons you to all the pride of pray'r." There, to the accompaniment of music and in a setting of near sensuous paintings, "the soul [may] dance upon a jig to heav'n." Religion so dispensed, according to the satirist, will never worry polite ears with mention of hell. Still more sybaritic is the dining hall whose appointments and service Pope represents as projections of the just ended "religious" ceremony:

> Is this a dinner? this a genial room?
> No, 'tis a temple, and a hecatomb.
> A solemn sacrifice, perform'd in state,
> You drink by measure, and to minutes eat.
>
> [155–58]

Luxury mockingly envisaged by Pope is a constant sacrifice to self-indulgence.

He had laughed at the rituals of social behavior in *The Rape of the Lock,* but in the *Epistle to Burlington* he is far more the didact. Although he ridicules the showiness of such as Virro, Visto, and Timon, his judgment is explicit, culminating in the angry line "I curse such lavish cost, and little skill" (167). At this point, however, a curious transition occurs, diverting the satiric and hortatory rebuke to a placid rationale for Timon's position:

> Yet hence the poor are cloth'd, the hungry fed;
> Health to himself, and to his infants bread

The lab'rer bears: what his hard heart denies,
His charitable vanity supplies.

[169-72]

Lest there be any doubt about his gray optimism, Pope annotates the first line (169) with the contention that those who *must* suffer suffer less because "a bad taste employs more hands and diffuses expense more than a good one." Reminiscent of Mandevillean ethics, Pope's system argues that in a well-ordered society benefits flow to the poor even from profligacy. That hierarchical ideology, first considered, is disturbingly shallow and has been attacked for facile, inconsistent morality. Pope understands that Timon's opulence, however blameworthy, should not monopolize attention. Looking for a philosophical balance, he responds to "the claims of a wider community"—a norm of British life that includes the very poor as well as the very rich.[21]

Thus interpreted, the poem is not exclusively satiric. Memorably, even spectacularly, Pope does force our revulsion; he does put the wealthy great man into an inviting posture for the kicks of an indignant audience. In addition, he strives for a more comprehensive, humane outlook than would be possible if we were not allowed to glance away from Timon to the hungry laborers and their kin. An integral part of the social scheme, the needy become the beneficiaries of Timon's vulgarity. His contribution, to be sure, is fractional and involuntary. The ironically "charitable vanity" of an uncharitable man is chillingly empty of social sympathy. No matter how ungenerous the giving, however, the useful consequence should not be dismissed. Pope at the same time wishes to reveal that wealth in other hands may be genuinely beneficial and therefore a fulfillment of moral necessity. Thus he can look to another, happier age (173) of rationally motivated pomp, as in the tranquil "country house ideal" celebrated by Jonson, Carew, Herrick, and Marvell. This is the posi-

21. *The Fable of the Bees*, p. A3ᵛ (pref.). Cf. John Dennis, *Vice and Luxury Publick Mischiefs: or, Remarks on a Book Intituled, The Fable of the Bees* (1724). See also Howard Erskine-Hill, "The Country House Ideal," *The Social Milieu of Alexander Pope: Lives, Examples, and the Poetic Response* (New Haven and London: Yale University Press, 1975), pp. 294-304; Bateson, *Twickenham Pope*, 3²:82n., 148n.

tive tradition of material elegance directed by reason and social purpose:

> 'Tis use alone that sanctifies expense,
> And splendor borrows all her rays from sense.
>
> [179–80]

The satire of Timon represents the breach of that ideal in the most conspicuous possible way. But his grossness contrasts with the admirable "use . . . that sanctifies expense" of Burlington and Bathurst. The satire dominating the first 170 lines gives way to praise for those who have steadfastly observed the moral and social—that is, the human—connotations of great wealth well disbursed. And in the final 30 lines Pope carries these beyond even the wise control of his friends. Invoking the genius of Jones and Palladio, he appeals to national pride for the construction of "new wonders" (and, judiciously, for repair of the old), such as churches and bridges. He calls out for public spending that will bring "honors, peace to happy Britain . . . These are imperial works, and worthy kings."

Pope's paean to private and public munificence has an aesthetic motive: to revitalize the "falling arts" and restore concern for productive good taste. That is the affirmative focus of his *Epistle to Burlington*. And so too is the fringe benefit derived from "charitable vanity." We have also seen the results of the negative impulse to castigate wanton extravagance like Timon's. Further, Pope had a calculated view of reckless luxury and its side effects informed by an age teeming in projectors and speculators whose get-rich-quick schemes collapsed with the bursting of the South Sea Bubble (1720). The *Epistle to Bathurst* (1733) apostrophizes ironically but "unambiguously . . . the world of City finance":

> Blest paper-credit! last and best supply!
> That lends Corruption lighter wings to fly!
> Gold imp'd by thee, can compass hardest things,
> Can pocket States, can fetch or carry Kings.
>
> [69–72][22]

---

22. Erskine-Hill, p. 260. The theological implications have been analyzed by Earl R. Wasserman, *Pope's Epistle to Bathurst: A Critical Reading, with An Edition of the Manuscripts* (Baltimore: Johns Hopkins Press, 1960).

Only a few years after publication of the complementary poems on the use of riches, Erasmus Jones in a pamphlet pursued the dangerous assumptions of "paper-credit." Indignantly, he equated profligate spending with everything self-serving, debauched, and oblivious to genuine need. It is "the mode," he complained, "to live high, to spend more than we get, to neglect trade, contemn care and concern, and go on without consideration; and in consequence it is the mode to go on to extremity, to break, become bankrupts and beggars."[23] This too was the disenchantment still being voiced some thirty-five years later when Goldsmith wrote in *The Deserted Village*, "Thus fares the land by luxury betrayed" (295).

In another country and in the time of Domitian Juvenal had roared against wanton opulence. *Luxuria* in his *Satire VI* has utterly pejorative associations of rankness, indecency, and riotous excess. The accusation beginning "Nunc patimur longae pacis male" (292–305) is an outcry against the delusions spawned in the wake of war. The peace that follows military triumph creates a sense of invincibility among the elect; and it also induces the lethargy of soft living. Profligacy, Juvenal intimates, asserts a maniacal ego that eradicates any vestige of charity. The wastrel is therefore able to treat poverty as a liability of the past, while he centers the comfortable realities, however he chooses to locate them, within his own experiences. The Roman poet concluded that the disaster of his times was one of national conceit smothered in luxury; and it was a conceit vested in the powerful few who had learned to banish altruism and compassion from their hearts and minds. Luxury so self-absorbed finally brings about the disintegration of reason, will, and morality. "Saevior armis luxuria incubuit victumque ulciscitur orbem" ("Luxury,

---

23. *Luxury, Pride, and Vanity, the Bane of the British Nation* [1735], p. 11. For an imitation of Swift dealing with city finance, speculations, projects, and the like see *A Voyage to Cacklogallinia: with a Description of the Religion, Policy, Customs and Manners of that Country* [1727], ed. Marjorie Nicolson (New York: Facsimile Text Society, Columbia University Press, 1940). A recent reprint (New York and London: Garland, 1972) appears with a brief introduction by Malcolm J. Bosse. The pseudonymous author of *Cacklogallinia*, "Captain Samuel Brunt," hints at the major entrepreneur of the South Sea Company, Sir John Blunt.

more deadly than any foe, has laid her hand upon us, and avenges a conquered world").

The same view of a "long peace" with its attendant "evils" was paraphrased by Dryden for his own age as prophecy come true:

> But wanton now, and lolling at our ease,
> We suffer all th' invet'rate ills of peace;
> And wasteful riot, whose destructive charms
> Revenge the vanquish'd world, of our victorious arms.
> No crime, no lustful postures are unknown;
> Since poverty, our guardian-god, is gone:
> Pride, laziness, and all luxurious arts,
> Pour like a deluge in, from foreign parts:
> Since gold obscene, and silver found the way,
> Strange fashions with strange bullion to convey,
> And our plain simple manners to betray.
>
> $[405\text{-}15]^{24}$

If an interlude between wars can be construed as peace, then, said Dryden, peace had come to England. What he saw was a paradoxically destructive end of fighting that encouraged the worst conditions of pride, a "deluge" of self-glorification. True to the spirit of Juvenal, he intensified his focus so that at war's end the nation dissolves into bacchanalian irresponsibility. As though staring through the aperture of an open-ended box, he confined within his field of mental vision an assemblage of moral atrocities. Less vivid and specific than the images of Juvenal, Dryden's are for the most part cast as epithets recalling sermons meant to awaken shame, fear, remorse, and abhorrence. Rationalizing an end of poverty, Dryden's profligates wallow in alternatives of pleasure and crime. The "gold obscene, and silver," along with the importation of French "fashions," have overwhelmed these traditionally good-natured Englishmen, turning them into monsters of lust and indolence. The manly will to endure wartime adversity has surrendered to the deceit and sensuous greed of contemporary dullness. In the eyes of the satirist, war is less deadly than luxury.

24. Loeb *Juvenal*, pp. 106–7; *The Satires of Juvenal*, trans. Rolfe Humphries (Bloomington and London: Indiana University Press, 1958), p. 74; Dryden, translation of *The Satires of Juvenal and Persius*, p. 105.

Although English writers inveighed against luxury at home, they blamed much of it on the influence of Continental decadence. They were mouthing a complaint familiar even when Donne in his first satire (ca. 1593) sneered at the courtier's praise of one who

> doth seem to be
> Perfect French, and Italian; I replied,
> So is the pox.
>
> [102-4]

Some of this disdain, implying scorn for mere appearance, can be heard in one of Polonius's many precepts to Laertes:

> For the apparel oft proclaims the man,
> And they in France of the best rank and station
> Are the most select and generous, chief in that.
>
> [*Hamlet*, I. iii. 71-73]

And Ben Jonson likewise noted the spread of French corruption with his epigram "On English Monsieur." After the Restoration, Francophobia not only continued to run high but was further exacerbated by King William's War and the War of the Spanish Succession. Incessant and rotelike, moving in step with Anglo-French military confrontations, Francophobia scarred the whole of the eighteenth century and the first few years of the Regency. Philosophically and culturally, French manners were once seen as the symptom of tyrannical monarchy. The prejudice outlasted kings, however, and simply rerooted itself in hatred of the permissive new society of revolutionary France. In 1791, for instance, Edmund Burke isolated what he called French degeneracy and attributed it to egalitarianism, whether it was found in political reigns of terror or in banal woodland retreats. Practitioners of trifling, unproductive occupations, encouraged by the edicts of a mindless legislative body, had achieved parity with the best of French society. What can be expected when "the females of the first families in France may become an easy prey to dancing-masters, fiddlers, pattern-drawers, friseurs, and valets-de-chambre." Under the influence of those who screamed "A la lanterne" and an earlier Rousseauan sentimentality, Burke lamented, the French were spending themselves in an orgy of inconsequential yet vicious leveling.[25] Long before the revolution, Gallic elegance inspired satirists in their tight little island to strike maliciously, representing the virile English in a symbolic if uneven passage at arms with effete adversaries. Ridicule and name-calling stereotyped a nation of syphilitics and effeminate opera singers. Should England suffer a moral and social collapse, its causes were certain to be located in a European setting. "I could heartily wish," said Mr. Spectator (No. 45), "that there were an Act of Parliament for prohibiting the importation of French fopperies." Too often, chauvinistic exuberance was funneled into invective and clichés. Witness the anonymous versifier of *A Satyr against the French* (1690), who in an "Epistle Dedicatory" professed "only to give a right idea of the French humor. What is generous and noble in them, I honor; but am something mortified, to see quality dote upon a dressing, cringing, complimenting monsieur; yet I am so charitable as to believe some esteem them as people do Merry Andrews, because they excite laughter; or, by a rule of contraries, love them as ladies do shock-dogs, for their ugliness."

On some occasions imaginative statement replaced scurrility. Swift, as an instance, indulged in French-baiting but made it metaphorically fresh: "I was asked at Court, what I thought of the French Ambassador and his train; who were all embroidery and lace; full of bows, cringes, and gestures? I said, it was Solomon's importation; gold and apes."[26] Swift orders his ironical whimsy in the juxtaposition of bedecked, posturing diplomats and the biblical sage. Broadly speaking, Solomon did not import gold and apes; these were tributes brought to him in symbolic acknowledgment that the wisest king on earth should also be the wealthiest. The French ambassador and his court, we may infer,

25. "A Letter to a Member of the National Assembly," 4:31; cf. 4:28. See also the once popular play by James Howard, *The English Monsieur* [ca. 1663], intro. by Robert D. Hume (Los Angeles: Augustan Reprint Society, 1977).
26. "Thoughts on Various Subjects," *Prose Works*, 4:247. From 1 Kings 10:22: "For the king had at sea a navy of Thärshish with the navy of Hiram: once in three years came the navy of Thärshish, bringing gold, and silver, ivory, and apes, and peacocks."

obtained splendors as inappropriate and artificial as their manners. In the midst of an apathetic English culture, their native decadence became strangely aggressive. They could buy finery and exotic household pets at will, but they did not earn them—as did Solomon—with wisdom. For the eighteenth century, further, the ape was a despicable, filthy beast with an unreasoning ability to imitate the movements of men. Consequently the Swiftian joke would have been appreciated by his countrymen, for whom simian and French gesticulations, motiveless and frenzied, were all one.

Fielding's essays and fiction also broadcast such bias. Everyone is familiar with the prefatory remarks of *Tom Jones* in which the author scores French (and Italian) affectation and vice. Nearly ten years earlier in the *Champion* (29 January 1740), he had set forth the qualifications of a liar, whose tutelage would be the responsibility of a French schoolmaster. Comparably tainted by trifling, immoral Gallic manners, the "French-English Bellarmine" of *Joseph Andrews* made seductive use of "gaiety and gallantry" (II, 4). And significantly named with a Renaissance term of contempt, the birdlike Beau Didapper was a petit gentleman "not entirely ignorant: for he could talk a little French, and sing two or three Italian songs" (IV, 9).[27] Satire like this thrives more on insinuating laughter than on reformist indignation. Certainly, Garrick in his one-act play *Lilliput* (1757) is, like Fielding, intent on exploiting the possibilities of the ridiculous. Through parody he mocks pettiness and degeneracy within a predictable French context. The Swiftian analogue gives Garrick's fun added affectiveness. Bolgolam, thus, to Flimnap: "Time was when we had as little vice here in Lilliput as any where; but since we imported politeness and fashions from Blefuscu, we have thought of nothing but being fine gentlemen; and a fine gentleman, in my dictionary, stands for nothing but impertinence

27. As an effeminate dandy, Francophile, and Walpole henchman, Lord Hervey made a good satiric study for Didapper. See Martin C. Battestin, ed., *Joseph Andrews* (Middletown, Conn.: Wesleyan University Press, 1967), pp. xxiii–xxiv, 112*n.*–13*n.*, 312 and 313*n.*; "Lord Hervey's Role in *Joseph Andrews*," *PQ* 42 (Apr. 1963): 226–41.

and affectation, without any one virtue, sincerity, or real civility" (p. 3).

Writing privately to Thomas Birch, Philip Yorke complained: "French men can never be quiet, & under all that outward gaiety & frankness, they conceal the fiercest rancour & most refined Malice." Yorke's opinion, as rancorous as that of any Frenchman under his attack, synthesizes the national *alienaphobia*. If some satirists like Fielding and Garrick chuckled wryly, others thought Continental manners too reprehensible for outright laughter. Notably, Johnson created in *London* the seamy image of a conduit through which flowed the leavings of a degraded French culture:

> Their air, their dress, their politics import;
> Obsequious, artful, voluble and gay,
> On Britain's fond credulity they prey.
> No gainful trade their industry can 'scape,
> They sing, they dance, clean shoes, or cure a clap;
> All sciences a fasting Monsieur knows,
> And bid him go to hell, to hell he goes.

> [110-16]

Although Johnson introduced some polished wit into these lines, their tenor is polemic. The presentation, sardonic rather than amiable, invites us to take painful stock of ourselves. That we grin at all is a tribute to his ironic isolation of human absurdities. *London*, if we relate it to Coleridge's generalization, predicates "serious satire" placing a moral check on "free and generous laughter."[28]

The "supple Gaul" emerges as a stock villain of satire and the Englishman as a stock dupe, closer to each other in temper and appetite than the satirist openly lets on. If French tastes appear brazenly profligate, those of the English are hardly less so. Political expedience may justify the sinister attribution of faults to the French; yet no one can argue seriously that the English enjoyed such naiveté as to eat the apple ignorant of consequences. From a satiric point of view, they too are culpable: even if we grant (dubious proposition) that the French had a more refined capac-

---

28. Yorke in a letter to Birch, 8 July 1744 (B.M. Add. MS 35,396, f. 219); *Coleridge's Miscellaneous Criticism*, pp. 118, 441-42.

ity for inventing and savoring perversity, their English imitators did not lag far behind in a desire to sample forbidden pleasures.

## III

Satiric carping about luxury and Gallic manners, although hyperbolic in its persistence, is faithful to a consensus of British morality. Eighteenth-century satire registers a widening discontent with the collapse of native culture and, conversely, a search for its own kind of moral vagility. The satirists were perhaps unduly dramatic in their depictions of Continental influence, but apparently they were responding to a popular clamor for British identity, whether in politics, in trade, or in social conduct. Through a large part of the century, extravagance and Gallicism were interpreted as parallel ills, the residue of morally depleted drones. Implicit in this criticism is the unacceptability of useless or lax effort to a society more or less prodded by an ambitious, ascendant middle class.

That class, in its own quest for reassuring solidity, joined the traditionalists who deplored the abandonment of any value that promoted integration, order, continuity. Inevitably, "new men" and landed gentry—in strange harmony—turned to the family unit as the epitome of durability, and to their alarm they saw a shift in the making, an incipient rebellion against the premises of sexual rank. Even as they took the social scheme to be built upon a foundation of hierarchy and benevolent subordination, so they expected the family to perpetuate structured order. But the usually submissive wife-mother appeared to be pressing for equality with the authoritarian husband-father. And marriage itself, hitherto formally inviolable, seemed to be on tottery ground. That at least was the impression fostered by satirists who liked to mirror a licentious age in which women kicked over the traces, defying the ancient rules of obedience. Garrick in *Lilliput* mocked a tentatively emergent feminism through Lady Flimnap confessing to Gulliver: "Though I have some children, I have not seen one of them these six months; and though I am married to one of the greatest men in the kingdom, and, as they say, one of the handsomest, yet I don't imagine that I shall ever throw myself into a fit of sickness, by too severe attention to him or his family" (p. 23). Any spectator would have readily understood (apart from the obvious political innuendo) that an entire social order was on trial by ridicule for breaking the sexual code and denying the sanctity of the family.

Lady Flimnap's rebellion against the role expected of women in marriage, though exaggerated, challenges convention; it also betokens the stirrings of a new sexual liberation to which the male was yet reluctant to capitulate and which he usually delineated as a petty contest of indignation moderated by polite wordplay. The breakdown of marriage and familial obligations could therefore be satirized in terms of conflicts whose weapons were inane chitchat and gaudy plumage. As satirist and socioliterary historian, Fielding took note of inflated "paper wars which hath lately broken out between the two sexes." Ironically detached in the *Champion* (1 January 1740), he sensed the threat of "an entire dissolution of the world."

None of this would have been news to the myriad pamphleteers who had long before discovered an insatiable market for sexist themes.[29] And then there was Pope, whose *Rape of the Lock* had established him forever as the historian of eighteenth-century wars of the sexes. By 1738, however, he deemed gender paradoxically irrelevant. His "tinsel insects"—masculine, feminine, and neuter—are everywhere committed to "folly, vice, and insolence." The corrupt political exercises of the times provided an appropriately dissolute environment for these trifling creatures—a court

> That counts your beauties only by your stains,
> Spin all your cobwebs o'er the eye of day!
>
> [221–22]

In such a context there is nothing to distinguish the manners of men from those of women. This is the dark vision of a middle-

29. Such various poems, as: Robert Gould, *Love Given Over: or, A Satyr Against the Pride, Lust, and Inconstancy, &c. of Woman, with Sylvia's Revenge, or, A Satyr Against Woman* (1710; 1st pub. 1682); Richard Ames, *The Folly of Love. A New Satyr Against Woman. Together with the Bachelors Lettany, by the Same Hand* (1701; 1st pub. 1691: on Ames and Gould, Foxon, *Catalogue*, 1:18, 312); Defoe, *Good Advice to the Ladies: Shewing, That as the World Goes, and is Like to Go, the Best Way for Them is to Keep Unmarried* (1702).

aged poet alienated by the social as well as the political trumpery of both sexes. But female conduct, he had argued only three years before (in *Epistle II*, which he addressed "To a Lady"), seems even more inconsistent and reprehensible than the masculine. Poetic adroitness and satiric bite turn what could easily be malice into a generalized essay against women. Sappho in "her dirty smock" shares unflattering prominence with Narcissa ("A fool to pleasure, yet a slave to fame"), the languishing Papillia, the notoriously willful Atossa, and even Queen Caroline:

> In men, we various ruling passions find,
> In women, two almost divide the kind;
> Those, only fix'd, they first or last obey,
> The love of pleasure, and the love of sway.
>
> [207-10][30]

As a result of their militancy, Pope hints, these female warriors could no longer complain about unchivalric men. Congreve had made the identical point in the dedication to Charles Montagu (later Earl of Halifax), that *The Double Dealer* (1694) had been criticized for false reasons, none more unjust than that he had misrepresented the social role of women. By "explaining" that he did not wish to offend, Congreve reiterated his argument and thereby strengthened it. Of the charge that he had portrayed "some women vicious and affected," he retorted: "How can I help it? It is the business of a comic poet to paint the vices and follies of human kind; and there are but two sexes that I know, *viz.* men and women, which have a title to humanity: and if I leave one half of them out, the work will be imperfect. I should be very glad of an opportunity to make my compliment to those ladies who are offended: but they can no more expect it in a comedy, than to be tickled by a surgeon, when he's letting 'em blood."[31] A relentless dramatist narrows the focus of his mockery. He describes *The Double Dealer* as a comedy, but his terms are indistinguishable from those associated with satire;

---

30. "Epilogue to the Satires, Dialogue II," *Twickenham Pope*, 4:325, and 3²: 44-71.
31. The surgical metaphor, we have seen, was a satiric commonplace. For example, Defoe, *The Present State of the Parties in Great Britain*, pp. A2-A3; Dryden, "To the Reader," *Absalom and Achitophel*.

and manners are on his mind as much as entertainment. His idiom, though one of ironic amusement, condemns as keenly as the harsher language of Juvenal in the sixth satire. The spectacle of life, especially that of women, gorgeous when seen from afar, becomes at Congreve's close range a dissolute world in rags and tatters.

As we have said, Pope saw a similar world in the closing years of his life. But neither the poet nor the social observer could be pinned down by consistency. His attitude toward women ran the gamut of the feeling mind: from appreciation to scorn, from gentle twitting to harsh rebuke. When as a buoyant young man he peered at fashionable peccadilloes, he could enjoy and certainly forgive their inanity. *The Rape of the Lock* set a standard for mock chivalry: "What mighty contests rise from trivial things."[32] Consistent with this "heroi-comical" reductivism, Pope claimed to have written "only to divert a few young ladies, who have good sense and good humor enough to laugh not only at their sex's unguarded follies, but at their own." From "a few young ladies," the poem's audience stretched out to nations and generations. And what Pope modestly called "trivial things" became the substance of philosophical truth. Perhaps, Johnson asserted, the poet had not "made the world much better than he found it," but he deserved public commendation for the insights of *The Rape of the Lock:* "The freaks, and humors, and spleen, and vanity of women, as they embroil families in discord and fill houses with disquiet . . . obstruct the happiness of life." What may indeed have begun as a *jeu d'esprit* outgrew itself. From a metaphoric cluster of feminine vanities it expanded into a set of exempla "that the misery of man proceeds not from any single crush of overwhelming evil, but from small vexations continually repeated."[33]

Few poems could be less overtly didactic than *The Rape of the Lock;* still it contains a thematic profundity that justifies Johnson's solemn judgment and that Pope himself quietly enun-

32. Cf. [Lady Mary Wortley Montagu and John Gay?] *Court Poems. Viz; 1. The Basset-Table. An Eclogue. 2. The Drawing-Room. 3. The Toilet* [26 Mar. 1716]; Robert Halsband, "Pope, Lady Mary, and the 'Court Poems' (1716)," *PMLA* 68 (Mar. 1953): 237–50; Foxon, *Catalogue,* 1:476.

33. *Twickenham Pope,* 2:140–206; *English Poets,* 3:234.

ciated in the final verses. Vanity, he could not resist saying, is as transient as mortality:

> For, after all the murders of your eye,
> When, after millions slain, your self shall die;
> When those fair suns shall set, as set they must,
> And all those tresses shall be laid in dust;
> This lock, the Muse shall consecrate to fame,
> And mid'st the stars inscribe Belinda's name!

[V. 145-50]

How sad to think that Belinda grown old could look back to a youth synthesized only by trifles. Warning is probably too strong a term for Pope's requiem, but the closing lines remind us that vanity cannot serve for a lifetime. Our follies may be tolerated only as exordiums—prefatory errors—from which, moving through dignified adulthood toward age, we should liberate ourselves. Pope preserves Belinda like a figure etched in crystal or fixed for eternity in the design of a Grecian urn. Here in the poem she remains everlastingly young, never—seemingly—to pass beyond the single girlish moment of outrage and petulant indignation. That is the central irony of the poem, for between the rising sun of Canto I and the impending darkness of Canto V Pope asserts his concern with a natural movement from youth to age, from life to death.

But does Belinda, to whom he speaks directly at the close, have the will or understanding to profit from his words? For this and all other Belindas instinct is a mightier influence than reason, and vanity remains. Once released from the ageless crystal prison of the poem, the "real" Belinda will again travel a trail of self-love and folly. Inevitably she must, like the principal of Allen Tate's "The Last Days of Alice," experience "decline upon her lost and twilight age." The same truth—sad and cruel—was satirized by the Earl of Dorset, whose verses "On the Countess of Dorchester" (1680) anticipate our Belinda grown old:

> Tell me, Dorinda, why so gay,
> Why such embroidery, fringe, and lace?
> Can any dresses find a way,
> To stop th' approaches of decay,
> And mind a ruin's face?
> Wilt thou still sparkle in the box,

Still ogle in the ring?
Canst thou forget thy age and pox?
Can all that shines on shells and rocks
Make thee a fine young thing?[34]

In Congreve's *The Way of the World,* a vain and imperious Lady Wishfort understands this cosmetic truth so well that she can satirize herself. To Foible, thus, who unkindly discerns "cracks . . . in the white varnish," her mistress stridently replies: "Let me see the glass—cracks, say'st thou? Why I am arrantly flay'd—I look like an old peeled wall" (III. i. 145–48). The outward decay of the mirror image is her painful reality; it is her perception of a disintegrated self reflecting the vanities of the fragmented society that binds her to its unnatural forms. Lady Wishfort may temporarily cover the ravages of aging ugliness, but art, she knows, cannot long repair it; and she cannot— indeed, will not—cancel the truth of nature as she now sees it.

Almost as explicitly as Congreve, Sir Fleetwood Shepherd ridiculed the "Old Affected Court Lady," who, when young, "was scarce thought more fair." Belinda had the advantage of beauty, but she was allowed to conceal her artifice no more than Lady Wishfort, or than Shepherd's "Fair Queen of Fopland":

Nature did ne'er more equally divide,
A female heart 'twixt piety and pride.
Her watchful maids prevent the peep of day,
And all in order on her toilet lay
Pray'r-books and patch-box, sermon-notes and paint,
At once t'improve the sinner and the saint.[35]

34. If, as Johnson maintained (*English Poets,* 1:308), Pope imitated "Dorinda," neither his vision nor his mood could embrace the cruelty of Dorset's closing lines: "So have I seen in larder dark / Of veal a lucid loin; / Replete with many a brilliant spark, / As wise philosophers remark, / At once both stink and shine." Fielding justified Dorset's reputation for being "the best good man with the worst natured Muse" on the grounds of satiric compulsion. *Champion,* 27 March 1740.

35. The "Old Affected Court Lady," attributed to Shepherd (also Sheppard, Shepheard), appeared in *A New Miscellany of Original Poems on Several Occasions* (1701), and again in Buckingham's *Miscellaneous Works,* 1:82–83. But for an attribution to Charles Montagu, Earl of Halifax, see Tillotson, *Twickenham Pope,* 2:155n. Cf. [Francis Chute] *The Petticoat; an Heroi-Comical Poem* (1716) [Foxon, *Catalogue,* 1:123]; [John Shirley] *The Triumph of Wit: or, Ingenuity Display'd in its Perfection; being the Newest and most Useful Academy,* 8th ed. (1724); *Whipping Tom: or, a Rod for a Proud Lady, Bundled up in Four Feeling Discourses, both Serious and Merry. In Order to Touch the Fair Sex to the Quick,* 4th ed. (1722).

Implements of church and salon come together indiscriminately, their "order" a jumble whose catalogue emphasizes the sinner rather than the saint. Pope's triumph of transience in *The Rape of the Lock* probably borrows from the earlier poem. Its derivation, however, becomes less important than its devastating confirmation of moral untidiness. Here, in symbolic disarray, are the significant and the trivial, the pious and the mundane, all thrown together with frugal indifference like the contents of a reticule that may one day be used.

The ridicule heaped upon female frippery and vanity hardly surprises in the male-dominated society of the eighteenth century. But under satiric scrutiny, such domination took on an unexpected and plastic dimension. Congreve had conceded that perhaps

passions are too powerful in that [female] sex to let humor have its course; or may be by reason of their natural coldness, humor cannot exert it self to that extravagant degree which it often does in the male sex. For if ever any thing does appear comical or ridiculous in a woman, I think it is little more than an acquired folly or an affectation. We may call them the weaker sex, but I think the true reason is because our follies are stronger and our faults are more prevailing.[36]

Grinningly ironical, Congreve grants men superiority in affectation by virtue of their greater corruptibility. By association, however, his remarks constitute an attack on indistinct sexuality. From the Restoration on through most of the next century, satire sought many of its victims in those men who denied or lost their masculinity. Neutral at best, they were figures in a contrapuntal sketch. Even as a newly aggressive order of women was nullifying an image of docility, their limp companions were fading away into lethargic caricature.

The satire of this period demonstrates repeatedly the pervasiveness of masculine hand-on-hip mincing. The affectation of men conveys a stronger moral taint than that of women. It may be laughed at in the latter—so went the implied argument—but it does not usually strain tolerance, if only because it *is* a feminine trait. Similar behavior in men, however, is "unmanly"— is contrary to the long fixed judgment of what constitutes mas-

36. "Concerning Humour in Comedy," ed. Spingarn, 3:250.

culinity—and therefore abhorrent. The heterosexual rake appears at intervals before the satiric glass, but not so often as the emasculated creature delicately lisping. Abel Boyer uses a heavy brush of ridicule for his portrait of a languishing male lover. "Bless me! how handsome, how tall! how well-shaped he is! how sweetly he quavers, how nicely his hair is curled."[37] The first impression of simpering effeminacy disgusts, for Boyer inflates posturing that counters the tradition of the aggressive male. Finally, indeed, the fop dissolves into a third, androgynous world: neither man nor woman, he combines a confusing and obnoxious mélange of the worst characteristics of both.

Boileau too renders the "fashionable fop," though more provocatively than does Boyer:

> D'autre part un galant, de qui tout le métier
> Est de courir le jour de quartier en quartier,
> Et d'aller, à l'abri d'une perruque blonde,
> De ses froides douceurs fatiguer le beau monde,
> Condamne la science; et, blâmant tout écrit,
> Croit qu'en lui l'ignorance est un titre d'esprit;
> Que c'est des gens de cour le plus beau privilége,
> Et renvoie un savant dans le fond d'un collége.
>
> [Satire IV, 11–18]

Boileau may agree with Boyer that fop and fool are virtually the same, but the lines of agreement lead in different directions. The French satirist emphasizes credibility, not caricature; he emphasizes defective reason, not a teasing femininity. The problematic sex of fops like Boyer's interests Boileau only as an aside, but the type's crippling foolishness is at the heart of his satire. The fop "fond of his folly" carries a birthright of inanity that isolates him from normal social pursuits even more than does physical posturing. The two may go together, of course, but Boileau has chosen to stress the flaw of imperception, which, once our laughter has ceased, we are more likely to find pathetic than funny. That quality helps to explain the personality of Will Honeycomb, the gallant dandy of *Spectator* 2, "who according to

---

37. *Letters of Wit, Politicks and Morality* [and] *Original Letters of Love and Friendship* (1701), pp. 44–45; cf. Beattie, *Essays . . . on Laughter, and Ludicrous Composition*, pp. 654–56, on foppish fashions.

his years should be in the decline of his life, but having ever been very careful of his person, and always had a very easy fortune, time has made but very little impression, either by wrinkles on his forehead, or traces in his brain." A beguiling man, untouched by maturity or talent, he prances elegantly about as the ageless youth with an uncanny instinct for feeling comfortable with women, and in fact comforting them.

Not too different is Florentulus of *Rambler* 109, who though a fool in his behavior has native capabilities. In Florentulus Johnson sees the pathos of the child and arrested adolescent subjected to smothering care. Reared with exceptional delicacy, he reports that even as a youth, "[I] silenced [my elders] by my readiness of repartee, and tortured [them] with envy by the address with which I picked up a fan, presented a snuff-box, or received an empty tea-cup." As long as he was the darling of the ladies, his alienation from male society did not seem to matter. But time left him behind and a new generation of beauties found him as laughable as did the men. Rejected by both sexes, except for "a few grave ladies," he dreamed away his final years "in stupidity and contempt." The fop presented by Johnson has become a psychological freak, a social grotesque. Like a dependent pet deprived of natural resources, he is isolated within the very society that had created him for its amusement.

Despite the hint of pathos, however, Johnson had little sympathy for the foppish tribe, distancing himself as much as possible. In the *Dictionary*, without amelioration, a fop is "a simpleton; a coxcomb; a man of small understanding and much ostentation; a pretender; a man fond of show, dress, and flutter; an impertinent." The implicit cruelty of that definition is consolidated by Nathaniel Lancaster in the epithet "pretty gentleman." He and his friends

do not indeed consume their hours in such points of vain speculation, wherein the pride of reason and learning has room to operate. And indeed there is something in the drudgery of masculine knowledge, by no means adapted to youths of so nice a frame, that it cannot be said, they are ever invigorated with perfect health. The enfeebled tone of their organs and spirits does therefore naturally dispose them to the softer and more refined studies; furniture, equipage, dress, the tiring room, and the toy-shop.— — — —What a fund is here for study! And what a variety of easy delights! Or, if the mind is bent upon manual exercise, the knotting-bag is ready at hand; and their skillful fingers play their part.[38]

What the reverend satirist lacked in subtlety he made up in a talent for assimilation.

In the final analysis the gender of those offending against public morality and manners was less significant, satirically, than the offenses *per se*. Indictments against women tended to be patterned rather than individualized. And similarly satirists isolated male foppery for attack much more frequently than they did specific male fops. The central issue, after all, remained that of vanity, the sediment of a privileged society.

IV

The kinds of vanity seen in the preceding section are futile and corruptive; they induce irrational devotion to dress, social ceremony, fashionable exchange, and the like. Translated into moral terms, such self-centered infatuation can be gained only by worthless conduct and wasted time. The vanities of diversion—those, for instance, of the salon, gaming table, theater, social round—have a parallel in vanities of the mind. These too clutter manners, both aesthetic and intellectual. Falling under the rubric "pedantry," they are culturally erosive affectations that often produce a twisting and tormenting of literary skill or erudition. Pedantry, in Johnson's description (*Rambler* 173), as much a failure of morality as of manners, "is the unseasonable ostentation of learning" and as such bears a striking resemblance to other marks of pride, which sacrifice truth or substance to imposture and superficiality. The pedant, having mastered recondite but not necessarily important lore, "obtrudes his remarks and discoveries upon those whom he believes unable to judge of his proficiency, and from whom as he cannot fear contradiction, he cannot properly expect applause." The pedant brands himself the presumptuous braggart, egotistical and indifferent to the comprehension of others. The intellectual

---

38. *The Pretty Gentleman: or, Softness of Manners Vindicated from the False Ridicule Exhibited under the Character William Fribble, Esq.* (1747), pp. A2, 10-11.

pretender, Steele writes of this favorite Spectatorial fool (No. 270), enjoys an arrogance "always founded upon particular notions of distinction in his own head, accompanied with a pedantic scorn of all fortune and pre-eminence when compared with his knowledge and learning." Deliberately patronizing, he assumes that none of his auditors is capable of meeting him on his own ground where erudition is sown like dragon's teeth.

Inevitably, Johnson's strictures against pedantry were turned against himself. Such was the case when Archibald Campbell, for instance, named him "Lexiphanes," in itself a pretentiously parodic borrowing from Lucian. Campbell had no apparent warrant for his satire other than personal envy and a desire to capitalize on Johnson's reputation. Ironically, "Horrible" Campbell's attack backfired, for the very fault he attributed to Johnson serves merely to call attention to his own pedantry. Johnson customarily ignored epithets. After the *St. James's Chronicle* for 14 June 1770 coupled him with Goldsmith as the pedantic Holofernes and the obtuse Dull of *Love's Labour's Lost*, Johnson impatiently brushed aside the similitude: "'Why, what would'st thou have, dear Doctor! who the plague is hurt with all this nonsense? and how is a man the worse I wonder in his health, purse, or character, for being called *Holofernes?*'"[39] Name-calling, Johnson knew, generally has little to do with actual guilt. Like Hamlet, further, he too knew "a hawk from a handsaw." Few were better equipped than Johnson to discriminate between malignant misrepresentations and justifiable reproaches against pedantry as an affectation destructive of morality and beneficial knowledge.

For the pedant the practice was mind-crippling, the failure of a flabby intellect to discern the genuine apart from the spurious, the important from the irrelevant. Addressing himself to the same error, Swift sometimes interpreted pedantry so broadly as

---

39. *Lexiphanes, a Dialogue. Imitated from Lucian, and Suited to the Present Time* (1767). The likelihood of malice is strongly urged by Sir John Hawkins, who wrote of the parodist, "as well for the malignancy of his heart as his terrific countenance, [he] was called horrible Campbell." See *The Life of Johnson*, p. 347; *Johnsonian Miscellanies*, ed. G. B. Hill, 2 vols. (Oxford: Clarendon Press, 1897), 1:270, 407.

to identify it with any kind of pretense or ostentation. If, as he once said, "there is a pedantry in manners," there is also one "in all arts and sciences; and sometimes in trades." Any excessive and unnecessary display of specialized knowledge offends. In this sense, the lady of fashion stands accused of pedantry along with the man of law, for both devote themselves to gossip, backbiting, or the accumulation of purposeless, piddling facts. Swift, however, comes closer to the generally understood meaning of the word when he satirizes pedantry as clumsy bookishness. What could be more absurd than the Homeric formality of the battle in a library, a battle so inept that its rewards were those of plagiarized plunder? "So Wotton fled, so Boyle pursued. But Wotton heavy-armed, and slow of foot, began to slack his course; when his lover Bentley appeared, returning laden with the spoils of the two sleeping ancients. . . . And, now ****** . . . *Desunt Caetera.*"[40] In related ways, through parody and mock mythology (for instance, in *A Tale of a Tub*, or *The Memoirs of Martinus Scriblerus*, or *The Dunciad*), Swift and his friends loved to display their contempt for learning that brought no one closer to grace, especially not its possessor.

One comic treatment of pedantry utilizes inversion whereby the satirist deliberately adopts techniques he intends to ridicule. The victim thus becomes the unwilling persona, as when Swift emulates the epic manner of Homer to suggest the pomposity of Wotton and Bentley and their elliptical emendations. As master of the volte-face, Pope pretends homage to a passage from Blackmore's epic poem *Prince Arthur*. The compliment is patently hollow: "The triumphs and acclamations of the angels at the creation of the universe, present to his imagination 'the rejoicings on the Lord Mayor's Day'; and he beholds those glorious beings celebrating their Creator, by huzzaing, making illumina-

---

40. Swift, *Prose Works*, 4:90, 215–16; also 1:164–65: "Hints towards an Essay on Conversation," "On Good-Manners and Good-Breeding," and *The Battle of the Books*. Cf. David Mallett's derision of Theobald and Bentley, in "The Scholiast's Art": "Hence Plato quoted, or the Stagyrite, / To prove that flame ascends, and snow is white: . . . / If Shakespeare says, the noon-day sun is bright, / His scholiast will remark, it then was light." For kinds of mock pedantry, see the *Spectator*, passim; Fielding, *Tragedy of Tragedies* (1731) and *Vernoniad* (1741); John Wilkes, *An Essay on Woman* (1763).

tions, and flinging squibs, crackers, and sky-rockets." In this context, the lines that follow are a model of bathos. Still unsatisfied, however, Pope mercilessly pursues Blackmore, among others, with pseudoscholarly apparatus: "*NB.* In order to do justice to these great poets, our citations are taken from the best, the last, and most correct editions of their works. That which we use of *Prince Arthur*, is in *duodecimo*, 1714, the fourth edition revised." The self-evident *non sequitur* magnifies the weakness of weak poetry and ironic judiciousness lays bare ostentatious scholarship.[41]

Pope's technique has the unconsciously burlesque undertones of certain sacrificial rites. Among primitive tribes, the anthropologists inform us, a young girl symbolizing a maize goddess would be flayed and an officiating priest would then squeeze himself into her skin, subsequently conferring her divinity upon the crops and the people.[42] In his sophisticated variation, Pope may be imagined the verbal priest reducing to nonsense the words of the condemned pedant. As in the totemic ceremony, he figuratively encases himself in the skin of the sacrificial figure and thereby transfers the latter's qualities to himself. That is, Pope the knife-wielder reemerges as Pope the pedant, even though we recognize him as the pedant mimed whose aim is not to sanctify but to derogate bad learning and literature. This he does by teasing his readers with pseudogravity about the same scholarly premises to which his victims address themselves.

In his further assault on pedantry—as in *The Dunciad*—he assumes a new role, that of implied critic:

> What Gellius or Stobaeus hash'd before,
> Or chew'd by blind old scholiasts o'er and o'er.

41. *Miscellanies by Dr. Swift, Dr. Arbuthnot, and Mr. Pope*, 4th ed., 4 vols. (1742), 2:145, 211 ff. It was Blackmore's lot, Johnson wrote (*English Poets*, 2:235), "to be much oftener mentioned by enemies than by friends." Appearing in the Pope-Swift *Miscellanies* (1732) with *Peri Bathous* was Arbuthnot's virtuoso piece, *Virgilius Restauratus*, an elaborate parody on Bentley's Latin scholarship. The title was an obvious spoof of Theobald's *Shakespeare Restored* (1726). Pope had first included Arbuthnot's essay with *The Dunciad Variorum* of 1729. *The Dunciad*, in the *Twickenham Pope*, 5:xxv and 217n.

42. Frazer, *The Golden Bough*, pp. 590–92. For an excellent discussion of satiric magic and ritual, see Elliott, *The Power of Satire*, especially ch. 2.

> The critic eye, that microscope of wit,
> Sees hairs and pores, examines bit by bit:
> How parts relate to parts, or they to whole,
> The body's harmony, the beaming soul,
> Are things which Kuster, Burman, Wasse shall see,
> When man's whole frame is obvious to a flea.
>
> [IV. 231–38]

Taken by themselves, Gellius and Stobaeus are too distant in time to be more than token culprits. As links in a scholarly chain, however, they contribute to a legacy that connects them with the moderns, for Gellius and Stobaeus exemplify arid learning. Having been lured thus far in the poem by the call to ancient authority, we quickly discover that the catch consists of the three moderns as successors tainted even further by sundry associations with Bentley, who in his turn is a stock *alazon* often pelted by Pope's friends, Swift and Atterbury. The ancients and moderns conjoined are proof that they can be equally absurd when they waste learning on speculation worthy of insect effort.

The appeal of pedantry as a satiric norm continued well on into the eighteenth century. Sterne heard the call and enlarged upon it notoriously in *Tristram Shandy*, that encyclopedia of classical and obscure learning.[43] Sterne is the consummate virtuoso manipulating his readers in a performance that, recalling the spirit of Swift and Pope, turns real pedantry upon itself to become the stuff of parody. Much of this burden is carried by two of the principal characters, Uncle Toby and Walter Shandy. If failure to communicate intelligibly distinguishes the pedant, then Uncle Toby surely becomes the archetype. For all his sentimentality, he is starkly wanting in knowledge of worldly manners, a naif who has stretched his innocence out to safely neutral morality. A whistled tune becomes his substitute for articulated exchange, immersion in the study of warfare and fortifications, his precipitate retreat from frightening reality or—more specifically—his way to elude the clutching Widow Wadman.

Equally paralyzed by inability to cope with manners and morals, Walter Shandy is so recessive as to be virtually incom-

---

43. For a good overview of this problem, see Fluchère, *Laurence Sterne: From Tristram to Yorick*, pp. 161–74, 193–200.

municado. Thriving on allusion as others do on food and drink, he has closed himself into a bewildering maze of abstract, frequently irrelevant information drawn from esoteric books. Typically if extremely the pedant, he is "a brilliant illustration of one who possesses knowledge but not wisdom. He is so lost in speculative philosophy that he has no thought of the genuine needs of those under his charge—his wife and sons. His theoretical concern for their welfare is so compelling that he has lost touch with the concrete reality of their human wants and desires."[44] Whenever a problem arises, Walter slides into a metaphysics of dissociated language and allusion. Supported by the sonorous authority of imaginary writers like Prignitz, Scroderus, and Slawkenbergius, Walter sets about proving his theory of noses. But he also advances the wisdom of Paraeus, Bouchet, Erasmus, and Rabelais, an absurd potpourri in which the pedant ceases to discriminate between fantasy and truth.

The Shandean world depends in large measure on the learning, genuine and fake, that Sterne brought to the novel. Like his predecessors, though perhaps even more consistently, he indulges in counterpoint, acting the pedant who in fact satirizes pedantry. Many of the familiar devices are present: learned documentation—for instance, the Tristrapaedia—translations from French and Latin texts, the inevitable corrective footnotes. But through it all Sterne never forgets that he is a novelist who must create and develop characters. Walter Shandy's digressive, allusive lore becomes the trait that makes the reader increasingly comfortable with him as a fictional acquaintance. My Uncle Toby similarly induces expanding awareness of personality by his simple obsessiveness. These are not complex characters but they are deepening ones whose quirks allow them to respond with intriguing versatility to their varied situations.

Tristram too should be mentioned in this context, for his role as Sterne's narrator-editor makes him a triumphantly pedantic recapitulator. It is Tristram's responsibility, finally, to bring Walter, Toby, and the others into a likeable, credible focus. And in

44. John M. Stedmond, *The Comic Art of Laurence Sterne* (Toronto: University of Toronto Press, 1967), p. 59.

reporting what they say and do he necessarily discloses a great deal about himself as the pedant-voyeur. Nothing is too trivial or obscure for his retentive keyhole curiosity. Playing many parts (*pharmakos, eiron, rhetor,* above all *virtuoso*), he sees a world teeming with petty absurdities and includes himself among those observed trifles.[45] To a large extent, then, Sterne defines Tristram's character by his function as persona, the perceptive mock pedant. He is the clownish victim who manages to survive by laughing at a society that has reduced manners and morals to the inconsequentiality of bits and pieces.

v

We have seen that in a time when religion and politics share tensions, the distinctions between them—although the critic makes them—need not always be broken down as are the chemical components of an organic substance. Likewise, diverse manners may be considered part of a social phenomenon that, if only for the moment, is examined separately from corollary religious or political meanings. The chameleon coloration of satire allows the critic thus to adopt as host a referential object without denying the existence or relevance of surrounding objects. A satire by Juvenal, for instance, may invite primary attention to degenerate manners that are nonetheless fixed within a frame of religious or political circumstances. Those circumstances are not to be ignored, but the satirist's comprehensive social purpose may be best served by the ordering of priorities—as legislated, of course, by the critic's understanding of the satire. Equal attention to every detail and ideal can merely compromise the whole.

That risk, it seems to us, is especially manifest in satire whose cast is distinctly social, for manners frequently range so broadly that they absorb us in the myriad parts to the exclusion of the end result. Given this complexity, no one satire can be wholly representative. Occasionally, however, a work does allow us to see with satisfying clarity a total pattern emerging from the artistic and logical fusion of the many elements. One such work by Charles Churchill, a dedicatory poem, affords an opportunity to

45. Stedmond, p. 177.

review recurring attributes basic to the satire of manners. A personal motif appears to rule the poem, in which an aggrieved satirist fabricates tributes to William Warburton, Bishop of Gloucester. Thus, the focus is at first deceptively religious, for Churchill emphasizes his own humble status as a parish priest, comparing it with the diocesan eminence of the adversary. As the poem progresses, however, the charges of Warburton's religious and clerical inadequacies compete with those of his secular failings—political, familial, and literary. The conflict is intensified by a dualistic tone complicating the intention. The satirist's reaction to Warburton is persistently and bitterly ironic. Opposed to that is the candidly confessional voice of Churchill, which without irony—though with hints of self-pity—laments his own vocational liabilities and lack of good fortune.

Thus Churchill universalizes the field of his satire from rancorous personal feelings to condemnation for moral disintegration. We are not permitted to forget the adversary, but before the end of the poem his importance is as equally symbolic as it is real. Without the identifying particulars, Warburton would be little more than a pasteboard figure. Churchill, however, has preserved the erring human dimensions, making valuable psychological use of himself as the confessional satirist, more sinned against than sinning. The victim of an unjust social order, he is disdainful of favors, less fortunate and also less ambitious than the bishop, whose overweening flaws are pride of self and place.

Warburton's portrait exaggerates, for Churchill has drawn a profile that shows only bad features. Most prominent is the egoism of a man so vain of his authority and accomplishments that he revels in pompous, ceremonious forms. "Dizzy, confounded, giddy with the height" of illusioned importance, he has lost the capacity "of knowing good from ill, / of sifting truth from falsehood, friends from foes" (172–74). As a literary critic, he has bartered originality for safer arbitrary rules, affecting ability he does not have and pedantically rejecting all judgments that do not square with his own. Represented as an incomplete man, Warburton qualifies for the role of the dullard who sees and lives life only in fragments, with no ability to make connections between himself and others. Thus, he plays the clergyman but proves himself the hypocrite whose lack of inner conviction paralyzes any will he might have had to lead others spiritually. If he makes any commitment at all, it is to himself. But in this act, he loses the opportunity to fulfill himself as a moral human being.

The animus cannot be brushed aside, but neither can the general ethical statement of the errors and irresponsibility that the profile projects. It would be hard to believe that Warburton crowded as much selfishness, ineptitude, and pride into his career as Churchill visited upon him satirically. Yet once we allow him to stand for generalized foolishness and error, we are able to suspend disbelief of the hyperbole and react not so much to the man as to the moral erosion he represents. Churchill similarly casts himself in a specific role. Vicariously, however, he transcends himself as complaining victim to become, as it were, a simultaneously hostile and compassionate observer-narrator who comments upon himself and his adversary.

Like Demas, in whom he saw his own image, Churchill was so addicted to worldly appetites that he sacrificed his spiritual office to them and in so doing destroyed his physical life as well. A hedonist perceiving the dangers of his devotion to pleasure, he extended this insight satirically and thereby became a commentator on his own faults. The confessional role, however, was calculated for the damage he could do his enemies (and Wilkes's) by comparing their blunders with lesser ones for which he held himself responsible. Churchill's feuds did not end when "this busy brain rest[ed] in the grave," for proof of which we have the posthumous *Sermons*, published by his brother a few months after his untimely death 4 November 1764. There, in the "Dedication" to Warburton, he perpetuated the well-known quarrel, the foundation of unyieldingly personal attack, which may now be viewed as a brilliant judgment on the corruptive nature of contemporary manners.[46]

46. "Dedication" (pp. i–ix), in Charles Churchill, *Sermons* [London: W. Griffin; for John Churchill (Executor of Charles Churchill) and William Flexney, near Gray's-Inn Gate, Holborn: 1765]. See also Churchill's *Poetical Works*, ed. Grant, pp. 429–35, 557–58; Wallace Cable Brown, *Charles Churchill: Poet, Rake, and Rebel* (Lawrence: University of Kansas Press, 1953), pp. 139–44. The allusion to Demas is in 2 Timothy 4:10.

The relatively brief poem (180 lines), though generally thought to be incomplete, is self-contained in its extant state.[47] The terminal asterisks and the phrase *cetera desunt* (if Churchill's) look suspiciously like a borrowing from Swift's *A Tale of a Tub* or *The Battle of the Books*, and consequently enhance the ironies that inform the entire poem. The ironies, further, are intensified by Churchill's conscious role-shifting as he weaves the articles of tension back and forth, between himself and Warburton. What catches the eye immediately is the traditional thrice-stated invocation: "Health to great Gloster . . . *Health* to great Gloster . . . To great Gloster, *Health*."

With history on our side, the mockery is implicit, for Churchill's aversion to Warburton was common knowledge in 1765. In *The Duellist* of the previous year, for instance, he had maligned him as one

> so proud, that should he meet
> The Twelve Apostles in the street,
> He'd turn his nose up at them all,
> And shove his Savior from the wall.
>
> [671-74]

Even without such crude documentation, the appraisal in the "Dedication" degenerates quickly from mock-panegyric to condemnation of a public man—"Doctor, Dean, Bishop, Gloster, and My Lord"—whose exalted rank masks "revolt from Grace." Rejecting misplaced titles and the exercise of high office unaccompanied by virtue, Churchill does not need to name the prelate as one "who deceives"

> Under the sacred sanction of lawn-sleeves,
> Enhances guilt, commits a double sin;
> So fair without, and yet so foul within.
>
> [42-44]

As drawn by Churchill, the enemy's career is an ignoble record of deceptions, failed obligations, and personal shame. The cuck-

---

47. Notice following the poem: "It is presumed the sudden death of the author will sufficiently apologize for the Dedication remaining unfinished." The holograph signature in the Huntington Library copy is that of "J. Churchill." Yvor Winters argues for the completeness of the poem in "The Poetry of Charles Churchill," *Forms of Discovery: Critical & Historical Essays on the Forms of the Short Poem in English* (Denver, Colo.: Alan Swallow, 1967), p. 143.

old and humiliated parliamentarian are as unworthy of esteem as the literary pretender and pious hypocrite.

Religious failure, in Churchill's treatment, is less a matter of theological shortcoming—he ignores the formalities of observance almost altogether—than of splintered communal and individual morality. And although he assumes blame for his own clerical shortcomings, he ambiguously claims to have retained a large spiritual vision: "Truth best becomes an orthodox Divine, / And, spite of hell, that character is mine" (7–8). Death, even as he wrote these lines, was an apparently encroaching reality. In its imminence, the indictment of Warburton supersedes churchly "Pomp and Pow'r" and raises questions about the manners and morals of a sheeplike society that endures his transgressions. The hearty toast fixes the ironic tone to follow; but it also insinuates doubts about the man's moral stamina and warnings about consequences. "Health to great Gloster" is a transparent jibe. But while it plays games with the reader, it also directs him to another purpose, one that isolates Warburton as a symptom of darker, more vexatious ills than the merely private. The individual, that is to say, is obviously guilty—in the eyes of the satirist—of serious deficiencies. The particularity of the charges, however, is so intertwined with generalized manners that the faults are extended beyond localized circumstance or person. Even as, tongue-in-cheek, Churchill declares he does not mean "to wound [Warburton] with flatt'ry," he is still less likely to apply this adulatory "villain's art" to mankind at large, whose moral health is very much at issue.

Innuendo is unmistakable when, utilizing a favorite technique, he drafts a catalogue of negative responses and traits associated with "Pomp and Pow'r": nor name, nor title, nor public authority, nor bishop's miter have won the satirist's heart. Contrarily, he rejects these as meaningless, vacuous tokens, the superficial panoply of unmerited distinction. Mockingly, he protests that Warburton needs more than personal charm, magnanimity, or "lineal glory" (his birth "is low as mine"). Understatement effects the cumulative force of Churchill's denials— "'tis not thy Name ... tinsel trumpery of state ... Title ... Mitre," "No, 'tis thy inward man," which the poet ironically celebrates: "Thy virtue, not thy rank, demands my lays." But the context makes it sufficiently clear that Warburton does not have those natural manners symptomatic of secular as well as sacramental worth: conduct conditioned by moral necessity, tolerance, and charity.

Moving from mockery to overt platitude, Churchill appears deliberately to sentimentalize his wayward position as a justification for the satire. From his "good father (on his bier / Let filial duty drop a pious tear)" the young priest ("Ordain'd, alas! . . . thro' need, not choice") had discovered the hardship and futility of the ministry. Countering that frustration was the strong call of poetry; but while he sought inspiration of the man he professed to admire, he vainly hoped for "a friend in him, who was the friend of Pope." As when one symphonic movement rhythmically and emotionally succeeds another, the new accusation flows from a plea for sacred and ethical dedication into the temporal and literary. The orchestration throughout draws its impulse from determinants, the specific charges against an individual that also reflect the guilt of an entire social order. The untrustworthy Christian, Churchill warns, is also the untrustworthy critic, strong in pretension, weak in ability:

> A judge of genius, tho' confest
> With not one spark of genius blest.
> [*The Duellist*, 799–800]

Seeking wise critical guidance from Warburton, he found instead a dependence on authority that never "rais'd 'bove the slavery of common rules," and that made him impervious to genuine art and taste.

Recriminating himself as a fool to expect wisdom of self-centered worldliness, Churchill belatedly recognized the error of surrendering spiritual values: "The cure of souls . . . For toys like mine" (118–19). Warburton and his kind, plainly, are the greater fools. Although Churchill, also the imperfect man, never seriously considered undertaking a reformation of manners, he means to win our regard for his confessional honesty. The moral apologist and stubborn recusant, he bows his head in a show of regret, if not of binding humility. He knew that he had failed as a clergyman and perhaps as a poet. Yet he could live (however briefly) with those failures, for by his own testimony he had learnéd to understand himself without resorting to "smooth hypocrisy."

In Warburton, then, we see a summation of mannered society, corruptly indifferent to ethical values, neglectful of spiritual duties for want of spiritual commitment, a dissembler who breaks faith with himelf as he does with all others. Churchill's Warburton emerges the perfect fool, dunce, poseur; authoritarian and intolerant:

> ... (should a world, perverse and peevish grown,
> Explode his maxims, and assert their own).
>
> [107–108]

Worst of all, "the false saint, and true hypocrite" (*The Duellist*, 810) has dissociated himself from the Christian fundamentals of sympathy, altruism, and humility:

> Let him not, gorg'd with power, and drunk with state,
> Forget what once he was, tho' now so high;
> How low, how mean, and full as poor as I.
>
> [178–80]

Adroitly ordering details between the personal and the general, between scorn and anger, the poet is almost always securely, rationally in control. He anatomizes a victim but he also intimates a social lesson: others may rebel against or even subvert manners up to a point; but when unthinking, selfish renunciation of communal values turns into hubris, the collapse of aspiration, dignity, and inner decency must follow.

Churchill, a modern critic notes, had gone as far as he could or needed to in the "Dedication." Critics of the satirist's own day thought he had gone too far, proving himself an "enraged wasp," the author of "a virulent libel," flagrantly sacrilegious. For the ultimate irony, which Churchill would have enjoyed, he was virtually accused of hypocrisy, damned for the very sin he thought damnable in others: "Churchill the Poet, and Churchill the Preacher appear to be very different characters. In his poems, he is an outrageous and merciless satirist; in his sermons a meek and placable Christian. Yet strange as the mixture may seem, in the present publication [the *Sermons*] he is *both* characters in one!"[48] Public reaction to Warburton's prominence and Churchill's notoriety obviously distorted initial readings of the "Dedication": contemporary imagination was quick to seize on the possibilities of a bitterly personal satire but reluctant to concede a larger social intention.

Time and distance have been useful correctives, though not—two hundred years later—without encouraging equally extreme opposing claims. The poem, Yvor Winters asserts, "is a horrifying judgment of moral ugliness.... [It is] the greatest English poem of the eighteenth century and one of the greatest in our language."[49] On the second count at least, we think the assertion farfetched. The depiction of the corruption wrought within a corrupt milieu is appalling, though no more affective or mind-stirring probably than many a judgment set forth by Swift, Pope, or Johnson. It is enough to call it an important poem, very likely Churchill's best, without forcing it into competition with *The Dunciad* or *The Vanity of Human Wishes*. Yet somewhere within a range of acceptable qualitative assumptions, we gladly concede, Churchill has in fact written an indictment of false manners that—for vigor, perception, and feeling intensity— deserves the closest scrutiny when we study the poetic records of man's sins and follies.

48. Winters, *Forms of Discovery*, p. 143; *Monthly Review* 32 (1765): 101–9; *Critical Review* 19 (1765): 117–19. The last laugh may be Churchill's, for there is some doubt whether he wrote the *Sermons*. They may be his father's. See Grant, *Poetical Works*, p. 557.
49. Winters, *Forms of Discovery*, p. 145.

# INDEX

SATIRE'S PERSUASIVE VOICE

Designed by Richard Rosenbaum.
Composed by The Composing Room of Michigan, Inc.
in 10 point Baskerville, 2 points leaded,
with display lines in Baskerville.
Printed offset by Thomson/Shore, Inc. on
Warren's Number 66 Antique Offset, 50 pound basis.
Bound by John H. Dekker and Sons, Inc.
in Holliston book cloth
and stamped in All Purpose foils.

**Library of Congress in Publication Data**
(For library cataloging purposes only)

Bloom, Edward Alan, 1914–
   Satire's persuasive voice.

   Includes index.
      1.   Satire—History and criticism.   I.   Bloom,
Lillian D., joint author.   II.   Title.
PN6149.S2B57       809.7       78-11668
ISBN 0-8014-0839-3